The New
Southern Girl

The New Southern Girl

Female Adolescence in the Works of 12 Women Authors

CAREN J. TOWN

McFarland & Company, Inc., Publishers

Jefferson, North Carolina, and London

LIBRARY OF CONGRESS CATALOGUING-IN-PUBLICATION DATA

Town, Caren J., 1957–
    The new Southern girl : female adolescence in the works of
12 women authors / Caren J. Town.
        p.   cm.
    Includes bibliographical references and index.

    ISBN 0-7864-1893-1 (softcover : 50# alkaline paper) ∞

    1. American fiction — 20th century — History and criticism.
2. Girls in literature.   3. Women and literature — Southern
States — History — 20th century.   4. American fiction — Southern
States — History and criticism.   5. American fiction — Women
authors — History and criticism.   6. Young adult fiction, American —
History and criticism.   7. Women — Southern States — Intellectual
Life.   8. Teenage girls — Books and reading.   9. Southern States —
in literature.   10. Teenage girls in literature.   11. Adolescence in
literature.   I. Title.
PS374.G55T69 2004
813'.6 — dc22

                                                2004009443

British Library cataloguing data are available

Cover photograph ©2004 Brand X Pictures

Manufactured in the United States of America

McFarland & Company, Inc., Publishers
  Box 611, Jefferson, North Carolina 28640
    www.mcfarlandpub.com

To my own adolescent girl,
Rosa Elizabeth Town,
with the hope that her bright future
will make her find all this discussion
of limitations faintly ridiculous

Acknowledgments

My gratitude falls into three categories: institutional, inspirational, and emotional. First, thanks to Georgia Southern University, which has supported me financially all these years and given me a place to work where both teaching and research are rewarded. In particular, I have received reduced course loads for research as well as a six-month academic leave in which to pursue my research on this book. I also was supported by my former department chair, Jim Nichols, who was everything one could want in a boss. Finally, GSU paid the salary of my proofreader, Michael McDonald, whose careful reading and constant cheerfulness made this project much easier — and cleaner.

My inspiration came, indirectly, from my graduate school professor Hazard Adams, whose stern, uncompromising, and unsentimental attitude about balancing the demands of research and teaching taught me, as he said (well before the Nike shoe company), to *just do it*. It also comes from the writers whose work I discuss and whom I have never met, but whose lucent prose and profound insights about being young and female inspire me continually.

Emotionally, I have been supported by my friends Mary Hadley and Barbara Weiss, who have helped me nourish the body as well as the mind; by Caroline McMillan, to whom I can always speak frankly; and by my colleagues and friends in struggle, Candy Schille and Marc Cyr, who have kept me (sort of) sane all these years. My father, James I. Town, taught me that I could do anything I set my mind to, and my mother, Carla S. Town, has always been my most loyal supporter.

Finally, of course, I would like to thank my husband, David W. Robinson, without whom ... but you know the rest.

Contents

Acknowledgments vi

Introduction 1

ONE. Narratives of Development/Developing Narratives . . . 7

TWO. "Becoming: Maybe So": Breakdowns, Setbacks, and Triumphs in Lee Smith's Novels 21

THREE. "Three Meal a Day Aftermaths": Anne Tyler's Determined Adolescents 41

FOUR. "One Layer Deeper": On the Road and In Country with Sam Hughes 57

FIVE. "People Have No Respect for Girls": Lucille Odom's Ride Through Adolescence 71

SIX. "The Hope of the Remade Life": Allison's and Gibbons' Rewritten Girlhoods 83

SEVEN. "Claim What Is Yours": Tina McElroy Ansa's Spiritual Journey 103

EIGHT. "Odd How Things Are and Then They Aren't": Janisse Ray's Identity of Loss 115

NINE. "A Whole World of Possibilities": Jill McCorkle's
       Troubled and Tenacious Girls 129

TEN. "Keep on Asking Questions": Tough Girls in Young
       Adult Fiction 145

Notes 171
Bibliography 181
Index 195

Introduction

Over the past decade, bookstore shelves have overflowed with books about America's troubled teens, in particular endangered teenage girls, although lately there has been an outcry about our embattled boys as well.[1] Works like Mary Pipher's *Reviving Ophelia* and many others have contributed to the general perception that contemporary young women are in a state of crisis. Parents, educators, social scientists, and other concerned adults worry that our nation's girls are losing their ambition, moral direction, and self-esteem as they enter adolescence, which can lead them to promiscuous sex, anorexia, drug abuse, and, at the very least, declining math scores.[2] However, although female adolescent development *has* come under considerable scrutiny in recent years, the gloomy prognosticators are rarely challenged, in spite of evidence to the contrary in life and in literature.[3]

A good place to begin dismantling this bleak picture of female adolescence may be with recent representations of young women, fictional and autobiographical, which show adolescent girls who are proud, stubborn and focused, who suffer from being female, but who also use their brains and good humor to work toward satisfying adult lives. For example, in Anne Tyler's 1987 novel *Dinner at the Homesick Restaurant*, heroine Jenny Tull says, "I don't see the need to blame adjustment, broken homes, bad parents, that sort of thing. We make our own luck, right? You have to overcome your setbacks. You can't take them too much to heart" (196). This comment speaks to an important attitude Tyler shares

1

with many other contemporary female writers — that "luck" of their own making (and not gender or family background) determines the futures of young women. Making luck, overcoming setbacks, not taking things too much to heart (all character traits usually associated with male protagonists) can now be seen as the legitimate inheritance of young women, too. Instead of collapsing under the burdens of gender limitations and troubled relationships with parents (especially mothers), these female adolescents are stubbornly asserting the right to create their own futures. Surprisingly, given the patriarchal flavor of the region, this transformation may be quite clearly seen in the works of Southern women writers. Drawing on the tradition of strong female characters and adding a more optimistic view of their future, these writers are creating new young women of the South who challenge both traditional Southern views of womanhood and recent prophecies of their impending doom.

Writers like Tyler and the other women discussed in this work — Lee Smith, Bobbie Ann Mason, Josephine Humphreys, Kaye Gibbons, Dorothy Allison, Tina Ansa, Janisse Ray, and Jill McCorkle, as well as a number of novelists writing for the young adult market — are creating adolescent female characters who challenge not just traditional expectations for the future but also contemporary theoretical explanations of their relationships and behavior. Their characters' actions and beliefs are frequently at odds with recent sociological studies and psychoanalytic criticism, however, which continue to insist that gender-based social inequities and psychological identification with the Mother, mothering, or maternal language explain the problems of adolescent girls — and the literary characters based on them. The fact is that the young women these writers have created over the last three decades refute most commonly held notions about the adolescent girl. This book explores their challenge to current orthodoxy about female adolescence and emphasizes the very different picture of young women that is emerging in recent fiction and autobiography.

The first chapter confronts the popular ideology concerning adolescent females, both in the world and the text. At issue are claims about adolescent girls' loss of confidence, their moral sense, and their relationships to their mothers, to language, and to writing. This chapter seeks to refute the claims made by such theorists as Mary Pipher, Carol Gilligan, and Nancy Chodorow, among others, who assert the existence of special categories for women's language, social behavior, and personal morality. Concentrating on theoretical and critical arguments against these ideas, Chapter One raises questions about the motivations behind feminist essentialist theories and the rhetoric of adolescent female crisis and suggests new directions for theory and criticism. It also outlines the history of the young adult (YA) novel and shows how contemporary YA women writers are both extending and transcending the tradition of the female *Bildungsroman*. Finally, it demonstrates the ways in which the writers discussed in this book extend the Southern literary tradition to create confident, contemporary heroines.

Chapter Two explores the novels of Virginia native and North Carolina resident Lee Smith. In her works *The Last Day the Dogbushes Bloomed* (1968), *Something in the Wind* (1971), *Black Mountain Breakdown* (1980), *Fair and Tender Ladies* (1988), and *Saving Grace* (1996), Smith works through the various trials and tribulations that face girls growing up in remote Appalachian mountain towns. Her young women cope with rape, death, infidelity, and mental breakdown, as well as restrictions imposed on them by patriarchal and fundamentalist Southern culture. For the most part, though, they emerge from their troubles with recreated lives and new ways of thinking about their futures. Smith's work provides an excellent starting place for a discussion of new Southern girls in fiction, as her work spans the decades from the 1960s to the 1990s, and her young women provide the models for nearly all the girl protagonists to come.

The third chapter discusses several works by Baltimore writer Anne Tyler (who grew up in North Carolina): *A Slipping-Down Life* (1970), *The Clock Winder* (1972), and *Dinner at the Homesick Restaurant* (1987). It shows the ways in which her adolescent heroines mature into confident women, in spite of dead, clueless, or abusive mothers, obsessive love, early pregnancy, multiple marriages, various false starts, career misdirections, and personal crises. Each of the main characters becomes the kind of woman she (if no one else in the novel) knew she could be — through a strange but compelling combination of aimless perseverance, willed good luck, and serious humor. Like Smith, Tyler's work is a basis from which many future Southern women writers will work.

Chapter Four treats Kentucky writer Bobbie Ann Mason's novel *In Country* (1985). In this novel, seventeen-year-old Sam Malone struggles with gaps in her personal narrative. Her father, who died in Vietnam before she was born, is obviously unable to provide her with any background, and her mother, who has remarried and has a new baby, is unwilling to talk about the past. Sam must confront the fraught legacy of Vietnam in order to move toward her future, which she does by the end of the novel. Like the characters in Tyler's novels, she is empowered (not handicapped) by the absence of her mother in her quest to discover her past and form her future.

Charleston native Josephine Humphreys' novel *Rich in Love* (1987) is the focus of the fifth chapter. The discussion here concentrates on the ways in which the main character manages to pull her life together in spite of (or perhaps because of) her mother's inexplicable disappearance. Like the characters in Smith's and Tyler's novels and Mason's Sam, seventeen-year-old Lucille Odom has her share of troubles: her missing mother, her distraught father, her pregnant and depressed sister, and her attractive new brother-in-law. Still, she manages to find a way to prepare for her future and to accept the inevitable changes to her family caused by her mother's abrupt departure. Lucille is no saint, and often blind about her own and others' motivations, but at the end of the novel she is moving toward a future that is bright with possibilities.

Shifting the focus to working-class characters, the sixth chapter compares two novels by writers from the Carolinas: Kaye Gibbons' *Ellen Foster* (1987) and Dorothy Allison's *Bastard Out of Carolina* (1992). These slightly younger girls have larger problems than the mostly middle-class heroines of the previous chapters. Their mothers are either dead or rendered helpless by work and love, and their fathers (or stepfathers) are drunk, angry, and physically and sexually abusive. In spite of these serious troubles, however, the two girls manage to create sustaining and safe lives for themselves. The heroine of Allison's novel, Bone, escapes to the home of an aunt, whose unconventional ways and personal strength provide her with a positive model for the future. Gibbons' Ellen is shuffled between a series of unsatisfactory homes after her mother dies and her father physically abuses and neglects her, but finally she chooses a foster home for herself and starts to enjoy the security and pleasure of a family. In spite of economic differences, however, Bone and Ellen do resemble the other heroines in their determination not to accept the cards that life has dealt them.

Chapter Seven explores the novel *Baby of the Family*, by African American writer Tina McElroy Ansa of Georgia. This chapter investigates the ways in which main character Lena Macpherson struggles with her metaphysical gifts, which both frighten and alienate her from friends and family. Eventually, like the other girls in this study, Lena learns to use her talents and not to fear them. She also learns important lessons from various surrogate mothers, both real and spiritual, and in this way she resembles many of the girls discussed here who must find inspiration and example from women other than their mothers.

Although it is certainly possible to read Ansa's and Allison's novels as indirectly autobiographical, Chapter Eight moves into more clearly autobiographical territory, with Janisse Ray's *Ecology of a Cracker Childhood* (1999). Ray's juxtaposition of the natural and the personal (she alternates the story of her childhood with the story of the Southeast Georgia pine barrens) shows us the ways in which a girl's development can be hampered by the destruction of her regional identity. For Ray, the landscape is destiny, and only through its reclamation is she able to grow. Though it is not a novel, it explores issues of identity, home, and region in ways very similar to the works of the other writers discussed in this book. *Ecology of a Cracker Childhood* clearly deserves a place among narratives of Southern female adolescence.

Chapter Nine considers two novels by Jill McCorkle, *The Cheer Leader* (1984) and *Ferris Beach* (1990), and discusses the ways in which McCorkle (like Bobbie Ann Mason) focuses on the lives of Southern girls struggling with the changing values and expectations of the New South. McCorkle is interesting, too, because she does not shy away from difficult issues — anorexia, mental illness, rape, violent death — while at the same time she shows her characters the ways in which they can escape, overcome, or reconceptualize their problems. Like Dorothy Allison's, McCorkle's characters view their lives with humor and with hope.

Chapter Ten focuses on novels written primarily for young adults. These works by Katherine Paterson, Mildred D. Taylor, and Cynthia Voigt feature young female protagonists who triumph over seemingly impossible odds: maternal abandonment, pathological jealousy, violent racism. Although they are geared toward the young adult market, these novels are complex and intriguing to adult readers as well, and they are important for the ways in which they both reflect and shape the picture of female adolescence.

Through its discussion of these contemporary narratives of female development, this book offers a partial answer to those wringing their hands about the dire state of girls in America. At least in the pages of these books (which are, of course, making their way into the hands of actual young women), teenage girls are strong, confident, funny, and clever. They meet the various challenges of their lives directly and usually have some success in changing whatever circumstances make them unhappy. True, they face abandonment by and loss of their parents, abuse by those parents who remain, early motherhood and divorce, confrontations with ghosts, and anguish over the destruction of their environment, but they emerge at the end of their stories setting up house for themselves, going off to college, moving in with new, extended families — in short, making lives for themselves that don't repeat the traumas of the past. If these girls can do it, one assumes, so can the girls outside the world of the text.

A final note: There are, of course, other interesting examples of female adolescence in contemporary Southern women's writing, but the purpose of this study is to explore fictional and autobiographical narratives that, either in first-person or intimate third-person voices, concentrate explicitly and at length on the development of young female protagonists. In other words, girls and the changes they undergo on the way to adulthood constitute the center of the works chosen for this book. The goal of this study is to show the ways in which new Southern girls *transcend* the limitations placed on them by society, so this book places attention necessarily on girls who remain alive and (relatively) confident by the end of their stories. In addition, I was looking for writers who were relatively unfamiliar to readers (in the case of Ansa and Ray, and perhaps McCorkle and Gibbons), or not discussed in terms of adolescence (Tyler and Smith), or works that I believe deserve another look (Mason, Humphreys, and Allison). Finally, it just isn't possible to discuss *every* new Southern girl: an analysis of the representations of female adolescence in the works of Southern women writers like Shirley Ann Grau, Gail Godwin, Doris Betts, Ellen Gilchrist, Jayne Ann Phillips, Alice Walker, and Mary Karr, for example, as well as the wonderful new young adult novels featuring Southern girls appearing every day, would probably provide a useful companion to this volume, as would a discussion of the new Southern male adolescent. My focus, however, is on *these* girls and how they successfully traverse the rocky path to adulthood. The heroines in this study are not disillusioned or destroyed; neither are they smug or ridiculous; nor are they pushed to the side in favor of more complicated adult characters and themes. These girls sit squarely in the center of their stories, and they ask that we pay attention.

ONE

Narratives of Development/
Developing Narratives

> To recognize the ways in which we surround ourselves with
> our fictions is a step toward finding new ways for thinking the
> organization of sexual difference as grounded in cultural and
> political reality without positing that reality — man or woman,
> for example — as somehow preexisting our thought and fictions
> [Alice Jardine, *Gynesis*, 47].

> If there is something right in Beauvoir's claim that one is not
> born, but rather *becomes* a woman, it follows that *woman* itself
> is a term in process, a becoming, a constructing that cannot
> rightfully be said to originate or to end. As an ongoing discursive
> practice, it is open to intervention and resignification [Judith
> Butler, *Gender Trouble*, 33].

Girls in Trouble: The "Problem"

We "surround ourselves with our fictions," says Alice Jardine, and
so we do — both with those books we *acknowledge* as fictions and with
ideas about gender, culture, and history that we assume to be true. The
key is to recognize which fictions are necessary, which merely useful, and
which are damaging to the ways we read the text *and* the world. Perhaps
no area of life is more weighted with fictions than adolescence — each new

coming-of-age novel or autobiography adds to an already immense corpus of *Bildungsromanen*, and the study of adolescence in psychology, sociology, and popular culture is cursed with clichés and rife with unsupported generalizations. Recently, *female* adolescent development in particular has come under considerable scrutiny, and commonplaces (about girls' lack of confidence, their relativistic ethical system, and their unhealthy attachment to their mothers, for example) are rarely questioned.

The popular conception of female adolescence — in life and in literature — has been shaped by recent essentialist and deterministic sociological and psychological theories. Books like Mary Pipher's *Reviving Ophelia* (1994), Carol Gilligan's *In a Different Voice* (1982), and Nancy Chodorow's *The Reproduction of Mothering* (1978) have helped to create three powerful late–20th century clichés about American girls: 1) their identities and self-confidence are in serious danger, 2) their ethical judgment is dramatically different from (and probably inferior to) that of boys, and 3) their development is thwarted by their psychological struggle to separate themselves from their mothers. Although Pipher and others base their arguments on statistically valid studies, their conclusions may explain more about current financial and social inequalities for *adult* women than they offer a full accounting of the experience of adolescent girls.[1] Nevertheless, the pervasiveness of such descriptions of female adolescence in popular culture necessitates both an examination of their arguments and an elaboration of possible alternative ways of describing the lives of young women.

Pipher's book is perhaps most familiar to a general audience, and her conclusions about the perils experienced by young adult women have struck fear in the hearts of parents and educators. The following is a representative passage from *Reviving Ophelia*:

> Something dramatic happens to girls in early adolescence. Just as planes and ships disappear mysteriously into the Bermuda Triangle, so do the selves of girls go down in droves. They crash and burn in a social and developmental Bermuda Triangle. In early adolescence, studies show that girls' IQ scores drop and their math and science scores plummet. They lose their resiliency and optimism and become less curious and inclined to take risks. They lose their assertive, energetic and "tomboyish" personalities and become more deferential, self-critical and depressed. They report great unhappiness with their own bodies [19].

It is hard to imagine grimmer scenario: Girls not only start making bad grades in math and science, but they also lose their ability to take risks, *and* they are miserable about their bodies. Given this dire forecast, one wonders how any young women could ever arrive at the shores of a safe and productive adulthood.

Carol Gilligan adds to this unhappy picture with her analysis of girls' morality. *In a Different Voice*, her best known work, claims that girls and boys accept "different truths," with girls embracing an ethos of "attachment" and boys endorsing "the role of separation as it defines and empowers the self" (156). In other words, when it comes to ethics, girls look to community, boys to themselves. The result is that girls make moral decisions based on connections and context while boys develop an individualistic, non-relational morality. Although Gilligan has insisted that this difference is not indicative of an undeveloped moral sense in girls, just a "different" one, the bottom line is that girls' relational morality at adolescence turns into a reluctance to take moral positions that threaten girls' connections to others. Relationships take precedence over morality, and essentially girls *have* no independent moral position, at least one that they are willing to articulate.[2]

After Gilligan, perhaps the most frequently cited formulation of gender difference in adolescent development — for literary critics as well as psychologists and sociologists — comes from Nancy Chodorow, whose *The Reproduction of Mothering* attempts to explain girls' social and psychological problems in terms of their relationships with their mothers. To summarize her position: mothers make mothers of their daughters, and not of their sons, and thereby create for them roles limited by their sense of an obligation to mother. The mother/daughter relationship becomes central, therefore, to the daughter's sense of self. Like Gilligan, Chodorow has carved out a separate sphere of nurturing for young women that justifies both their motivations (to mother or escape mothering) and their primary dilemma (to free themselves from their maternal role model). The problem with this, of course, is that young women who seek other futures or who have few difficulties with their mothers are not adequately explained, or often even included.

Consistent with these sociological studies, although probably more limited in scope and public influence, the work of linguists and literary theorists in the 1970s and '80s suggests that the adolescent female struggles under gender-specific linguistic and psychological burdens, most frequently originating in the maternal/child bond. According to this line of thought, mothering reproduces itself, creates female linguistic origin, forms individual psychology, enforces social mores, and even engenders a particularly female literary style. Not surprisingly, then, much criticism of women in literature — both authors and characters — has, in the last two decades, concentrated on the alienation of daughters from maternal origins, or, conversely, on the imbrication of mother/daughter identity. The effect of this emphasis has been that works (and authors) unconcerned with the pernicious effects of maternal influence or not employing a self-consciously female voice or narrative structure have been ignored — or misread — by the critics.[3]

So what motivates these theories of embattled girlhood in the world and in fiction? It would be mean spirited to say that social theorists in particular are motivated by the potential notoriety of such doomsday scenarios. It would be simplistic to say that these theories are merely the result of fin-de-siècle gloom or feminist sentimentality. Most likely, the need to manufacture gender differences in life and literature arises from a residual essentialism that wants to create a separate category of nurturing, caring, sensitive females in order to remove girls (and by implication women) from the uglier aspects of modern life — high-tech warfare, global capitalism, environmental disasters, violence of various sorts. It also provides a convenient way to set off literary productions by and about women from contamination by male-dominated structures of knowledge and language. Most problematic, however, is that, whatever their motivations, these readings of real and fictional girls fail to account for the diversity in moral, social, psychological, and physical responses of adolescent girls in literature and in life.

A (Partial) Theoretical Solution

There *have* been a number of negative responses to the essentialism, maternalism, and determinism of this area of feminist theory. One group argues that no privileged position exists outside of "male" discourse from which one could speak about a maternal female language,[4] while another counters maternalist discourse with deconstructive cultural criticism. Judith Butler's thorough critique of the reification of gender provides an excellent example of the latter. In *Gender Trouble*, Butler offers an important reevaluation of a pre-symbolic maternal identity, arguing that mothering is not a pre-cultural activity; it is itself a cultural institution, through which the action of culture is inscribed as originary. Thus, culture/language creates motherhood; motherhood (or exclusion from it) does not create language.

Butler bases her critique of mothering on her theory of gender, which claims that gender creates sex or sexual identity; gender doesn't follow as a cultural overlay from original sexual difference, and, paradoxically, the sense of the "natural" associated with sexual difference is in fact a creation of culture. Gender, she says, "is itself a kind of becoming or activity, and ... ought not to be conceived as a noun or a substantial thing or a static cultural marker, but rather as an incessant and repeated action of some sort" (112). This notion of gender as "incessant and repeated action" or as "a kind of becoming or activity" is useful for those who study culture and literature, and especially for critics of the novel of adolescence — a period that is itself "a kind of becoming." Sexual identity (and by implication overall identity) becomes in Butler's terms a transitory, flexible matter, a series of choices, many of which are reversible.[5]

In another equally productive direction, several literary critics have begun to reexamine maternalist psychoanalytic approaches to literature (and development narratives in particular). They have shown that while the psychological approach may seem well suited to — and is frequently used with — texts featuring adolescent characters (who are often in the process of forming adult identities and dealing with various psychological problems), the method has several potential limitations. Psychoanalytic critics may be blinded by their own demons to the complexities of the texts in front of them, exclusive critical attention to mother/daughter relationships may limit the analysis to texts that foreground this aspect of development, and even more importantly, formal and political questions may be ignored in the quest to explore female characters' psychology.

Nina Baym, in "The Madwoman and Her Languages: Why I Don't Do Feminist Literary Theory," offers a provocative example of this kind of critique. Implying that feminist critics who rely on Freud are masochistic, she argues that Chodorow's insistence on the importance of the maternal "must have satisfied a need among literary feminist critics for it has inspired numerous readings of women writers based on the assumption of their less organized, more connected and fluid personalities" (52). For

Baym, the pre–Oedipal (a unity Chodorow stresses between mothers and daughters that precludes adolescent conflict) "is an interested fantasy of the maternal. Its purpose — to contain and confine mothers and hence women within the field of the irrational — is evident; to espouse such a fantasy is to accede to a male appropriation of the mother and her language" (55). Although it satisfies the wish to keep motherhood free from the limitations of the rational world, Baym says, the notion of the pre–Oedipal acquiesces in a traditional male/rational female/irrational dichotomy. Rather than creating a new space for female relationships and language, this "fantasy" merely reifies the old, confining ones, and thus literary readings thus have no means of accommodating the new.

Perhaps even more provocatively, Baym says that feminist theory about mothers and daughters "provides testimony, often unwitting and in contradiction to its stated intentions, of the deep-seated hostility of daughters to mothers" (56). To put it bluntly, critics hate their mothers and assume their authors do as well. She continues: "Even at the moment when the daughter-writer or daughter-feminist claims that she is seeking the mother in order to make strengthening contact, she reveals that the mother she seeks is not *her* mother, but another mother, preferably an imaginary mother" (56). Literary mothers, then, can become surrogate "good" mothers for the critic. Finally, Baym wonders about "what a theory deliberately developed from childhood fantasies describes other than childish fantasies, and how such a theory serves feminist intentions" (58). Baym is concerned about the ways in which critics are satisfying their own unmet needs in their readings of texts. Her message to feminist critics, stated less diplomatically, might be, "Grow up."[6]

Marxist theorists offer another critique of a psychological approach to literature. In much the same way as Butler analyzes gender, Jane Flax argues that our ideas of the family are conditioned by social relations that constitute it. Rather than focusing on internal family dynamics, Flax suggests, the critic should concentrate on the forces that created those dynamics. For texts about adolescence, this might mean thinking about the social structures that subtend the particular problems in individual families and the struggles adolescents have to escape and incorporate those structures.

Jane Gallop continues this attack on the psychoanalytic critic's emphasis on family in *The Daughter's Seduction*. "One of psychoanalysis's consistent errors," Gallop says, is to reduce everything to a family paradigm. Sociopolitical questions are always brought back to the model father-mother-child.... This has always been the pernicious apoliticism of psychoanalysis" (144). The "pernicious apoliticism" of psychoanalysis resembles, not surprisingly, feminist essentialism, and Gallop's call to contextualize and historicize recalls Butler's argument, as well as criticism of Gilligan. Families exist as part of large social matrices, Gallop and these other critics remind us, and so do feminism, gender, and the text.

This study uses the insights of Gallop, Baym, Butler and others to a emphasize the ways in which adolescent girls — both within and outside of novels — participate in, and react against, the larger contexts of the worlds in which they live. Rather than reifying the mother/daughter bond (and therefore giving it supernatural power), rather than creating a separate sphere for girls' morality, language, and identity, and rather than giving into despair, this book attempts to show the ways contemporary novels about young women both reflect *and* shape a more hopeful picture for adolescent girls. A brief look at the history of the young adult novel and its reception is probably the best place to start this process of reassessment.

Reading the Novels of Adolescence (and For Adolescents): A Way Out

In her essay "The Novel of Awakening," Susan J. Rosowski sets the standard for how novels of female development have been read until recently. Rosowski's study of 19th-century development novels describes a "pattern in literature by and about women: movement is inward, toward greater self-knowledge and the nature of the world;" this pattern, she says, amounts to an "awakening to limitations" (49). In these kinds of novels, Rosowski finds that "[c]onflict is largely internal, between two selves; an inner, imaginative self of private value is at odds with an outer, conventional self of social value" (49–50). She continues:

> All present protagonists who seek value [*sic*] in a world that
> expects a woman to define herself by love, marriage, and
> motherhood. For each, an inner, imaginative sense of personal
> value conflicts with her public role: an awakening occurs when
> she confronts the disparity between her two lives [68].

Granted, Rosowski is describing the world for 19th-century women, writers and characters, but many readings of 20th-century women's fiction follow this model, especially when the heroine is an adolescent. The formulation goes like this: Young women, initially filled with a sense of unlimited possibilities, grow into an awareness of an increasingly circumscribed existence, either because of estrangement from their mothers, responsibilities for mothering themselves, or societal expectations. Such a scenario is enforced on the novel, whether or not it fits the pattern. Novels where heroines escape — or reject — societal limitations are usually ignored.

Many recent novels featuring young female protagonists have come a long way from the "novels of awakening" described by Rosowski, however. In these works, young women, while aware of possible limitations due to gender, economics, and/or race, nevertheless find ways to overcome or circumvent those limitations.[7] The novels in this study written about adolescents but not necessarily for them show girls overcoming their limitations, persevering in spite of obstacles, and awakening to *possibilities*. In the novels written specifically for the young adult market, there is even a more explicit emphasis on redefinition — of gender, of family, of self. All the novels discussed in this book feature characters whose lives are works in progress and whose gender does not interfere with that process.[8]

In the young adult novel, especially, the idea of female development as an ongoing process may in fact have been a part of the genre since its inception. What is commonly regarded as the first young adult novel, Maureen Daly's *Seventeenth Summer* (1942), has, as Virginia Carroll says, "a strong, unlikely heroine in a complex novel of female development" (12). The novel is, she says, "a type of female *Bildungsroman* that assumes that reader is more interested in the emotional and intellectual development of the young woman than in the romantic relationship depicted on the cover" (15). The novel succeeds, Carroll says, "because it is rooted in the ordinary but allows readers access to an extraordinary process of development. It is distinctly feminine in its narrative structure, avoiding the linear models of organic growth in the male-centered *Bildungsroman* tradition and focusing instead on the recursive, tentative, spiraling process of female development" (18). Novelists like Paterson, Taylor, and Voigt, then, can be seen as following in the path laid by Daly more than 60 years ago, but what Carroll says about young adult novels applies equally well to the other novels of development discussed in this book.

Unfortunately, Daly's book was followed by decades in which traditional feminine characteristics — deference, helplessness, feigned ignorance, attention to external appearance — were privileged. The 1970s inaugurated a sea change in young adult fiction for girls, however. Indeed, Anne MacLeod correctly points out that "[R]ecent portraits of girls have a variety, individuality, and ease that contrasts with the narrowness of pre–1970s literature and, equally, with the self-consciousness of many early efforts to strengthen girls' literary images" (213).

Joanne Brown and Nancy St. Clair even say "there has been an explosion of young adult novels with female protagonists whose sense of independence and assurance contrasts sharply with that of their predecessors" (22). These girls "make a place for themselves through meaningful contributions to it, nurturing others without sacrificing their own selves. They come to know themselves well, both their strengths and their weaknesses, and they resist letting themselves be defined by others.... They are courageous, enthusiastic, and determined"(49). "Courageous, enthusiastic, and determined" clearly describe the young women in this book and the ways in which they "defy socially approved but oppressive behaviors and values" (49).

The novel of adolescence may in fact usually have been about defying conventions and beating the odds, in spite of occasional detours into the traditional. Unlike novels about adults, children's and adolescent novels, according to Lissa Paul, assume that the protagonist can and will escape the limitations, either physical or psychological, imposed upon him or her:

> [P]rotagonists in children's literature transcend, and, for the most part win, even when the endings of stories are not conventionally happy. Though they have to deal with the same (often overlapping) forms of physical, economic and linguistic entrapment that women do, they are not yet closed in by the rules of adulthood [188].

Children can escape the various sorts of entrapment that ensnare adult women, as the rules don't yet apply to them. Thus, adolescent literature, either about or for young people, is particularly suited to representing the active female self. Girls like the ones in this study do seem able to slip under the radar of the adults around them trying to force them into conventional femininity.

Perhaps more than the protagonists, the *readers* of these novels reconstruct their notions of female identity. Not simply seeing these determined girls as role models for their own lives, readers begin to think about what being female will mean to them. In other words, what they see novels modeling is the disturbing of the universe through asking questions and demanding answers. One could argue that books treating female development are especially valuable to young women readers, who feel the walls of gender expectations closing in on them. Books such as those by Tyler, Allison, McCorkle, Paterson, Taylor (and the others discussed here) give their readers both adventures *and* options.

Angela Hubler's study of adolescent female readers has borne this out. Interviewing 42 adolescent girls about their reading practices and attitudes, she found that girls in her study "commonly focused on aspects of texts that confirmed female behavior they found desirable while ignoring or forgetting aspects that undermined those behaviors" ("Can Anne Shirley" 270). Hubler calls this "liberatory reading," and she insists that their "descriptions of their favorite female characters manifest their rejection of the stereotype of women as quiet, passive, dependent, compliant, weak, and timid, as well as their desires to be 'different' from the social norm" (272). Hubler hopes this kind of reading will help to counteract simplistic notions of gender identity and female agency found in feminist psychology and manifesting itself in places like women's studies' textbooks (280).[9]

In a similar essay, Hubler says readers she interviewed "are not passively shaped by their pleasure reading, but, as reader-response critics argue actively construct the meanings of the texts they read." "[G]irls' reading," she says, "can play a role in their construction of female identity" (90). This kind of active reading suggests that girls do not need, and in fact may be harmed by, literature that self-consciously represents positive female role models. Indeed, Hubler argues that some feminist literature for girls has been too focused on depicting positive images of individual girls at the expense of social structure. "At the same time, in an attempt to encourage the depiction of strong female images in novels that will somehow construct female readers as similarly strong agents, feminist criticism has paradoxically overlooked the agency of adolescent female readers" (92). The writers in this study, on the other hand, show girls struggling with the social and historical forces of sexism and racism, as well as with difficulties faced by children abandoned — or abused —

by their parents, suffering from mental illness, and burdened by poverty. In each of these novels, the reader is made aware of the impact of social institutions on these girls' lives.

Since many writers both *about* female adolescents and *for* adolescent girls seem to be doing their job — creating strong girls and providing opportunities for their readers to reassess and reconstruct their gender identifies — what remains is for critics systematically to recognize these changes and respond to them in new ways. Carolyn Heilbrun, novelist and literary critic, provides inspiration for this kind of critic. "We live our lives through texts," she says. Until now, there has been "no script to follow, no story portraying how one is to act, let alone any alternative stories" (39). Contemporary critics, teachers, and parents have an obligation to discover and discuss the texts that provide such scripts for the girls — and boys — in their care. Criticism of these works needs to take into account differences in gender, region, social class, and race, and perhaps most importantly, attitude, when discussing the young women and men portrayed in contemporary fiction and autobiography.

The works in this study (and I hope my readings of them) provide these "alternative stories" — each young female protagonist accepts new roles expected of her as she grows to maturity, not with a sense of loss, but with a confidence in her ability to determine her own destiny. Smith's many girls, Tyler's Jennie, Humphreys' Lucille, Mason's Sam, Allison's Bone, Gibbons' Ellen, Ansa's Lena, Ray's Janisse, and McCorkle's Jo and Kate, as well as the heroines of the young adult novels discussed here, struggle with abusive, absent and mystifying mothers (and sometimes fathers), with boyfriends and lovers, with school and with work, but they emerge with a sense of making their own luck, determining their own destinies. These texts reflect what recent social scientists and literary critics are slowly coming to recognize about the lives and attitudes of adolescent girls in the very last part of the 20th century: they take on the challenges of their lives with chutzpah and skill. They also will provide "the script to follow," for girls — and critics — in the 21st.

A Note on Southern Precursors

It cannot be ignored that the writers in this study all come from the South — those states below the Mason-Dixon line that share (at least in theory) a sense of regional identity. Therefore, it seems negligent to completely ignore the ways in which these writers extend the literary tradition of *Southern* coming-of-age stories. Therefore, the last section of this introduction will briefly trace the ways in which these authors benefit from and move beyond earlier writers from their region.

Following in the paths laid by Ellen Glasgow, Carson McCullers, Eudora Welty, Harper Lee and Elizabeth Spencer (among others), the writers in this study enrich the landscape left by their Southern precursors. While their characters frequently *resemble* the stalwart Dorinda Oakely, adventurous Mick Kelley, and tomboyish "Scout" Finch, these new young women enhance the fictional portrait of Southern womanhood with their intrepid confidence and faith in the future. These contemporary heroines are not dogged by their pasts, troubled by traditional gender roles, or even, for very long, undermined by the catastrophes that befall them. They are complex, optimistic and capable, tackling the difficult task of growing up without becoming either victims or cynics, using their adolescence as a time to make mistakes, to learn, and to grow strong. These women represent part of a new wave of Southern female writers who, while building on an existing tradition of self-determined heroines, are striving to portray contemporary young Southern women as confident, resilient, and independent.

Clearly, though, contemporary Southern female writers have benefited from Southern literary history. From Glasgow's 1932 novel *Barren Ground* to Elizabeth Spencer's Marilee Summerall stories in the 1960s and 70s, Southern woman writers have been exploring the paradoxes and prisons of gender. Yet while they have created strong, determined, iconoclastic heroines, these earlier writers seem unable to fully separate their characters from the expectations of their societies, or from their destinies as Southern women. Many of the young female characters of the past find themselves feeling lost, hopeless, or at best aimless at the end of their novels, as they fail to fulfill the wishes of their parents, the expectations of their communities, and the demands of their traditions. They start out brave and brash — and end up being isolated by their community, guilty for their "transgressions," or stoic in the face of their losses.

For example, Dorinda Oakely in *Barren Ground* gives the impression early in the novel of "arrested flight, as if she were running toward life" (3). Life, unfortunately, beats her down, leaving her in the middle of the novel thinking that "in the security of her disenchantment there was the quiet that follows a storm" (321). The novel ends with her believing that "While the soil endured, while the season bloomed and dropped, while the ancient, beneficent ritual of sowing and reaping moved in the field, she knew that she could never despair of contentment" (525). Dorinda has moved from a young woman "running toward life" to someone who has settled for "contentment" in the passage of the seasons. In another Glasgow novel, *The Sheltered Life* (1933), Jenny Blair Archbald is introduced to the reader as someone who thinks the characters in *Little Women* are "just poky old things" and who exults in her difference from other girls, but her passionate abandon ends disastrously with the murder of her married lover (3). Both characters must accept the limitations of their lives as Southern women: Dorinda gets the farm but loses what she discovers (too late) is the real love of her life, and Jenny learns that indulging her physical passions leads to death.[10]

Mick Kelley, featured in Carson McCullers' *The Heart Is a Lonely Hunter* (1940), makes plans for "when she is seventeen years old and very famous," but she winds up at 15 working in the Woolworth's and feeling "like she was cheated" (269). Although McCullers' other adolescent protagonist, Frankie Addams in *The Member of the Wedding* (1946), feels an "instant shock of happiness" at the end of the novel, she moves through her story with a sense of fear that gradually metamorphoses into terror. Virgie Rainey in Eudora Welty's *The Golden Apples* (1947) is, as a young adolescent, "full of the airs of wildness," but she seems to accept her life in Morgana by the end of the story cycle (43). Clearly, in McCullers and Welty, the young women start out brave and unconventional and end up feeling cheated, afraid, or resigned.[11]

Although the "starched walls of a pink cotton penitentiary" appear to be closing in on Harper Lee's Scout in *To Kill a Mockingbird* (1960), it looks like she might escape from it in the world of men, which she clearly prefers (136). Nevertheless, Scout finds herself drawn into the ladies' realm, and finally, trapped inside a ham, she is unable to protect herself without the strength of her brother and the determination of Boo Radley. The most contemporary of these earlier Southern women writers, Elizabeth Spencer, creates an engaging and independent character in Marilee Summerall, although Marilee never leaves her home town, feeling the need "of a land, of a sure terrain, of a sort of permanent landscape of the heart" ("A Southern Landscape" 52). As a grown woman, she is overlooked in family discussions because "a girl in business, their assumptions went, was somebody that had no right to be and did not count in thinking or in conversation" ("Indian Summer" 390). Although Marilee is sardonically funny and often wise, she seems to have little control over her family or her fate. Lee and Spencer's slightly more contemporary adolescents *do* have more confidence and success than the young women in McCullers, Welty and Glasgow, but in the end they find themselves protected (and controlled) by the men in their lives.[12]

This brief glance at these novels of the first half of the 20th century makes it clear that characters of the writers discussed in this book have been anticipated by the determination of Dorinda Oakely, the spunk of Mick Kelley and Frankie Addams, the defiance of convention of Virgie Rainey and Scout, and the good humor of Marilee Summerall. These contemporary writers have gone a step or two further, though, allowing their Southern girls to escape from places like Morgana, Queensboro, Port Clairborne, Maycomb, and all the other small towns "in the middle of the deep South" (McCullers 5). More importantly, they have also allowed them out from under the expectations that they remain dutiful daughters, respected citizens, and, most of all, good girls.

Learning from the past but looking toward the future, these contemporary Southern writers are forging a new view of Southern womanhood, which, as novelist and critic Doris Betts says, is "heard-earned, increasingly unsentimental, and rendered via Dickinson's concrete particulars" (8). Or, as Lucinda MacKethan puts it, these writers and characters "seek an integration of mind and place that both celebrates and transcends gender" (11). These young women of the South, and the women who created and recorded them, indeed offer a new way, one that both "celebrates and transcends."

TWO

"Becoming: Maybe So": Breakdowns, Setbacks, and Triumphs in Lee Smith's Novels

> The steps were solid under me and it was all right [Lee Smith, *The Last Day the Dogbushes Bloomed*, 180].

> [I]f you're entirely a passive person, you're going to get in big trouble [Lee Smith, "An Interview with Lee Smith," Edwin T. Arnold, 4].

> I know myself as the girl I was, who used to love stories so much [Lee Smith, *Saving Grace*, 272].

Terrible things happen to the girls in Lee Smith's novels: they are raped, seduced by family members, manipulated and hectored by religious fanatics; they live in desperate poverty, endure the death and suicide of parents and lovers, and lose track (sometimes permanently) of who they are and what they want in life. Still, most of them manage to find ways — practical, spiritual, sexual, or psychological — out of the traps they have been cast (or cast *themselves*) into. More often than not in Smith's works, these girls mature into self-reliant women who manage, in spite of the odds, to find both peace and joy in their lives. That they do this within the confines of a resolutely patriarchal Appalachian culture is even more amazing.

For more than 30 years, Virginia native Lee Smith has been chron-
icling the often rocky development of Southern girls into women, from
The Last Day the Dogbushes Bloomed (1968), the story of nine-year-old
Susan Tobey's cataclysmic summer, to Brooke Kincaid's confused development in *Something in the Wind* (1971), to the horrific tale of Crystal
Spangler in *Black Mountain Breakdown* (1980), to Ivy Rowe's epistolary
narrative of self-discovery in *Fair and Tender Ladies* (1988), and finally to
Florida Grace Shepherd's journey of religious awakening in *Saving Grace*
(1995). In these novels Smith shows the ways in which young women are
oppressed by gender expectations as well as their own passivity, how they
escape their individual dilemmas, and, most importantly, how they re-write
the script of young womanhood in Smith's particular part of the South.

Because of the length of her career and the number of her books
featuring adolescent protagonists/narrators, Lee Smith is the perfect writer
to begin this study. Smith also has strong affinities with many of the
women to be discussed in future chapters, having been influenced by and
a model for many of them. Jill McCorkle, for example, was a student in
the first creative writing course Lee Smith taught at North Carolina
State, and Smith shares with her pupil a concern for the disastrous effects
of passivity on young girls (McCord 166). Smith's Crystal can be seen
as a precursor to McCorkle's Jo in *The Cheer Leader*, and her treatment
of sexuality, both violent and transformative, also clearly resembles
McCorkle's. An avowed admirer of Anne Tyler, Smith shares with her a
love of society's outcasts, as well as a fascination for the ordinary aspects
of life (Arnold 16). With their often cheerful determination to keep going
in spite of serious obstacles, Smith's female characters resemble Tyler's
Evie in *A Slipping-Down Life*, Elizabeth in *The Clock Winder*, and Jenny
in *Dinner at the Homesick Restaurant*.

Tina Ansa and Smith are both interested in the intersections between
the supernatural and the natural world and the impact — both positive
and negative — of spiritual life on the psychology of young women. She
treats the same Appalachian region as Bobbie Ann Mason and admires
the spare quality of her style, and Smith shares with Mason and Josephine
Humphreys an attention to the loss of a distinctive culture in the South
(Arnold 14). Like Janisse Ray, Smith recognizes the importance of the
natural world for the human one and regrets the losses to culture and
identity caused by the destruction of the Southern landscape in the name
of progress. The violence done to Smith's girls is reflected in the work of

Dorothy Allison, and her identification with those people, who, for economic reasons, are disenfranchised from mainstream society, is a link between her and both Alison and Kaye Gibbons. As these examples show, then, Smith represents a shaping voice in the literature of the New South, and her treatment of young women's development has been a model for many writers who have followed her.[1]

Smith is also a good starting point for a discussion of the complexities inherent in trying to define Southern fiction in the latter-half of the twentieth century. First of all, as a writer from the Appalachian mountain town of Grundy, Virginia, Smith is clearly writing from a subset of the area and concentrating on issues particular to that region: geographic isolation, mountain folk traditions, and a lack of racial or social diversity. In fact, Smith tells interviewer Daniel Bourne that she writes with a sort of "insular vision" that is the result of growing up in the Appalachian mountains (15). Her Southernness, then, is complicated by the particularities of her regional identity, as is the case with all of the writers in this study.

However, Smith is linked to other Southern writers by a strong sense of the *loss* of specific Southern identities following the introduction of modern technology. On the other hand, Smith admits that the changing of region can't be stopped, in part because "it's all equated with progress in this funny and terrible sort of way" (Arnold 9). She also recognizes that whenever any writer goes back to the past, "all you ever get is your interpretation of it" (Arnold 5). Finally, Smith says that contemporary Southern writers can't copy earlier literary traditions "if we are to register the world accurately, if we are to find new images for what already exists." The best writers can do, she says, "is try to find some common ground between the past and present, and proceed from there" ("Driving" 123). Regional identities, then, are always inflected by individual identities, and complicated by personal world views, and Smith feels it is her job — and the job other Southern writers — to reflect those differences and complications.[2]

Literary critics have long recognized the ways in which Smith has sought regional common ground and moved forward. For example, Paula Gallant says that Smith's main concern is not with "preserving the past, but with examining, deconstructing, and ultimately redefining the past" (121). Smith treats Southern tradition as merely a starting point in reconstructing a vision of (usually female) identity. In her extended treatment of Cherokee elements in Smith's novels, Katerina Prajznerova comments on the relationship between the Southern landscape and identity. Prajznerova says that "changes in the natural environment go hand in hand with the changes in the local culture." Thus, she says, Smith's novels "represent an ecological history of the region" (20). This "ecological history" has much to say about economics, identity, and gender. Smith's novels, she says, suggest that "human life and history are cyclic, organically connected to seasonal cycles and the rest of the universe" (99). In an interview with Prajznerova, Smith agrees that much of the rural culture of the South was once "tied to the seasons, and what you were planting when, and then the various rituals that would celebrate planting." When these rituals disappear, she says, much is lost from the culture, especially for women (103).[3]

As well as rewriting the narrative of Southern life, Smith has also been engaged in revising the traditional gender script for young women. Smith tells Dorothy Combs Hill that she is interested in "the difference between image and reality and the faces [especially women] present to the world" (28). According to Rebecca Smith, Smith's characters "search for identity against a backdrop of the myth of Southern womanhood" (8). Smith's work, she says, "reflects and subverts her society's belief systems about gender" (7). This is the key: Smith is able, through her young female characters, to both reveal and challenge gender stereotypes, especially as her work progresses over time. Nancy Parrish puts it well: Smith's early novels, she says, "describe girls and young women who have been literally or figuratively silenced, limited or raped. Her later novels, by contrast, reveal women who resist cultural restraints, find their own voices, and succeed at unique life goals that oppose conventional expectations" (576–77). Throughout her corpus, then, Smith is trying to figure out how to give voice to her silenced and abused young women, a goal that will take her decades to accomplish.[4]

The Last Day the Dogbushes Bloomed

Smith's first novel, *The Last Day the Dogbushes Bloomed*, tells the story of Susan Tobey, a nine-year-old girl posed at the threshold of what will turn out to be a harrowing summer. *The Last Day the Dogbushes Bloomed* is the first of three novels, that, as Lucinda MacKethan says, "chart the rites of passage of girl protagonists entering the world of womanhood and its consequences, from dawning sexuality, to commitments, to desertions, even to death" (4). Even though this work is less polished and complex in its narrative structure than Smith's later novels, many of Smith's familiar elements are already present: gender/identity formation, dysfunctional family structures, the importance of both the natural and supernatural worlds, and the very real threats — physical and psychological — to young girls in rural Southern society. Smith calls it "a quiet, tasteful little novel" (Walsh 29), but Nancy Parrish's study of the changes Smith made between the short story and the novel versions of Susan's story show that Smith "developed a broader and more complex vision of the ways in which innocence is taken away from young girls" as she revised and lengthened the work (195).

Because of the first-person narrative, Susan is unable to see what the reader, with increasing distress, comes to recognize: that her father is cowed by her mother's imperious manner, that her mother is unfaithful to her father, that her parents' expectations for how Susan will grow into womanhood are increasingly at odds with Susan's desires and experiences, and that the world is a very frightening place. The narrative structure insists that readers "are meant to be held exclusively in the mind of a child in order to respond as she must, [while] observing her limitations" (MacKeathen 10). For example, Susan calls her mother "The Queen" and says she is "everything she should be" (5), but, in fact, Susan is so alienated from her mother that when people refer to "The Queen" as her mother, Susan has difficulty figuring out what they mean (40). Her use of the title "The Queen," Rebecca Smith says, is "a linguistic signifier of Susan's anxiety about the mother-daughter relationship and about her own identity as a female" (15). This is probably true, but it is equally likely that calling her mother "The Queen" also offers Susan some necessary distance from her mother as she chooses her own path toward adulthood. Such positive distancing will be seen in nearly all the mother/daughter relationships discussed in this book.

Re-naming her mother is just one of Susan's many namings in the novel. Her mother's lover is the "Baron," her sister is the "Princess," and her best hiding place is the "dogbushes." In general, naming things is Susan's way of both covering and uncovering her world. Harriette Buchanan says that Susan is a "self-centered child who in the course of the story is forced to the realization that the world is not as she imagines it" (326). However, she is also a child in the process of coming to understand her world and take part in recreating it. As Anne Goodwyn Jones says, Susan's namings "explain her experience ... protect her from painful knowledge ... and allow the magical numinous into her world" (122). In her namings, her re-appropriation of identities and meanings, Susan protects and enhances herself and her surroundings.

Such revisions are necessary, as Susan's proper Southern society doesn't offer her many options other than obedient Daddy's girl and/or male-dependent woman. After watching her older sister and her mother, Susan decides that she doesn't really want to grow up, that she can't think of anything worse than "to have big blobby things flopping around all the time in front of your chest and to kiss boys" (41). Instead of longing for a fully-developed female body, Susan takes pride in being "Susan with all the muscles in my legs and arms" (41–2). Seeing clearly the consequences of female sexuality, Susan decides that she wants to remain boyish. From her first novel, then, Smith explores the conflict between what girls *want* to be (strong and independent) and what society will *allow* them to be (queenly and remote or sexually available and vulnerable).

Not surprisingly, then, the major conflict in the novel will center around sexuality. Early in this ill-fated summer, Susan meets Eugene, a strange child with "flat white" eyes that have "secrets" behind them (20). Susan grows increasingly afraid of Eugene, who has a sinister imaginary friend called Little Arthur, throws rocks at mice, kills a kitten, and encourages the local children to engage in games that become more and more sexualized and dangerous as the summer wears on. One day, Eugene brings an "art book" to the kids' club house and forces them to hit the body parts of the naked people in the pictures. Realizing that the price of "beauty" (or sexuality) is violence, Susan decides that she "didn't even want to get beauty if I would get punched" (95). She wants out of the club, but she knows that "you have to finish a summer the way it starts," and as she says this, the reader recognizes that a final encounter with Eugene is inevitable (105).

At Eugene's insistence, the children play "Iron Lung," which culminates in Eugene raping Susan with the other children watching. As the rape concludes, Susan feels that "the dirt was coming up from all round to cover me, cool and friendly, coming up to cover me because I was dying" (163). The dirt floor, detached tone, sense of inevitably, and refusal (or inability) to acknowledge, or perhaps even recognize, what has happened will reappear in the rape of Crystal Spangler in *Black Mountain Break-*

down. The adults intervene, but as Rebecca Smith says, "Susan is forced to tolerate silently society's acceptance of her rape, and so she succumbs to a final linguistic repression" (19). Because she has no words for what has happened to her, Susan is unable to make either moral or psychological sense of it. Still, although Susan doesn't yet have to vocabulary to process the experience as either bad or good, her reference to the dirt shows that at an emotional level she is aware that some sort of death has occurred.

The rape, fortunately, is not the end of Susan's story. Shortly after the assault, Susan's mother leaves the family for her lover, and Susan gets a mysterious communication from God, as will Crystal and several of Smith's later female characters. In this early novel, though, God doesn't really offer much in the way of spiritual guidance or practical help. At the end of the story, Susan has another sort of epiphany that will prove to be much more useful — she recognizes her connection to the natural world. Sitting outside her house, Susan feels an intimate spiritual connection to the things around her, believing that "Everything talked to me, it was all the same, they wrapped me up in their green talking like a Christmas present. I could pray to anything" (180). Susan realizes that she doesn't have to talk only to God, who is notorious for his silences; she can pray to the world. She also knows that while Little Arthur will always be with her, as a reminder of her rape and her helplessness, "it didn't scare me" (180).

Acknowledging both the inherent beauty and immanent danger in the world, Susan decides that "the steps were solid under me and it was all right," and she goes upstairs to "put on my new yellow dress and my new red shoes without straps" for a dinner date with her father (180). Susan may not have reached an adult understanding of the world or the violence in it, but she is ready to go out and face it, unafraid, in her new shoes and dress. She is still Daddy's little girl and conforming to gender stereotypes, but she has learned some important lessons during the summer that may help her grow into a woman very different from her sister and her mother.[5]

Something in the Wind

Smith's second novel, *Something in the Wind,* features an older adolescent main character, 17-year-old Brooke Kincaid. Although Smith told interviewer Charlene McCord that she hasn't re-read the novel "because it's so *awful*" (169), she also says that Brooke's "spirit, in a way, was like mine" (169). Indeed, the first-person narrative, combined with Brooke's references to herself in the third person, creates both intimacy and distance. Readers see Brooke's confusion and frustration, as they recognize her increasing alienation from herself. Brooke shares with Susan an inability to understand what is going on around her, and she also seems unable to act with the apparent confidence of her family and friends. At the start of the novel, Brooke is returning home for the funeral of a childhood friend, Charles. Brooke says Charles "made her mind," and indeed it seems that Brooke is cast adrift without him, unable to decide who she is or what she will be (5).

Brooke's solution, unfortunately, is to slavishly copy those around her, to develop a "life plan" based on the behaviors of others (24). "All of them, every one of my classmates," she says, "knew the secret [of how to cope with death, among other things] and I had no idea what it was, no clue" (21). By imitating those around her, Brooke thinks, she will come to know what they know. "The only thing I knew about the life plan at first was that it was to be concerned with this secret that everybody else seemed to know," Brooke says (24). The result is, not surprisingly, that she "split [her] mind into two equal halves" (31). "I was real," she says, "and the other half was only apparent" (31). In her dissociation, her uncertainty about her "real" female self, Brooke resembles Tyler's Evie and Ansa's Lena, as well as the troubled heroine of McCorkle's *The Cheer Leader.*

Lena, however, can turn to her mother (or other mother surrogates) for validation and guidance, while Brooke's mother, Carolyn (like Susan's mother), is at best a problematic role model. As the "Amazing Perpetual Hostess of the World," Brooke's mother enjoys crises and crowds, neither of which Brooke likes. Still, like Susan, Brooke is drawn to her mother: "There was nobody, in spite of everything," Brooke says, "that I liked better than Carolyn" (6). Nevertheless, Carolyn only offers Brooke the rather limited role of charmingly scatterbrained Southern Hostess, and she is no help in finding the answers to the questions that plague her daughter.

In her search for a stable and satisfying female identity, Brooke first copies her sorority roommate Diana, but she finds it impossible to keep up her meticulous appearances, especially since unlike Diana, Brooke doesn't think virginity is "all that important." (81). Also unlike a good sorority girl, Brooke freaks out her fraternity boyfriend Houston with her sexual aggressiveness. Her next model is her new roommate Elizabeth, whose multiform personality, paradoxically, makes her easier to imitate. The result of this imitation is that Brooke feels she is "well adjusted." because "with Elizabeth any variation was fine" (127). Of course, Brooke is merely copying Elizabeth's variations, not creating her own coherent personality.

While imitating Elizabeth, Brooke also starts sleeping around, becoming, as she says, "a professional virgin," who tells each boy she sleeps with that he is the first and who has no regrets about her sexuality (127). Nancy Parrish says that Brooke challenges the "social definition of what a Southern lady should be," and that when Brooke cavalierly loses her virginity (over and over again!), she also loses "her belief in the clichés that have guided her life to that point" (577).

This is of course good and bad. As Lee Smith says, "Breaking the shackles is great ... but the price of autonomy often is a certain kind of isolation" (Loewenstein). Having gotten good at imitation, Brooke comments that her mind is now "white and blank." "I had gotten so good with the life plan," she says, "that a lot of what I said was always reflex" (138). The end result is that Brooke views her life as if it were a movie: "I leaned back in the car seat and enjoyed it all" (142). In her amused detachment from her life, Brooke most clearly resembles McCorkle's Jo and Tyler's Jenny.

This detachment, of course, can't — and shouldn't — last. Brooke's new boyfriend Bentley distracts her briefly, but then strange things begin to happen (probably caused by Bentley's jealous previous lover), and neither of them is willing to make a final commitment to one another. "I could feel something changing," Brooke says, "but I wasn't sure what the change was or what form it would take" (192). Brooke comes to feel that her life is being eaten up, filled with holes, and that it is at the same time strangling her. Most importantly, she wants to discover her real self, but she still doesn't quite know how to do it.

Such confusion could result in disaster, but, surprisingly, it doesn't. Brooke goes home for her brother Carter's wedding and gets involved with an old love and neighbor John Howard, but she decides at the end not to marry him. She realizes she could "step into my place" as proper Southern wife and mother, but she chooses not to. "I had come full circle myself," she says, "and now there were new directions" (243). With the resilience heretofore reserved for male adolescents, Brooke emerges from her college years not exactly with a fully-developed personality, but at least she has started down a path toward an individual identity not dependent on imitation of others or on traditional values. As Rebecca Smith says, Brooke "at least begins to question the language and the patriarchal ideologies enclosing her" (21).[6] As with *The Last Day the Dogbushes Bloomed*, the ending of *Something in the Wind*, while not entirely positive, at least shows the possibility of a self-directed future for the main character.

Black Mountain Breakdown

The next of Smith's young women is by far her saddest: Crystal Spangler of *Black Mountain Breakdown* loses her beloved father, withdraws from her practical, stoical mother and her brothers, is raped by her uncle, leaves town with an insane boyfriend who eventually commits suicide, returns home and is briefly satisfied teaching high-school English, marries an old boyfriend, has a breakdown, and finally ends up comatose in her childhood bedroom. From this brief synopsis, it is difficult to see how Crystal's experience, described by Parks Lanier as "a long journey to breakdown," resembles in any way the qualified hopefulness of Susan and Brooke's stories (58).

Still, Crystal's life can be seen as a morality tale of what happens when a young woman can't — or won't — take charge of her life and find ways to accept (or laugh at) those things she cannot control. Lee Smith says that Southern women in particular "are raised to make themselves fit the image that other people set out of for them," and that Crystal's tragedy is that "she wasn't able to get her own self-definition" (Arnold 4). As Nancy Parrish puts it, Crystal is "a woman so completely defined by social roles and male expectations that she literally paralyzes herself" (577). Readers watch Crystal's unhappiness and passivity with mounting anxiety and growing understanding. The narrative style contributes to this response: the third-person narrative, combined with present verb tense, as Lucinda MacKethan points out, "achieves a tension between closeness and distance crucial to both mystery and meaning in the novel" (11). Thus, readers are both frustrated with and sympathetic toward Crystal's responses to the various trials and tribulations in her life.

From the beginning of the novel, Crystal has problems. Her father, an alcoholic slowly dying of drink and emphysema, lives in the now-disheveled front room, while her mother Lorene has taken over the kitchen and refuses to interact with her husband. Crystal wishes she lived in one of her neighbor's houses, where life was familiar, rather than in her home, which one critic calls "a paradigm for dissociate sensibility" (Hill 41). Crystal adores her father, with his poetry reading and his tragic demeanor, but, unfortunately, he also provides her with a powerful example of passivity in the face of life's challenges. Although her father represents Crystal's link to literature, the past, and "another sensual human being" (Byrd 209), Smith also exposes in the novel "the exhortative nature of the father's voice and his story as violent and destructive to the daughter" (427). Crystal's father seduces her into inaction just as he numbs himself with alcohol, poetry, and isolation.

The fault is not entirely her father's, however. Crystal seems almost pathologically too fragile to survive the slings and arrows of outrageous fortune. As her practical best friend Agnes comments, "Crystal seems to lack something hard inside her that Agnes and Babe [Agnes's sister] were born with" (16). Agnes will grow up to become a successful business woman, and even as a child, Babe says she will never let a man control her (60). Crystal, on the other hand, has no idea what her future will be, and she likes school not for the intellectual challenge (although she is an outstanding student) but primarily because it is "something regular, a schedule to hold on to" (62). She also has trouble deciding what kind of romantic life she will have — safe and boring Roger Lee Combs or dangerous and thrilling bad boy Mack Stiltner.

While she is still in high school, Crystal's mentally disabled Uncle Devere rapes her in his toolshed, forgetting what he has done immediately afterward and leaving her on the "damp dirt floor" (70). Her father dies the same night, and Crystal (like Susan) doesn't talk about the rape with anyone. At her father's death, "the whole world falls away from her by degrees until nothing at all is left" (72), and in her grief she buries the memory (and the psychological effects) of the rape. In spite of her repression, or perhaps because of it, this cataclysmic event will return to haunt Crystal in later life.

After her father dies, Crystal dumps safe Roger Lee and takes up with Mack. "With Mack she feels like she can be herself," Crystal thinks, "Whatever that means!" (97). Even though he is not of her social class,

Mack gives her a sense of freedom and choice that may or may not be real, and their sexual relationship gives her life at least a temporary intensity. At around this point, Crystal also takes part in a beauty contest, but, not surprisingly, it does little for her self image. Preparing for the contest, Crystal thinks that "she doesn't look like herself in the mirror," and afterward she comments that the picture on her driver's license "doesn't even look like anybody's she's ever seen before" (117). Neither sexual passion nor social triumph helps Crystal to overcome permanently the profound dissociation between her internal self and outward appearance.

Desperately trying to feel *something*, Crystal attends a religious revival and is "saved," which makes her feel "like she felt when she was with Mack — alive, fully alive and fully real, more than real" (123). In spite of this, Crystal doesn't "feel real when she's by herself," and she becomes promiscuous, in part because the boys she sleeps with make her feel "pretty, or popular, or fun" (136). She begins to see herself in the desire she generates in the boys: "In the way they talk to her and act around her, Crystal can see what they think of her, and then that's the way she is" (136). Like Brooke, Crystal becomes what others want to see in her; she is the projection of their fantasies or expectations.

Like Susan, too, Crystal also thinks she might be called by God, this time at a Girls' State meeting, but once again it doesn't really come to anything, and shortly after Crystal leaves home — and the narrative. Agnes takes over the story, and her practical good sense and stoic wisdom relieves the reader of a pervasive sense of doom. Agnes thinks a lot about Crystal and her weaknesses, commenting that people need to "salvage what you can and keep ahold of what you've got, and not be looking off in the clouds someplace" (148). Her levelheadedness provides a much-needed antidote to Crystal's gloomy passivity.

Almost as if she has heard Agnes' advice, Crystal returns home and soon engages in meaningful work for the first time in her life — teaching English. She has her students keep journals, and when one of them writes that she is "becoming," Crystal thinks it is an apt description for herself: "Becoming: maybe so," she muses (182). The uncertain process of "becoming" is what all Smith's girls and young women are engaged in: trying to become something other than what their parents and communities expect of them, trying to find out what it might mean to be a woman who is not dependent on men, trying to live a life that is both sexual and safe.

With her new career, Crystal appears close to finding that unified identity. Unfortunately, however, Roger Lee Combs, now married, re-enters her life, insisting that they must get back together. Crystal eventually gives in to him, although "some part of her is screaming, or almost screaming," and she quits her teaching job to follow him (200). John Kalb says that Roger Lee's relentless pursuit of Crystal constitutes "a much more violently debilitating attack than the rape at the hands of the slow-witted Devere" (27–8), which may be true. Certainly, Roger's reappearance, and his aggressive pursuit of her, derail's Crystal's single attempt at independence, at "becoming." They eventually marry, but a traumatic encounter at a psychiatric facility reminds Crystal of her rape, and things start to fall apart.

The rape, it appears, has been waiting to claim Crystal all along. "Ever since the beginning [of her new relationship with Roger Lee]," Crystal thinks, "she has been conscious of the end" (210). This is the end not only of her relationship but also of Crystal's ability to control *any* aspect of her life, including, finally, speaking and even moving. Strangely enough, however, complete passivity is what "Crystal always wanted," Lee Smith says, so her end is, in fact, a "culmination" (100). In her refusal to take control of her life, Crystal has been heading for just such a breakdown. However, it is also possible to see Crystal's catatonia as a choice, an alternative to a life with Roger Lee telling her what to do, what she wants, and what she should be. In her complete passivity, Crystal has refused to accept a life on someone else's terms.[7]

With Crystal silent, Agnes gets the last word, and she provides a more positive ending, both for Crystal and herself. Reflecting that no one knows what the future will bring, Agnes says that "Crystal might jump right up from that bed tomorrow and go off and get her Ph.D. or do something else crazy" (227–28). Agnes recognizes that Crystal's state may be chosen and temporary, merely one of the many "crazy" things she has done in the past. Even if she doesn't "jump right up from that bed," Crystal may be content where she is. In the final sentence of the novel, Agnes says that "Crystal is happy, that she likes to have Agnes hold her hand and brush her hair, as outside her window the seasons come and go and colors change on the mountain" (228). Crystal may, after all, be living in an ideal world: no unwanted responsibilities or difficult choices, someone to "hold her hand and brush her hair," and a view of the mountains — a life that the hard-working and self-sacrificing Agnes even may envy. However, Lee Smith has said that Agnes is her "favorite character" (Arnold 3), and her hard-headed optimism provides a necessary counter to Crystal's passivity, while at the same time showing that even a life of action has its limitations.[8]

Although critics correctly point out that Susan, Brooke, and Crystal "are alike in that they are not so much actors as they are choosers, called upon to balance opposing demands, conflicting needs" (MacKethan 4), they also need to be seen as crucial stepping stones to the sorts of girls and young women Smith will develop in later novels. Smith archly points out to interviewer William Walsh that a "breakdown" in banjo playing is "the same refrain played over and over again, but it's augmented each time" (32). In some very important ways, then, Crystal's story is merely one breakdown, one kind of life choice that will be augmented again and again throughout Smith's novels. Writing Crystal's life thus becomes one means through which Smith will be able to create strong and self-determined characters like Ivy Rowe and Grace Shepherd.[9]

Fair and Tender Ladies

Fair and Tender Ladies is Lee Smith's seventh novel and her most critically acclaimed. Told entirely in the letters of Ivy Rowe to her family and friends (living and dead), the novel chronicles her life from 14 to her deathbed. Through telling her story, her triumphs and tragedies, Ivy writes herself into being as a strong and independent woman. Rebecca Smith says that Ivy "creates her own sense of self by filling the blank page, literally" (105). Most of the novel concerns Ivy's adult years and therefore is not directly related to the focus of this study, but of particular interest here is Ivy's attitude about her sexuality, which is consistent with those of Brooke and Crystal. These young women believe that while patriarchal society will try — through coercion and violence — to limit or control their sexuality, they must nevertheless step outside the language (and thereby the perceptions) of such limitations.

For example, Ivy sleeps with Lonnie Rash, becomes pregnant, and Lonnie, whom she doesn't love, dies in the war before they can marry. Since she is pregnant and unmarried, Ivy is officially "ruint," as she says, but, surprisingly, she says she is glad of it: "If you are ruint, like I am," she says, "it frees you up somehow" (167). Because her illegitimate pregnancy has placed her outside the mainstream, Ivy is able to act—and think—in ways not available to more conventional woman. Rebecca Smith says that "ruint" is "a position fixed by the ideology of femininity," and that Ivy "questions this ideology so explicitly and honestly that she unravels the word from its dominant meaning" (109). Like Susan, Ivy decides to appropriate words and meanings for her own purposes.

This attitude that one is not limited by social sanctions propels Ivy out a life of "disgrace" into the arms of rich wastrel Franklin Ransom, and eventually into a respectable marriage with Oakley Fox, a childhood friend. Being "ruint" has made it easier for Ivy to makes choices about her sexuality, rather than having them made for her. However, it may also be what leads her to Honey Breeding, a bee keeper with whom she has an affair. Although the affair nearly destroys her marriage and coincides with (as perhaps some kind of divine punishment) the death of her daughter, Ivy learns and grows from the experience. For example, Ivy and Honey hike to the top of Blue Star Mountain, and there she realizes that she could have climbed that mountain by herself, that she didn't need a man to take her there (233). The affair also jolts her out of depression and stagnation in her marriage. With Honey Breeding, Dorothy Combs Hill says, "we have come as far from the rape of Susan and Crystal as possible" (111) . Rather than being forced into violent and dissociative sex, Ivy has used sex successfully for transformation, just as many of the young women will in later chapters of this book.

Eventually Ivy comes home to her husband, but she still wishes she could "ride hell for leather down the high road of life" (245). Later, she counsels her daughter not to be too quick to marry, although she should "love him all you want" in the interim (253). Most importantly, she tells her daughter not to forget. "A person can not afford to forget who they are or where they came from, or so I think," Ivy says, "even when the remembering brings pain" (265). Toward the end of the novel, Ivy's husband dies. Although she mourns his loss, Ivy thinks at his death that "I can make up my own life now whichever way I want to, it is like I am a girl again, for I am not beholden to a soul" (277). In her attitude about sex and her desire to remember even the difficult moments, Ivy resembles Lucille in *Rich in Love* and Sam in *In Country*. Through her sexuality and her letters, Ivy has acted and written herself into independence, and she has provided a model for transformative sexuality that many Southern young women characters will follow.[10]

Saving Grace

Perhaps the most provocative of Lee Smith's novels featuring a young woman is *Saving Grace*, which tells the story of Florida Grace Shepherd, a "Holiness" girl raised by a saintly (but cowed) mother and a snake-handling preacher father who is drawn to demonstrations of faith *and* the attractions of sin. The book begins in 1949, when, after an early childhood on the road, Grace and her family settle in Scrabble Creek, North Carolina, and make a life for themselves, and her father slips further and further into charismatic religion and self destruction.

Grace's life is dramatic: she is seduced by her half brother, her mother commits suicide, she goes on the road with her father (who finally backslides once again and leaves her), marries a much-older and far-too-serious minister, has two daughters and loses one son, cheats on her depressed husband with a house painter, leaves her family for a life of self gratification, and finally returns briefly to Scrabble Creek, where she has a religious awakening. Throughout the novel, Grace's refrain is "My name is Florida Grace Shepherd, Florida for the state I was born in, Grace for the grace of God," and throughout her life Grace explores the importance of place and the healing power of grace (3).[11]

Early in the novel, Grace describes herself as "contentious and ornery, full of fear and doubt in a family of believers," and this is characteristic of her attitude throughout her childhood (3). Like many of the girls in this study, Grace wants to be a boy so she doesn't "have to stay home all the time and help Mama" (13). On the other hand, she also craves her mother's love, but hers is a mother who "loved Jesus [but] loved Daddy even more" (24). Her mother loves and cares for them — as well as their very limited income and her husband's religious prohibitions will allow — but she doesn't have a lot of emotional room for her children. Grace, like many other new Southern girls, will have to look elsewhere for her role models.

By seventh grade, Grace's typically adolescent desire to have "normal" friends leads her to keeping secrets, especially from her father. Eventually, Grace is "so full of secrets" that she thinks her "head would burst and they all fly out into the room like hornets from a nest, stinging everybody" (49). One of her biggest secrets is the admiration she feels for her friend Marie Royal's very worldly mother. Sounding very much like Mo Rhodes in McCorkle's *Ferris Beach*, Mrs. Royal has a "pixie haircut," "made-up eyes pointed down at the end," and "pale pink lipstick and tight black pants" (45). Nothing at all like her own dress-wearing, make-up free mother, Mrs. Royal is an artist with paint-stained hands who smokes and drives a car. She also represents a type of woman who is not bound by the dictates of her husband or father. Her attraction to Mrs. Royal makes Grace feel guilty — and thrilled. Even though she is "fairly sure [she] was going to hell" (68) for all her secrets and her disloyalty to her father *and* mother, Grace nevertheless says she would "rather be me than anybody" (58). Keeping secrets helps Grace begin to free herself from the emotional stranglehold her family has on her.

Grace's most important secret is that she is having sex with her half brother, Lamar. Although she says that Lamar can "sniff out like a bird dog" the bad in her (81), Grace still feels that in loving him, her "senses had been turned up — colors were brighter, sounds were louder, and everything seems so important" (77). Sneaking off with Lamar, Grace thinks she is "living in a mystery, which I was about to solve" (77). As with Ivy, sex has given Grace access to a more complex and sensual adult world. The down side to this, however, is she that starts living solely for Lamar, going to school only because he wants her to and abandoning her friends. At this same time, her mother commits suicide over her father's infidelities, but Grace blames herself and her liaison with Lamar. "I felt dirty," she says. "Nasty. I felt like anybody could just look at me ... and see what I had done with Lamar" (115). As with Ivy, sex doesn't come without a price, even though it offers important benefits.

Guilt over her mother's death (and her own sexuality) leads Grace to follow her father on another of his proselytizing journeys, feeling that it was her "due" because of what she had done. When father abandons her, however, Grace decides to move forward, rather than back. "I simply thought that I had come too far along the road that I was on, to turn back now," she says. "I had to keep on going" (15). After the experiences she has had in her young but troubled life, it seems impossible for her to return to an earlier state of innocence. Still, moving forward is *moving*, after all.

Grace is rescued from her father's neglect and taken in by Travis Word, a dour older man who will become her husband. When she arrives at Travis's house, Grace looks in the mirror and sees a girl who "looked healthy and strong," and she winks at her reflection (160). In spite of all she has been through, Grace is still tough and pleased with who she is.

During this time, Grace gets "a reputation for sweetness, well deserved" because for once she is being taken care of, rather than taking care of others (169). Travis turns out to be a loyal, hardworking, and sexually conflicted husband, and while she enjoys her children, Grace is still, as she was as a child, "prone to question and agonize" (202). Grace remains uncertain that there is a purpose to life, even though the thought makes her feel "a great bottomless empty feeling would rush through me, scaring me to death" (202). Although she is afraid, Grace is nevertheless willing to look into the abyss.

Like Ivy, Grace takes up with another man, in part to prevent herself from turning into a ghost-like woman, with "nothing left of her but a little mist" (212). Still, the affair leaves her feeling "like I was being whirled around and carried away by some mysterious current, sucked down down into a deep blue hole of my own making" (222). Given these choices — between disappearing in her own life with Travis and drowning in the "mysterious current" of her sexual and emotional desires — Grace, like most of Smith's women, chooses the current. As always with Smith, movement — climbing up or even being sucked down — is the better choice; her successful female characters are constantly in a state of "becoming."

Her somewhat sordid (albeit necessary) affair is not the end of Grace's story either. Deciding that she is "not real good at modern life," Grace leaves her painter behind and returns to Scrabble Creek (239). On the journey back she feels "suddenly, completely alive in a new way, a way that made me realize I had only been walking through my life" (253). Although she doesn't even seem able to remember why she "left a good man, a man who loved me, for a bad one," Grace can see that Travis's life of endless sacrifice and duty will end in despair (262). Packing up, she thinks that she is "traveling light," and like the female characters in Tyler's novels who are always ready to travel, Grace recognizes that it is important for her to keep moving — even if it means going back to where she started — if she is to move forward in life (270). Until she returns to her childhood home, Grace is stuck in an adolescent mode, reacting to the domineering father, now replaced by her husband. In order to become a fully functional adult, Grace has to put her father — and her mother's self sacrifice — behind her.[12]

Given her family history, Grace finds her transformation through charismatic religion, the source of both her most intense and frightening childhood memories. Back at her family's old cabin, Grace has a religious epiphany, putting her hands in the fire as a test of faith (something her mother used to do) and not being burned, and she feels "a joy which spreads all through my body, all through this sinful old body of mine" (271). She assures her mother that she is happy, and this appears to be true, at last (272). As Grace prepares to go back to her adult life (and children and grandchildren) the novel ends like this:

> [M]y name is Florida Grace, Florida for the state I was born in, grace for the grace of God. Just before I drive around the bend, I stop to look back one more time at the little house by Scrabble Creek and the long white sweep of snowy ground where me and Billie Jean [her sister] made angels in the snow [273].

Once again, Grace "claims her name" (Smith 176) and claims her childhood self, her family, and her religion, but on her own terms. Like Susan, who finds God in the bushes and the steps, Grace is now able to see "angels in the snow" and to get on with her life.

Rebecca Smith says that in *Saving Grace* Smith "create[s] female characters who can move beyond the constraints imposed by a patriarchal society and a patriarchal religion, who can find identity and spiritual fulfillment because God speaks to them in a feminine voice," and this may be where Lee Smith has been leading all along in her novels about young women (11). She has discovered in Grace a way to combine faith and sexuality, family and individual identity. The girls in her earlier novels have been clearing the way for Grace, who survives the restrictions not only of Southern traditions but of fundamentalist religion as well. Truly, Grace's story ends in a moment of grace, and redemption.

From *The Last Day the Dogbushes Bloomed* to *Saving Grace*, Lee Smith explores the ways in which girls grow into young women, how they survive tragic circumstances, and how they succeed (although not always) in constructing or *reconstructing* their lives. Most of her young women find ways to rise above or work around the restrictions their rural, Southern societies create for them, and through claiming their own names and namings they redefine what it means to be female and Southern. Susan, Brooke, Crystal, Ivy, and Grace, as well as many of the other minor women characters, both young and old, in Smith's novels and short stories have faced high walls and deep holes and, for the most part, have found their ways to higher ground. Smith, along with Tyler in the next chapter, thus stands as a link between the previous generation of Southern girls of O'Connor, Welty, Lee, McCullers, and Spencer, who more often than not bowed to the gender restrictions placed on them, and those new Southern girls created by McCorkle, Ansa, Humphreys, Mason, Alison, and many others, who leave those limitations behind.

THREE

"Three Meal a Day
Aftermaths": Anne Tyler's
Determined Adolescents

> There was a period in my life, starting at 17 or 18, when I seemed determined to do whatever seemed the most contrary thing. And I suppose that any decision I make is more or less like that even now [Anne Tyler, Interview with Clifford Ridley, 23].

> The fact is that for every woman writing metaphorically about her imprisonment, you can surely find at least one man writing metaphorically about his imprisonment — and neither imprisonment is necessarily sex-related [Anne Tyler, "Women Writers: Equal but Separate," 21].

Given her iconoclastic approach to life and literature, it is not surprising that Anne Tyler's fiction is filled with plucky (and sometimes difficult) female characters: women who in near middle age decide to leave home and family, older women who are willing to be outrageous to break out of their routine, and young women, who, in spite of abusive or dead mothers, absent or useless fathers, unexpected pregnancies, attempts on their lives, scars real and psychic, and/or broken early marriages emerge at the end of their novels with a sense of determination and purpose, if not hope. Adolescent characters Evie Decker (Casey) in *A Slipping Down*

Life (1970), Elizabeth Abbot ("Gillespie" Emerson) in *The Clock Winder* (1972), and Jenny Tull (Baines Wiley St. Ambrose) in *Dinner at the Homesick Restaurant* (1987) are not deterred in their optimism about the future by their troubles in the past. These young women share with many of Tyler's other characters — male and female — a sense of their ability (and *responsibility)* to shape their own lives. Being female in a Tyler novel is unique (female protagonists *do* have to contend with unexpected, and often multiple, pregnancies and limited opportunities), but most of the other issues in their lives — fraught relationships with their mothers (and fathers), romantic troubles, and eventual solutions to their problems — seem less influenced by gender than by temperament.[1]

Her characters of both genders are most affected by their stubborn refusal to be permanently sidetracked by events in their lives and their unflagging determination to form relationships with others. Novelist and perceptive Tyler critic Doris Betts notes that while there are crises of various sorts in many of Tyler's novels, "climactic events become early cause; her characters work through them toward later denouement or conclusion. She remains more interested in how her people survive and persist *beyond* crisis during their long, steady, three-meal-a-day aftermaths" (2). The frequency with which Tyler's characters continue beyond tragedy, abandonment, and disappointment makes her vision, Betts says, "more classic than romantic" (3). Also, although many of her novels do contain strong female main characters, Tyler's perspective is not traditionally feminist. In her novels, "No rebellious Nora goes slamming out of her doll's house in the conclusion; no woman is swimming out to where the horizon meets the sea or going mad from seeing creatures swarm inside her yellow wallpaper" (11). According to Betts, Tyler is neither simply romantic nor strictly feminist and believes that "The real adventure is not to light out for the territory with Huck Finn but to function as the Hallmark card advises, even with all the risks of sentimentality that affirmation entails, to 'Bloom where you are planted'" (12).

Her adolescent characters *do* bloom. This is in part because they find support and solace outside their original families, which, for one reason or another, often fail them. As I have said in an earlier essay on *Dinner at the Homesick Restaurant*, Tyler's characters construct new families for themselves to replace the ones that have — for various reasons — become unsatisfying. Their ability to imagine — and bring into reality — sustaining families helps her characters escape the confines of the Patriarchal traditional family (14). This imaginative recreation of family is particularly important for Tyler's adolescent girls. Without designing satisfying alternative families (which may contain some biological family members), they can never fully develop nor escape traditional gender expectations. Southern women, especially, have a need to find a way out of the traditional family.

My view shares much with Mary F. Robertson's argument in "Medusa Points and Contact Points." Tyler's novels, she says, are unlike more traditional family novels, in which "a kind of binary thinking rules the narrative," compelling characters to completely accept or reject their families values, while keeping "the concept of the private, inward-turning family ... coherent and ideologically definitive" (121). Tyler's novels, on the other hand, are not conventional in this sense; familial order (and narrative order) are disrupted by moments of miscommunication (what Robertson calls "Medusa points") and connections to extra-familial characters ("contact points"). "Because the boundary between insiders and outsiders is continually transgressed," she says, "the progress of Tyler's novels is felt more as an expansion of narrative disorder than as a movement toward resolution and clarification"(122). Yet this disorder is productive, showing "the healthy partial escape from total petrification" (127). According to Robertson, Tyler's novels "enact thematically the growth from adolescent notions of identity to the adult willingness to live with unachieved situations of involvement with people's otherness" (138).[2] Of course, this movement outward, away from the family, can happen at any age for Tyler's characters, but it is especially clear with her adolescent characters, and extremely important for her young women.

Tyler's adolescents must survive when parents are absent, abusive, distracted, dim-witted, and resolute in their refusal to acknowledge what their children want and need. Particularly for her female characters, as Elizabeth Evans points out, "mothers rarely serve their daughters well" (92). Daughters in Tyler novels frequently "suffer because their mothers neglect them, or fail to guide them, or remain unaware of the lives the daughters lead" (93). This is certainly true of Evie Decker's mother, dead before the novel begins, Elizabeth Abbott's well-meaning but distracted mother, and Jenny Tull's abusive and angry mother, Pearl. Interestingly, however, although the young female protagonists are often not well served by their mothers, they do find surrogate mothers — of various ages and genders — who provide the necessary balance between caring and distance.[3]

A Slipping-Down Life

Neither escape nor balance seems likely for the characters at the beginning of Tyler's third novel, *A Slipping-Down Life*. Joseph Volker describes them as

> self-absorbed in the manner of people usually found in naturalistic fiction, robotically pursuing ends that strike the reader as ill-defined, grotesque, and self-destructive. They do not so much live their lives as get enmired in them, and they struggle with the leaden awkwardness of terrapins to get free [41].

Robotic, self-absorbed, and trapped in self-destructive behaviors clearly describes the main character, seventeen-year-old Evie Decker from Pulqua, North Carolina, "a plump drab girl in a brown sweater that was running to balls at the elbows" (3). Evie is aptly described as "one of the least attractive teenage girls ever to heave her bulk and insecurities onto the twentieth-century page" (Gulette 100). Abandoned by her mother — "the last woman in Pulqua County to die of childbed fever"(42) — Evie is saddled with a father who is "a high school math teacher, a vague, gentle man who assumed that Evie would manage just fine wherever she was" (10).[4] Using a fairly typical pattern for a novel of adolescent development, Tyler saddles Evie with a dead mother, hapless father, and no real friends, leaving her to fend for herself.

Not surprisingly, Evie feels lonely and at loose ends:

> She walked most places alone. She carried her books clutched to her chest, rounding her shoulders. Her face, which was pudgy and formless, poked itself too far forward. And like most heavy people, she had long ago stopped expecting anything of her clothes [8].

"Formless" in her appearance and hopeless about her clothes and her life, Evie tries (and fails) to "brighten her complexion" and make an impression, but she is frustrated by a "swallowed sock" or "knotted laces" and is unable, because of her self consciousness, to connect with others (9).

Untidiness coexists with loneliness for Evie, and she even fails to find comfort in her one friend, Violet, as much of an outcast as Evie, or in the family housekeeper, Clotelia, a brusque woman more invested in her soap operas than in Evie's life. Evie, like most of Tyler's heroines, is "shockingly alone" (Evans 90). In her loneliness, she resembles many of the young women (Sam, Bone, and Kate, in particular) discussed in the following chapters of the study.

Throughout the first part of the novel, Evie struggles — in typical adolescent fashion — with her clothes and what she sees as her dismal future. Her clothes (folded waistband, untucked blouses, and slipping sandals) seem to be conspiring with her attitude to make Evie feel depressed and hopeless (18). However, in spite of the many strikes against her, Evie does manage to take charge of her directionless life, albeit in a somewhat haphazard (and self-destructive) fashion. She becomes obsessed with Bertram "Drumstrings" Casey, a musician she first hears on local radio and goes to hear Casey at a concert and then at a local roadhouse. It is at the roadhouse that she is discovered (the passive tense is crucial here) in the bathroom with Casey's name carved (backward) into her forehead.

Her response to the mutilation is, surprisingly, one of joy. She says to Violet while she is recovering in the hospital, "I believe this might be the best thing I've ever done.... Something out of character. Definite. Not covered by insurance. I'm just sure it will all work out well" (40). She continues: "While I was walking through that crowd with the police-man, I kept thinking of my name: Evie Decker, *me*. Taking something into my own hands for once. I thought, if I had started acting like this a long time ago my whole *life* might have been different" (40).[5] Of course, her assertions of self-determination are undercut by the ambiguity sur-rounding the carving of the letters on her forehead (there is some spec-ulation that another girl did it), but at least in Evie's reformulation of events, the mutilation takes on the quality of a transformation.

In spite of her exhilaration in literally taking her life into her own hands, Evie finds herself unable to leave the house following her return from the hospital. She dreams of being transformed (losing weight, hav-ing the scars removed), her dreams always leave her "feeling hopeless and betrayed" (63). Clearly, Evie's first step toward independence has left her feeling depressed, anxious, and apparently even more hopeless than before. Her solution to her temporary paralysis is to offer Casey her forehead (and her presence) at his performances for publicity, thereby exchanging her mutilated body for his career. This could be seen as a step backward in her movement toward independence, but it could also be a (somewhat misguided) attempt to turn a momentary lapse in judgment into a more concrete benefit for herself and the new-found object of her affections. At least she is *doing* something, rather than just waiting for life to happen to her.

Evie is aware, however, of the ethical — if not yet the feminist — implications of what she is doing. She decides it is "all right to take money for lifting a scarred face toward a rock player every Saturday night but only if what she did was real, without a single piece of playacting" (85). If she is sincere, Evie decides, she can't be doing wrong. However, Evie now has the difficult task of distinguishing between what is "real" in her life and what is not. Her scars and her presence are real, she thinks; awed hero worship and girlish enthusiasm are not. In the process of selling herself to Drum, she is, paradoxically, discovering her ethical boundaries, an important step in adolescent development.

The publicity arrangement breaks down after a fight with Drum, however, and Evie begins the process of finding a new center for her life. After the argument, Evie feels "as if she had returned from some long hard trip that no one else knew about" (108), and she seems determined to start anew. If it were a typical young adult novel, the story could end here, with Evie using insights from her strange relationship with Drum to give direction to her life, but Tyler intends for her to learn much more — about herself and others. Typically, Tyler is interested in what happens after: after a traumatic event, after a marriage, after any life-changing experience. Even her adolescents are not allowed to sail off in a haze of unlimited possibilities and (conventional) happy endings.

For reasons not exactly clear to Evie or to readers, but obviously part of Tyler's plan to enhance Evie's emotional development, the couple reconciles, and Drum (after being thrown out of his house) begins sleeping on her porch. Evie expects her dreams to be disturbed by his presence, but all she experiences is vague anxiety (114). On the one hand, she wishes he would leave, but n the other, Drum is a patient listener (119). Unlike her life with her father, which had been straightforward but boring, spending time with Drum makes her feel luxurious, if a little guilty. With Drum on her porch, Evie has received the gifts of time and attention, neither of which she could get from her father.

Improbably, at least from her clueless father's perspective, the young couple decides to get married. Drum's proposal is somewhat less than romantic — not surprising for someone whose songs consist of cryptic message fragments — but it is pointed (and poignant). He says his life is "petering out all around" him, and he wants to marry "someone I like and have me a house and *change*" (130). Evie's response is "Oh, well. Why not?" (131), which in its cavalier tone resembles both the response to proposals by *Dinner's* Jenny Tull and Tyler's own attitude toward marriage and life.[6] Still, although Evie's reaction seems somewhat passive, by marrying Drum she is acknowledging *her* need for change and her responsibility for making that change happen.

In spite of its rather undramatic beginning, their marriage seems to work out. Their first house is a $24-a-month tarpaper shack on the outskirts of town that Evie thinks is "a wonderful place to start out in" because in its emptiness and abandonment, "[n]othing she could do would hurt it" (144). The blankness of her house, and of her future, is what appeals to Evie. There is no model for the future to follow, no past to mess up. This is the perfect way — at least in fantasy — for the adolescent to begin adult life, with no models or restrictions.

Drum, too, is the perfect husband, "the easiest person" Evie had ever known (151).). In her surprisingly peaceful relationship with Drum, Evie has finally found a way "to feel as sure and as comfortable" as the classmates who ignored her in school.... She has a husband who listens to her talk about domestic details, loves her cooking, and, best of all, keeps "cheerfully silent and mend[s] chairs" (151). The problem is that Evie has achieved this perfection by absorbing the conventional image of the happy housewife, complete with apron and pincurls, which by 1970 Tyler knew was rapidly becoming a dangerous illusion.

This women's magazine paradise doesn't last, of course, based as it is on a 1950s nuclear-family fantasy, which positions women inside the home and men in the world, to both their dissatisfactions. Drum, as the sole family provider, becomes increasingly unhappy with his career prospects: "I'll never get anywhere. I ain't but nineteen years old and already leading a slipping-down life, and hard rock is fading so pretty soon nobody won't want it" (170). Evie gets a job at the library to help out, which she enjoys, but Drum does not, and their peaceful life slips away.

Predictably, given the parameters of this particular fantasy, Evie begins thinking about having a child as a way of making her marriage stronger. "The thought of a baby sent a shaft of yellow light through her mind, like a door opening," the narrator says (170). For Evie, having a baby, like getting married and supporting Drum's music, represents another way to jump start her life. Getting pregnant proves more difficult that Edie imagines, however. Drum, exhausted and depressed, falls asleep the minute he hits the bed. Evie stays "awake for hours with all her muscles tensed, as if she were afraid to trust her weight to the darkness she rested on" (171). The fantasy baby is light; her real marriage, unfortunately, is dark.

In spite of logistical and emotional problems, Evie does manage to get pregnant, but at the same time her father dies of a heart attack. After his death, Evie decides to move into his house, but Drum doesn't want to go, saying it isn't the right time. "Right time or not," Evie responds, "we are going to have to make some arrangements. ... Start a new life. Give some shape to things" (210). When Drum refuses to leave with her to start that new life, Evie makes plans to go without him. Although she feels "something pulled out of her that he had drawn, like a hard deep string," Evie is determined to go, "squar[ing] her corners as if she were a stack of library cards" (211). The library card simile is not random; Evie has been working at a library (her first real job), and Tyler has positive memories of her own work in libraries. For both author and character, library cards (and libraries in general) represent making order out of chaos, just as Evie is trying to do with her life.

Desperate to prevent her from leaving, Drum tries to string out the conversation by asking Evie what she will tell her child about the name on her forehead. Evie replies that it *is* her name, which, of course, it is, now that she has married him. Drum responds, exasperated, "Now that you have done all the cutting... and endured through bleeding and police cars and stitches, are you going to say it was just for purposes of *identification?*" (212). Evie then tells him that she didn't do it, that someone else carved the name in her forehead, although this may be a way of cutting off communication or hurting him. Still, there is a sense that Evie *has* done it for identification, that carving the name into her forehead helped to make her who she is now. She has identified herself as Drum's loyal supporter, then his wife and the mother of her child, and finally as an independent woman.

Missing Evie's point, or perhaps inadvertently supporting it, Drum says, "Life is getting too cluttered," to which Evie responds, "Didn't I tell you so?" (213). Their life has been cluttered by traditional expectations about marriage, home, and family. Drum holds out the hope that she will return, but Evie's last words to him, "I never back down on things" (213), indicate that she has a far stronger will than he imagines.[7] She drives away, left with "a trace of his cool, slick surface and a smell of marigolds and a brief tearing sensation that lasted long after she had rolled out of the yard toward town" (214). Evie is sad, but she is moving on in spite of it. Drum, on the other hand, is stuck in the past. The novel ends with him asking questions during his performance, even though "the only person who could have answered him was not present" (214).

In spite of its melancholy tone, the novel's end does not represent failure for Evie, in spite of Stella Nesanovich's position that Evie's father's death and her separation from Drum "leave her even more bereft than before" (26). Instead, Evie remains firm in her resolve to "never back down on things" like her identity or her chance for a new life. Her self-mutilation is for "purposes of identification," as is her decision to leave Drum when he won't live in her father's house, and her decision to raise her child on her own.[8] At the end of the novel, Evie clearly plans to "give some shape" to a life that had, up until the final moment, been slipping down.[9]

The Clock Winder

In Tyler's fourth novel, *The Clock Winder*, the main character is a troubled, or at least troubling, late adolescent, who has problems with clothes and men and other difficulties caused primarily by her refusal to accommodate herself to gender stereotypes. Nineteen-year-old Elizabeth Abbott arrives out of the blue to help Mrs. Emerson with her house, not as a housekeeper, but as a handyperson. When matriarch Mrs. Emerson first meets her, and Elizabeth agrees to work for her on the spur of the moment, the elder woman wonders, "what kind of person would let herself get so sidetracked. Weren't there any fixed destinations in her life?" (11).

Like Evie Decker Casey, Elizabeth first appears as someone with no direction, no plan, someone moved, by forces she doesn't quite understand, into taking particular actions. Later on in the novel, Mrs. Emerson says to her, "It's just that you seem so — aimless. You don't make any distinctions in your life" (85), and her son Timothy asks Elizabeth, "Why is everything you say so *inconsequential*? Can't you understand when something serious is going on?" (96). These traits, according to Volker, are typical for Tyler's characters, who are "forever engaged in writing [their] autobiograph[ies], composing apologias for attitudes and gestures that are deeply ingrained, irretrievable in origin, and often a little compulsive" (48–49). Thus these criticisms sit lightly on Elizabeth, who seems satisfied with her approach to life. For example, when Timothy reproaches her for "seeing life as some kind of gimmicky guided tour where everyone signs up for a surprise destination" Elizabeth smiles at the word *life* "as fondly and happily as if he had mentioned her favorite acquaintance" (123). Life — aimless, without fixed destinations or distinctions — is quite enough for Elizabeth, if not for those who care for her.[10]

As well as criticizing her world view, Elizabeth's new-found family also thinks she should take more care of her appearance, but like Evie, Elizabeth isn't concerned with how she looks, although Mrs. Emerson is. When she first meets her, Mrs. Emerson worries that Elizabeth isn't wearing makeup, is ruining her feet with moccasins, and is wearing an inappropriately masculine white shirt (11). Mrs. Emerson, who knows the language of clothes (and gender), thinks that Elizabeth's problems would be solved by lipstick and high heels and is unable to understand why Elizabeth so effectively resists being feminized by her, or the world. In fact, much of the two women's struggle early in the novel will center around Mrs. Emerson's desire to make Elizabeth into more of a lady.

Timothy, who is attracted to Elizabeth, nevertheless reacts to her clothes in much the same way as his mother, annoyed by her ill-fitting jacket and her lack of obvious feminine qualities. Thinking that her appearance is "a joke played on him by the universe," Timothy wants Elizabeth to smell like something more feminine than wood shavings, or at least be delicate in some way (53). Like his mother, Timothy needs Elizabeth to fulfill his vision of femininity, which consists of smelling sweet, being graceful, or having "at least one romantic quality." Getting ready for a date with Timothy one night, she attempts to match his vision, with unsurprisingly disastrous results. Her dress fits "haphazardly," and her wrinkled nylons and "squashed-looking" purse make her look to Timothy like a waitress just getting off a long shift (61). Trying to fit herself to someone else's model, Elizabeth ends up bulky, flaking, wrinkled, and squashed looking. In spite of— or perhaps through — her apparent aimlessness and her careless appearance, Elizabeth's sense of self is clearly defined.[11] Only when she tries to be something else than her plain, unadorned self does she appear vaguely ridiculous.

Actually, in her new life Elizabeth feels "amazed all over again that she had finally become a grownup. Where to go and when to sleep and what to do with the day were hers to decide — or not to decide, which was even better. She could leave here when she wanted or stay forever, fixing things. In this house everything she touched seemed to work out fine. Not like the old days" (38). With the Emersons, Elizabeth has a clear sense of who she is and what she does — and doesn't — do. "I *always* go where I'm asked, " she says, "It's a challenge: never turn down an invitation" (42). And, she says, "I would never change someone else's affairs around" (63). Because she is not restricted by her family history and expectations, Elizabeth is free to develop a carefree and idiosyncratic personality. With her family, however, things are different: "At home I break things more than fix them," she says (64). Again, Elizabeth, when not forced to act in the traditionally female ways her family expects, finds herself competent and confident.

In a tipsy moment at a party, Timothy extends Elizabeth's accidentally happy situation to all parents and children, picturing "a gigantic migration of children across the country, all cutting the old tangled threads and picking up new ones when they found the right niche, free forever of other people's notions about them" (71). Being "free forever of other people's notions about them" *is* a kind of paradise, especially for female characters, who are often the victim of "notions" about how they ought to look and act.

This paradisiacal vision cannot last, of course. Timothy is kicked out of medical school, and in a struggle with Elizabeth, whom he has kidnapped, shoots her and kills himself. Elizabeth leaves the Emersons and returns home, where "everywhere she looked seemed parched and bleak and glaring, but at least she was back where she was supposed to be" (151). However, she is plagued by vague unremembered nightmares, which end in a comforting, if exhausting, dream about sorting buttons (144–45). The work of mending buttons is "boring and comforting," much like the work Elizabeth did for the Emersons. The Elizabeth of "quiet calm," who took "joy in doing her job so well," is lost at home and must return in dreams to the kind of work she finds satisfying.

Eventually, she finds a job that appears to resemble her work for the

Emersons. She tries nursing ancient Mr. Cunningham, but watching him
sleep, "It was as if she were asleep herself, or in that space on the edge of
sleep where people make plans for some action but only dream they have
carried it out" (186–87). When Matthew (the other Emerson brother
who loves her) comes to visit, he remarks that "Everything about you
has changed. I don't understand it. There's something muffled about you"
(192). Outside the Emersons' house, Elizabeth is no longer herself, no
longer the confident and capable handyperson but instead a drifting
"muffled" caretaker for someone who can't appreciate her skills. This is
also a much more feminine job, caring for the elderly, not at all like fixing
things around the house and taking care of the yard.

Ignoring the Matthew's worried comments, her sleepy depression,
and her anxious dreams, Elizabeth makes plans to marry her high-school
sweetheart, Dommie Whitehall. On her wedding day, her clothes on
again reveal her discomfort with the role imposed upon her. As a bride,
Elizabeth loses "all her style," clumping along the aisle in oversized shoes
and looking like a peasant (221). Not surprisingly, she doesn't go through
with the wedding and gets a job teaching arts and crafts in a reform
school. Had the novel ended there, Petry says, "It would be a virtual *Bildungsroman,* tracing Elizabeth's emergence as an artist and as a self-reliant
adult" (91). But it *doesn't* end there; Elizabeth is cajoled back into the
Emerson's house when Mrs. Emerson has a stroke, and Elizabeth's fate
becomes much more complex, and interesting to those studying Tyler's
representation of female development.

The first thing that changes is her name. When Mrs. Emerson's
slurred pronunciation turns her name into "Gillespie," she gains a new
identity as well, become "someone effective and managerial who was sum-
moned by her last name, like a WAC." The new name is "contagious,"
and soon the entire household begins using it (271).[12] With her new name
and her new identity, Elizabeth can become "effective and managerial,"
almost military in her competence and control. Since this new identity
is also contagious, it becomes the way others see her as well.

Having become indispensable to — and inseparable from — the Emerson family, Elizabeth eventually marries Matthew, and when youngest son
Peter returns after a tour in Vietnam, he sees Elizabeth, now known to
everyone as Gillespie, "her face a little broader and more settled looking
but her fingers still nicked by whittling knives and her manner with
babies still as offhand as if she were carrying a load of firewood" (296).

Elizabeth has become more traditionally feminine in her appearance, but she hasn't become more femininized in her behavior. More associated with firewood and knives than with housework, Elizabeth is still both the most domestic and competent member of the family.

Unable to adequately interpret what she sees, Peter's wife, P.J., in a moment of anger, renders her judgment on Elizabeth and the family she manages:

> That little closed-up family of yours is closed around *nothing*, thin air, all huddled up together scared to go out. Depending on someone that is like the old-maid failure poor relation you find in some places, mending their screens and cooking their supper and fixing their chimneys and making peace — oh, she ended up worse off than *them* [307].

P.J.'s description looks ahead to closed up families of *Dinner at the Home-sick Restaurant* and *The Accidental Tourist,* but she is wrong about Elizabeth's relationship to this family. Peter recognizes this as he leaves the house near the end of the novel and sees Gillespie/Elizabeth as "juggler of supplies, obtaining and distributing all her family needed" (310). At the end of the novel, Elizabeth is both mother and provider, homemaker and manager, matriarch and patriarch, giving her family all that they need.

Elizabeth "Gillespie" Emerson has made herself into the person she wanted to be from the moment she showed up at Mrs. Emerson's door. She has become someone who resists traditional gender expectations and nevertheless finds a way to belong in what looks like a traditional family. As with Evie, she moves from indecision to decision, from dependence to competence, from competence to identity. It is well known that Tyler, who thinks the ending is sad, is surprised when others do not, although she admits that what Elizabeth does "is the happiest and best thing for her" (23).[13] Perhaps this is what readers must come to understand about Tyler's novels — that what is best for the character may be as difficult for them to accept as it is for their families.

Dinner at the Homesick Restaurant

A later novel, *Dinner at the Homesick Restaurant* is still concerned, as are most Tyler novels, with family dynamics and personal development.

It tells the story of the Tull family: Pearl, the mother, and her children Cody, Ezra, and Jenny; it is also her most fully developed treatment of the mother/daughter relationship. Pearl, who has been abandoned by her husband Beck, is a violent and unpredictable mother, who sees herself as a woman struggling to provide for her family alone, and her children, most particularly her daughter, have to find ways to grow up in spite of her complicated legacy.

Jenny, the only daughter, moves through a series of unhappy relationships only to settle into domestic (but untraditional) bliss as mother to a brood of unruly but lovable step-children. In her multiple marriages, names, children, and occupations, Petry says, "the young Jenny Tull [is] barely detectable in the series of accumulated identities" (195). And this is precisely the point.

Jenny has constructed for herself and her husband's kids a family she believes to be, in its chaotic but loving environment, diametrically opposed to her own. In *her* childhood, she dreamt of a mother who

> laughed a witch's shrieking laugh; dragged Jenny out of hiding as the Nazis tramped up the stairs; accused her of sins and crimes that had never crossed Jenny's mind.
> Her mother told her, in an informative and considerate tone of voice, that she was raising Jenny to eat her [70].

Yet while these dreams reflect the tension that inhabited her waking hours, these nighttime stories also exorcize her fears and begin the process that allows her to separate herself from her mother and to imagine a different life for herself. The devouring mother, in this passage, is both threatening and transformative, representing absorption *and* alteration. Here, especially, in a novel centered around the preparation, presentation, and pleasures of food, the metaphorical connections between eating and imagination established by the devouring mother become emblematic of productive story making. With her dreams, Jenny begins the process of becoming a mother transformed by creative imagination.

Another opportunity for creative rewriting (and perhaps escape) arises with Jenny's first marriage:

> What appealed to her more [than her initial emotional attraction] was the *angularity* of the situation — the mighty leap into space with someone she hardly knew. Wasn't that what a marriage

ought to be? Like one of those movie-style disasters — shipwrecks or earthquakes or enemy prisons — where strangers, trapped in close quarters by circumstance, show their real strengths and weaknesses [89].

Jenny has moved from fairy tale to movie melodrama, and while this new story is powerful enough to propel her from her troubled home, it is not complex enough to sustain her or her marriage.

Nor does it differ sufficiently from her mother's "mighty leap into space" with Beck. Jenny finally settles happily with a second husband, who brings with him "his padding, his moat, his barricade of children, all in need of her brisk and competent attention" (213). She has created for herself, both in her marriage and career as a pediatrician, a story in which she can be "brisk and competent" and extremely "padded" against the bumps and bruises of life. Most significantly, she has combined her two fictions — fairy tale and disaster film — and become the princess behind the "moat" and "barricade" with children "all in need of her." Rapunzel meets Florence Nightingale. According to Gullette, "A person can *learn* to be the most responsible kind of adult. Jenny did it by going around watching people who did it better" (102).

In fact, Jenny becomes reconciled to her past, advising stepson Slevin's teacher, when the boy has been having trouble in school, "I don't see the need to blame adjustments, broken homes, bad parents, that sort of thing. We make our own luck, right? You have to overcome your set-backs. You can't take them too much to heart..." (196). She tells Ezra, "if you catalogue grudges, anything looks bad. And Cody certainly cat-alogues; he's ruining his life with his catalogues. But after all, I told him, we made it didn't we? We did grow up. Why the three of us turned out fine, just fine!" (200)[14]

In this novel, Tyler shows how each member of this family creates for her/himself a fictional family that is, finally, like the food that Ezra's restaurant serves, both nostalgic and nourishing, providing both long-ing and satiety. And the novel is satisfying in the same way. Because it calls attention to its own fiction making, it relinquishes the control over the narrative so characteristic of other family-saga novels and undermines the premise that it is ever possible to tell *the* story of a family. This loss of control can leave a reader longing at times for the authority of a cer-tain kind of narrator (a paternalistic one who knows what he thinks the reader needs to hear), but it also facilitates potential re-writings, where the reader *seems* to remember things the way they *ought* to be. A family history, Tyler shows her reader in this novel, belongs to whoever is telling the story.

Jenny Tull, Elizabeth Abbott, and Evie Decker are three young women making their way in haphazard fashion toward adulthood, but when they arrive they find a world governed by the rules they have created. For these characters, as well as many others in Tyler's large corpus, "It's not *getting* what you want," as Gullette says; "it's knowing what you want" (107). This is, of course, particularly important — and difficult — for her adolescent characters, male or female. Knowing what you want, however, doesn't mean a static adulthood. As Sweeney says, Tyler's characters "continue changing and developing — a process that remains always unfinished" (80). The implication is that for Evie, Elizabeth, and Jennie, achieving adulthood is only the beginning of a life filled with "making your own luck."

FOUR

"One Layer Deeper":
On the Road and In Country
with Sam Hughes

> Everything in America is going on here, on the road. Sam likes the feeling of strangeness. They are at a crossroads: the interstate with traffic headed east and west, and the state road with north-south traffic. She's in limbo, stationed right in the center of this enormous amount of energy [Bobbie Ann Mason, *In Country*, 17].

> Like me, these characters are emerging from a rural way of life that is fast disappearing, and they are plunging into the future at a rapid saunter, wondering where they're going to end up. I realize we are making the journey together and that I am privileged to discover their loves and sorrows and confusions. I want to see how they are going to face the future, and I am excited to meet them at a major intersection. It makes me hopeful [Mason, Introduction to *Midnight Magic*, xii].

Like Elizabeth in the previous chapter and Lucille Odom in the next, Samantha "Sam" Hughes is apparently "in limbo": stalled between high school and college, between childhood sweethearts and grown-up lovers, between loyalty to family and identification with the wider world.

Sam, of course, is literally at a crossroads as her novel begins — on the road with her grandmother and uncle, heading toward the Vietnam Veterans' Memorial in Washington, D.C. There she hopes to find listed the name of her father, killed in Vietnam before she was born, and, more importantly, discover a way out of the slump into which her life has fallen, much as Elizabeth turns to the Emersons to give direction to her meandering life. In her new (to her) VW bug, she wants to "glide like this all the way across America," driving toward her future in the same spirit as Lucille rides her bike and Elizabeth hammers nails (3). In particular, Sam, unlike other adolescent characters in this book, is also at a "major intersection" between a rural Southern life and a generic American life. All of these crossroads and intersections, however, leave the reader, as Mason says, "hopeful" and excited about her future.

Also like Lucille, Sam feels the loss of her mother, who has moved to Lexington to be with her new husband and is preoccupied with Sam's new half sister. Thinking that the trip "would be so different if her mother could have come," Sam wishes her mother could be as interested in the past (her father, Vietnam, the Beatles, the '60s) as she is (5). Repeatedly, she tries to engage her mother in her quest (to no avail), and repeatedly her mother tries to minimize its relevance to Sam's life. As Elizabeth does, Sam comes to realize that her past will offer her few answers. So while Mason says in an interview with Lila Havens that she is "very interested in mother-daughter relationships, and it seems like I'm always writing about that," Sam's search for her past — and her present — identity will (literally) leave her mother behind (88). However, like Lucille and Elizabeth's stories, the ending of Sam's tale promises the recreation of a family tie, albeit not the original mother/daughter dyad.

The structure of *In Country* differs from many of the other novels discussed in this book, which either start with life-changing events or move slowly toward them. Sam's story begins *in medias res* in Book One, with her father's death and mother's departure already long over. Still, regardless of when in the narrative each young woman experiences her own personal crisis, something *beyond* the loss (or abandonment) of their parents must occur in every novel for the main characters to move ahead with their lives. Just as Evie's pregnancy forces her to take action, and Elizabeth/Gillespie is shocked out of her drifting by Timothy's suicide, so Sam is finally motivated by her new knowledge about her father. Each of these events, more so than their loss of their mothers or fathers, leads these young women toward change. Sam, who "shudders at the idea of growing up on a farm, doing chores, never getting to go to town" (13), wants to get lost, to "wake up and not know where I was" (6), to escape her home town of Hopewell, Kentucky, her family, and her new-found knowledge of her father's past.

The summer the novel begins, after the revelations (still unrevealed to the reader) about her father, Sam "feels like letting loose. She has so much evil and bad stuff in her now. It feels good to say shit, even if it's only under her breath" (8). She feels "that everything is more real to her, now that they are on the road" (19). Although the reader has no idea at this early point in the novel what has happened to propel Sam "on the road," it is clear she is headed in the right direction, or at least in *some* direction, which is better than being stranded.

As Mason says about *In Country,* her characters "are on the threshold of possibility. Their lives are being changed, and they're very excited by it" (Rothstein 102).[1] Sam says that on the road "everything seems more real than it has ever been." She likens the peeling away of layers of experience to an exercise in gym, when the aerobics instructor tells the girls to "squeeze one layer deeper" when they were doing the pelvic tilt (7). Although this gymnastic image is deliberately silly, it is an appropriate one for an adolescent, drawn as it is from the adolescent's attention to the body and to sexuality — psychological (or perhaps even philosophical) truth arising from a "row of girls with their asses reaching for heaven" (7). There is something serious at work here (beyond buns of steel), however; Sam is trying to understand what lies underneath the surface of her life. She is working at becoming an adult, uncovering what is mysterious to children — who their parents really are, where they came from and why, how they fit into the world. Consequently, the novel is equal parts mystery and coming-of-age story.[2]

Clearly, with its emphasis on quest and education, *In Country* fits the pattern of the female *Bildungsroman,* and, in fact, much has been written about this aspect of the novel as well as its commentary on gender and regional identity. Mason recognized the potential richness of the development theme *as* she worked on the novel, which she has said many times did not begin as either a Vietnam or a coming-of-age story. In an interview with Dorothy Combs Hill, Mason says that when she "realized that Sam's father had died in Vietnam — that's when I knew I had a novel. ... Because it had been just enough time for a child to come of age and to start searching. Making the archetypal quest for the father" (100). Sam literally came of age in the middle eighties, when it would have been possible for the child of a Vietnam veteran to have graduated from high school, and her search both follows and remakes "the archetypal quest for the father," although what makes this novel unique is that the father Sam sets out to find is dead. Thus her search is for an understanding of her father's history and not his identity, for an explanation of the past that will guide her future.

Critics have emphasized both the ways in which the novel conforms to the traditional structures and themes for this genre and the ways in which it resists those forms.[3] The novel is traditional — with its coming-of-age and quest motifs — but the subject matter (Vietnam, the dead father) and the characterization (the female protagonist) set it apart from those more familiar structures. Barbara T. Ryan correctly stresses the ways in which the novel deconstructs traditional notions of the self and of development, using the *Bildungsroman* "to reenact the twentieth-century shift from the modernist quest for authority and coherence to a postmodernist recognition that neither exists in the way we had supposed" (199). Unlike the traditional *Bildungsroman,* the character in this novel reconstructs her *world* rather than *herself.* This does not lead to an existential crisis, however. *In Country*, she says, "suggests that a recognition of the duality of authority and seeker, text and reader, other and self is, paradoxically, a step toward a kind of self-affirmation and wholeness in a conflicted, fragmented world" (200). Sam becomes more integrated as a result of this disintegration of authority.

Whether it is a traditional *Bildungsroman* or postmodernist deconstruction of identity/history, the novel is also a story concerned with the structures of gender. According to Ellen Blais, "a subtextual preoccupation [in the novel] with gender definitions weaves itself in and out of the questions raised by America's experience in Vietnam" (107). Nothing that happens to Sam, Blais says, can be seen as separate from her gender. Yet it is possible to read the story as blurring the lines of gender, with Sam assuming the traditionally male quest motif. Mason, however, appears to believe in the importance of gender distinctions, saying that *In Country* may be appealing to so many readers because it documents both the "quintessential male experience" of war and the female experience of child birth (Hill 98).[4] The novel does muddle the distinctions between these "quintessential" experiences, however. Sam "goes to war" and realizes women who have abortions kill; men nurture the young and are emotionally vulnerable.

Another complexity in the novel is its attitude about the "New South." Although *In Country* takes place in one of the border states, Kentucky, many critics have seen it as an allegory for the changing South, for good or ill. One group reads the references to generic, national culture as a destruction of unifying Southern values. Leslie White, for example, calls the novel "a kind of white trash chic," which "reads more like the destruction of white trash" (71). Others see the lack of cohesive values as a catalyst for change.[5] The culture of the South can be seen in the novel as a restrictive legacy, a regional backwardness that must be thrown off, or as a fast-disappearing cultural landscape that creates identity and meaning for its inhabitants. For Sam it is both — the connection to the past with her grandparents and the promise of the new with her trip across America.

The opening of Book Two shows clearly shows this combination of confidence in a shared contemporary national culture and an anxiety about the loss of distinctive Southern values:

> It was the summer of the Michael Jackson *Victory* tour and the Bruce Springsteen *Born in the U.S.A.* tour, neither of which Sam got to go to. At her graduation, the commencement speaker, a Methodist minister, had preached about keeping the country strong, stressing sacrifice. He made Sam nervous. She started thinking about war, and it stayed on her mind all summer [23].

The Michael Jackson and Bruce Springsteen tours represent national cultural events, which Sam hasn't been able to experience, although she recognizes their importance. The Methodist minister at the high school graduation (as well as his message of patriotism and sacrifice) is a peculiarly Southern tradition, but he makes Sam "nervous." Sam both does and doesn't participate in shared national or regional identities; she can't go to either concert tour because Hopewell is too isolated, and she can't accept the minister's call to sacrifice. She is and isn't Southern; she is and isn't American.

Sam does find a link to the wider world in the way of many isolated small town dwellers — through watching television, in particular *M*A*S*H*. Watching this show, she is linked to other viewers across the country, and she is, for better or worse, conditioned by it to have particular emotional responses. When one of the main characters, Colonel Blake, was killed, Sam is "so shocked she went around stunned for days" (25). Blake's TV death, while seeming "more real to her than the death of her own father," helped to drive home the reality of her own loss (25). It is possible to see this inability to feel except through the prosthetic effect of television as a horrific commentary on Americans' crippled emotional sensibilities. However, we can also read this as the therapeutic function of television, helping viewers to experience emotions they would otherwise deny or repress. Clearly, Mason wants us to consider both the positive and the negative effects of popular culture's artifacts, like television. Sam can *only* respond to the loss of her father through television, but through it she finally is able to come to terms with his death, which, regardless of the means, is a good thing.[6]

*M*A*S*H* also allows Sam's Uncle Emmett to mitigate some of the bad effects of his Vietnam experience. Using the cross-dressing Klinger in the series as his model, he re-fashions himself as a woman, rather than a troubled veteran. He wears a skirt, he cooks, he mothers Sam, he tries on moves and behaviors associated in our culture with women, sporting all the time "a gleeful expression that said he had gotten away with murder" (27). The "murder" that Emmett is getting away with is transgressing the lines of gender; by "pranc[ing] like Boy George" (another female impersonator from '80s popular culture); he is gleefully experiencing the freedom from self that acting like a woman gives him.

Later in the novel, Sam describes him looking "stately in his skirt — tall and broad, like a middle-aged woman" with several children (32). This image of Emmett as a matron, which will reappear later in the novel, suggests dignity and wisdom, attributes Emmett is unable to achieve as a man. This is undercut, however, by the slightly ridiculous image of Emmett "fluffing up his skirt." Pretending to be a woman can be embarrassing — and lonely. Sam and her boyfriend Lonnie can have "their hands on each other's thighs" while Emmett sits alone letting "air flood his legs" (32).

Emmett's playing with gender roles is also embarrassing to Sam, who wants her uncle to be "normal," not realizing that Emmett's freedom from gender stereotypes allows Sam a similar freedom. When Sam is uncomfortable thinking about her uncle in a skirt, she conjures up images of traditional families as an alternative, ones with "nice houses and wives and kids" (46).

Yet Sam doesn't fit the typical model of femininity, either, refusing to step into her assigned role of daughter-in-law in her boyfriend Lonnie's family. Sam realizes that such a "perfectly well" adjusted life is not for someone like her, who "loved to run because it set her apart from the girls at school who did things in gabby groups, like ducks" (75). She also knows that gender is in many ways a role one tries on, which often doesn't fit as well as one might like. When she meets Emmett's friend and fellow veteran Pete at K-Mart, she notices that he is "sentimental, no matter how tough he talked about women" (136). Even though Pete is "covering up his feelings" in a typically male way, Sam can see through his charade because of her growing awareness of gender as performance (136).

In spite of Sam's resistance to femininity, Lonnie tries to force her into a more traditional role, in particular into a dress for a family wedding. Sam is thinking about black leather pants and "a lot of metal" when Lonnie tells her that her problem is that she reads too many war books and watches too much television. The books and TV are "just fantasy," he says, and not "how it is here." Sam's response is, "I don't care how it is here. I don't want to stay here" (187). For Sam, TV is not just escapism — it's escape — escape from limited options for young women in Hopewell, from small-town isolation, from the necessity to wear dresses instead of "black leather pants." TV represents that one layer deeper, the wider realities of life beyond the gender limitations of rural Kentucky.

Sam's friend Dawn, with her teenaged pregnancy, represents one of the limited choices for young women in Hopewell. Sam and Dawn are similar in that they "lived with no other women in the house," which makes them both unusual and independent. However, "Dawn was much more domestic than Sam, and she was a good cook," and Dawn wants a future (including children) with her boyfriend (40). Dawn's pregnancy, which she first fears and then accepts, literally becomes a nightmare for Sam. She dreams of a baby that "had to be pureed in a food processor and kept in the freezer" only to be thawed out every morning. Although this is a "happy arrangement" in the dream, Sam nevertheless wakes up with "its horror rushing through her" (83). Clearly Sam horrified by the thought of having a baby; not yet having come to terms with her childhood, Sam isn't ready to become a parent herself. Instead Sam's "baby" is her struggle with her father's peculiar legacy; her "delayed stress of the Vietnam War" becomes "her version of Dawn's trouble" (89).

When Sam's mother and new baby sister show up at the house (to bring back Emmett from a drunken escapade), Sam finds herself sickened by the idea of babies in general. She thinks having a baby is equivalent to having your body — and your mind — stolen (155). Unlike the dream baby who could be parked in the freezer, a real baby has to be taken everywhere. Not surprisingly, Sam tries to talk Dawn into having an abortion. Dawn refuses, saying that having a baby "would be as wild as anything [she] can think of." Sam furiously tells her that "Having kids is what everybody does. It doesn't take any special talent" (177). Of course, Sam hasn't found out what her "special talent" is, but she does know that she prefers doing something *truly* wild to having a baby, which "everybody does," at least in Sam and Dawn's world.

Instead of making a baby, or at least cultivating Lonnie and attending weddings (which both Lonnie and Dawn think she should do) or planning her college career (as her mother wants her to do), Sam puts her energy into finding out about her father, perhaps looking to the past as a way to avoid what is to her an unappealing future. She looks first in her mother's old room, which is a treasure trove of early '70s kitsch: "a fondue pot, a hot-curls set, two old hair dryers, a Dutch oven, a pair of framed pictures of chickens" (178). The level of detail here (the passage goes on for a page) may seem unnecessary and distracting, but it is possible to see the details as aesthetically and thematically significant as well.

Barbara Henning says "minimalists" like Mason need elaborate detail to create "a metaphoric frame for comparison and reflection, an afterthought for grappling with meaning, a hope for resolution" (690). As is the case with all masterful realistic writers, the accumulation of detail creates a frame for understating character and purpose. The details are the means to narrative movement. Henning also says that we "must be willing to be emphatic readers" who can make connections between details and meaning and come therefore to an understanding of the characters (698). In this case, the things in Sam's mother's room are her cast offs, wedding gifts from her first, short marriage, tacky decorative items and crafts, old sexy underwear no longer needed in her practical, matronly new life. Sam, too, has been cast off, left behind in the old house with the fondue pot and hair dryers, equally stuck in the past.

According to Majorie Winther, Sam's reactions to the artifacts of culture "supply the chiaroscuro that gives her character three dimensions. Mason's careful choice and placement of these cultural elements within the story does the same for the novel — gives an added political and analytical dimension to a straightforward narrative" (200). In this particular case, Sam's reaction is significant. Rather than respond to the artifacts as useless junk (as many readers might), Sam sees them as potentially profitable in a yard sale — *good* junk, that is. Although she can't profit from the items in any emotional way (they don't tell her what she wants to know about her father), she can still use them. This is key to Sam's character: she spends much time in the novel finding ways to make use of cast-off things, much as Lucille in *Rich in Love* finds and refurbishes old furniture, Elizabeth Abbott in *The Clock Winder* makes the old Emerson house function again, and Bone's aunt recovers trash from the river by her house in *Bastard Out of Carolina*.

Among her mother's things, Sam finds her father's letters, but reading them plunges her deeper into confusion and anger, in particular with her father for refusing to communicate with her. "The dead took their secrets with them," she thinks. "She wondered how far to go in honoring the dead if the dead offer you nothing except a little mindless protection, by keeping their secrets from you" (182). Without sufficient knowledge, Sam can neither understand nor honor her father, which makes her angry. She begins to form conclusions about her mother and father based on this anger, to think that she had overestimated the time her parents had spent together, and to decide that her conception was merely the result of their "simply having a good time in bed, or in the back seat of a car" (192).

Although her new attitude sounds cynical, it may mark the beginning of Sam's progress toward adulthood, the beginning of her realization that she is not the center of the universe, a childish perception, and is actually the accidental (although not unwanted) product of brief contact between two separate people. She is, after all, not much different from Dawn's baby, although her parents were married, however briefly, at the time of her conception. This is, although she doesn't realize it at the time, a liberating notion. If one is not the center of the universe for anyone, one is much freer to take chances, and make mistakes.

Sam is not quite ready for such positive insights, however. After she is given her father's Vietnam diary by her paternal grandparents, she begins to uncover the mystery surrounding him. Like all mysteries, however, there is a corpse — in this case the dead bodies of several Vietnamese. As she reads about her father, Sam is outraged by her perception of his ignorance, insensitivity, and casual brutality. For awhile, her anger at her father extends to herself: "She recalled the dead cat she dug up once in Grandma's garden, and she realized her own insensitive curiosity was just like her father's. She felt humiliated and disgusted" (205). By identifying with her father's less positive traits, Sam is allowing herself both connection to him as an actual person and distance from his behaviors. She discovers she is like, and unlike, him. Until reading his diary, she has no clear image of her father to love — or to hate — and no clear sense of herself.

She decides to strengthen the connection between herself and her father by simulating his experience in Vietnam at Cawood's Pond, a place "so dangerous even the Boy Scouts wouldn't camp there" (208). Camping out in such a dangerous place will be her equivalent of his "humping the boonies" (210). She concludes that although men go to war, women are really no different in their desire for power and violence. This is important to Sam, and to young women in the late 20th century — to be like men and to accept the consequences of making oneself more masculine. Soldiers and women, fathers and daughters, mothers and children come together: "Soldiers murdered babies. But women did too. They ripped their own unborn babies out of themselves and flushed them away, squirming and bloody" (215). Abortion and war are equated but not exactly condemned; both become necessary and equivalent evils. Sam is learning that her father's killing is not fundamentally different from the killing she would probably do if she found herself pregnant — and the killing she has recommended to Dawn.

In a reversal of roles, Emmett comes to rescue Sam, who has been taking care of *him* for years, and tries to convince her that her night in the pond is nothing like Vietnam. He says: "What have you got to be afraid of? You're afraid somebody'll look at you the wrong way. You're afraid your mama's going to make you go to school in Lexington. Big deal" (220). He tells her, "It's childish, to go run off to the wilderness to get revenge. It's the most typical thing in the world" (221). Here Emmett is telling her, rightly, that she is still a child, even as she takes what she thinks are adult risks. But this adult insight leads to childish behavior on Emmett's part — he bursts into tears. It also leads to a breakthrough and to his realizing "I came out here to save you, but maybe I can't. Maybe you have to find out for yourself. Fuck. You can't learn from the past. The main thing you learn from history is that you can't learn from history. That's what history *is*" (226). His final conclusion is, "There are some things you can never figure out" (226). Cawood's Pond may be like Vietnam, after all, where nothing is every really clear. Regardless of the ambiguity of the message at dawn, for both Sam and Emmett, Cawood's Pond represents a dark night of the soul.

Still, the end of this wrenching passage and of Book Two shows the possibility of redemption. Walking ahead of her on the path out of Cawood's Pond, Emmett looks "like an old peasant woman hugging a baby." As he moves away from her, Sam sees him float. "like a pond-skimmer, beautiful in his flight" (226). Although until now she has been helping him, Emmett is now leading the way through the woods and poison ivy; on Sam's journey he has become her guide. He has also become the woman he has merely pretended to be earlier — the "old peasant woman" who will help Sam on the final leg of her voyage of discovery. He has become both woman and bird, "beautiful in his flight," whom Sam will follow.

In Book Three, the novel returns to the beginning and the now redemptive trip to the Vietnam Veteran's Memorial. Sam, her uncle, and her father's mother each hope to find something important at The Wall. Sam is looking for clues to her father's (and her own) identity, Emmett needs tangible proof to absolve his guilt for still being alive, and Mamaw needs to know that her son's sacrifice has been properly recognized. During the preparation for the trip, Sam is shell-shocked from her night at Cawood's Pond, "still stunned, waiting for her head to clear, wondering what will hit next" (229). Emmett has taken over the role of manager, and she has adopted his role of the walking wounded: "They had changed places, she thought. She had post–Vietnam stress syndrome" (229). Still, as they start traveling, she "begin[s] to recover her sense of direction" (230). Sam has lost all understanding of her past self and must create a new identity on the road.

The initial part of her journey, however, is tempered by her recent traumatic experiences: "It is a good country. But she keeps getting flashes of it through the eyes of a just-returned Vietnam soldier" (231). Her identification with the alienated Vietnam veterans makes her feel disconnected, too; she thinks she doesn't "fit in" anywhere (231). Sam is clearly moving toward her future by moving away — literally and psychologically — from her small town. She abandons her high-school job, her hangout, her friends, her past, and the South.

The trip is eventful, as are all spiritual journeys: the transmission breaks down, they have to stop for lengthy and expensive repairs, they eat at Howard Johnsons and sneak bourbon in hotel rooms. Finally, though, they arrive in Washington, and Sam has a moment of painful insight, thinking that the Washington Monument is a "big white prick" and the Vietnam Memorial "a black boomerang, whizzing toward her head" (238–39). Sam is personalizing and politicizing the monuments around her. Although the Washington Monument is clearly male, Sam envisions a way to render the monument harmless, with a "big rubber" of pink plastic, turning it from a symbol of neo-colonial male domination to a toy, or at least a safe-sex icon. And the Vietnam Memorial will also change from a weapon directed at her head to one which will come, eventually, to heal her (and her family's) wounds.

Perhaps most importantly, the child who was born *in spite* of the destruction caused by Vietnam will be transformed into a young woman at the memorial. Staring into its blackness, Sam notices the Washington Monument and the American flag reflected on its surface, "like the country giving the finger to the dead boys, flung in this hole in the ground." Sam's emotions at this point are " like a tornado moving in her, something massive and overpowering," and she feels like she is "giving birth to this wall" (240). This "massive and overpowering" feeling is the creation of self, separate from parents and family. Sam has found a way to take the sterile "prick" of American patriotism and turn it — and her loss — into something generative, from death to birth, in spite of the "big rubber." Her growing awareness is enhanced by finding her own name on the wall. (244) Sam has found what she was looking for — verification that she exists as part of the Vietnam story. She has proof that she has shared in the American experience of the war.

Her grandmother and uncle also find what they seek. Noticing a white carnation "blooming" in a crack in the wall, Mamaw feels hope in the middle of her sadness (244–45). Like Sam and Mamaw, Emmett is looking for something as well, verification or hope, perhaps, or more likely absolution (it is never clear if he does or does not find the name of the buddy). He needs to be able to let go of the guilt that he feels for surviving the war, and it appears at the end that he does. Mamaw asks, "Did we lose Emmett?" and "Silently, Sam points to the place where Emmett is studying the names low on a panel. He is sitting there cross-legged in front of the wall, and slowly his face bursts into a smile like flames" (244–45). Emmett's "smile like flames" is his transfiguration back to the world of the living. Emmett is no longer lost, as Mamaw fears.[7]

Robert H. Brinkmeyer, Jr., sums up the ending: "From a simplistic and emotional understanding of the Vietnam War and human evil, Sam here at the end possesses a deeper knowledge of the dark complexities that shadow all human experience" (30). In other words, Sam is on her way toward adulthood, which is necessarily filled with "dark complexities." Her father's death and her mother's absence have shaped her path, but her destination is the same as the other heroines discussed in this book. Sam, with her androgynous name and traditionally male quest for a lost warrior father, differs little from young male protagonists from Telemachus on. What makes Sam unique is less her gender than the particular tragedies of the American experience with the Vietnam War and her location in the rapidly disappearing American Southern landscape.

For Sam, unlike for Emmett, verification is enough. Throughout the novel she has needed to know that she existed, not just as a forlorn byproduct of a difficult time but as an individual with a past — and a future. It matters less that Sam is a girl than she is a legacy, a living record of the losses America suffered in Vietnam. Thus her growth to adulthood cannot take place without coming to terms with Vietnam. She must reach down to that deeper layer, which includes taking responsibility for — and at times resisting — the expectations of national, sexual, and regional identity. Sam, like all of America, is in "limbo" until she can understand what she has lost and what she has been given by her country's troubled history. Sam has to move from limbo to the crossroads, from a state of suspension to a state of decision (which it appears that she has done by the end of the novel), so that readers can be as hopeful for her as Bobbie Ann Mason is for all of her characters. Like the other young women in this study, Sam has taken a hard road toward independence and identity.

FIVE

"People Have No Respect for Girls": Lucille Odom's Ride Through Adolescence

"Lucille," Rae said, leaning past me to crush a cigarette in my saucer, "you live in your own little world." I didn't respond. She was half right: it was my own. But it was not little [Josephine Humphreys, *Rich in Love*, 45].[1]

Lucille Odom, the 17-year-old heroine of Josephine Humphreys' novel *Rich in Love*, begins and ends her story on her bicycle, which is perhaps an even more perfect vehicle for an adolescent than Sam's VW bug, as it provides movement and a small element of danger, while not being as adult — or as risky — as an automobile. Lucille's novel starts as she rides home "on an afternoon two years ago," when her "life veered from its day-in-day-out course and became for a short while the kind of life that can be told as a story — that is, one in which events appear to have meaning" (1). Her mother Helen has left the family — "betrayed the rest and set off a series of events worth telling" — and the rest of the novel recounts Lucille's growing understanding of her mother and father (and their relationship), her pregnant sister Rae (and her new husband), and, finally, what her own story means (1).[2] Although she feels abandoned by her mother, responsible for her father Warren, mystified by her sister's pre-natal depression, and guilty about her affair with her brother-in-law Billy, she nevertheless will emerge at the end of the novel confident about her future. Like the plucky female characters in Tyler's novels, Lucille will pick herself up and get on with her life, making her luck as she goes.

What frustrates her especially as the novel begins, however, is her realization that "People have no respect for girls. People think girls are brainless. Even someone who has recently been one has no respect for girls..." (68–69). Lucille is right, of course, about what people think; girls are doubly cursed in American society, by their youth and their gender. No one takes them seriously, not even other women, like Rae, who criticizes her fellow female workers in Washington for their weakness when they leave, and who thinks Lucille's dilemmas are merely cute. Her father ignores her in his obsession with his missing wife, even forgetting her graduation, and her boyfriend and brother-in-law think her (and their) problems can be solved by sex — with them. Lucille's struggle in this novel is first to find a way to convince those around her that she is a major player in this drama and finally to accept that she is not.

Her touching naïveté, her passionate love for her family, and her confident (but sometimes mistaken) pronouncements about those around her endear her to the reader in spite of her self absorption, somewhat annoying preciosity, and occasional ethical blind spots. Humphreys admits in a 1991 interview that Lucille is "not an entirely likable creature, especially at the beginning of the book" (797); however, in general Humphreys' adolescent characters strike her "as insistent presences who will show up whether I plan them or not, as bearers of hope in an adult world of despair" (794). This combination of over-confidence and optimism, arrogance and hope, creates a kind of ironic sympathy for Lucille: the reader wants her to succeed in pulling her family back together while being fully aware (as the character is not) of all the reasons why she might fail. Adolescent characters like Lucille are "bearers of hope in an adult world"; readers want them to believe in abstract values like family when they do not.

Since Lucille is both a girl and an adolescent, it is tempting to explain her innocent desire for order and her inability to move forward with her life as consequences of her mother's disappearance. There is evidence for this position in comments the author has made to interviewers. Humphreys told Mickey Pearlman that while writing *Rich in*

Love she found herself "drifting back to thinking about girls, thinking about the relationship of a girl and her mother" (122), and she says in another interview that Lucille's "life has stalled. After her mother disappears, she doesn't grow. I blamed her mother's absence for Lucille not moving past that; she's sort of stuck, when she could be going into a new phase" (797).

Following this line of thought, critic Shelley Jackson says that Humphreys "develops the relationship between a mother and daughter by examining both the semiotic and symbolic communication between them. She creates a maternal metalanguage" (278). This "metalanguage" is denied Lucille when her mother leaves her, putting her at the mercy of years of Southern patriarchal history. Lucille, she says, "has sought permanence above all else in her life; change is the ultimate threat" (280); for Jackson, change is associated with the maternal, stasis with the paternal. The novel, she says, offers "a feminist view of the South for the postmodern world," with the mother and daughter's world view coinciding at the end and embracing change (285).[3]

It would be a mistake, however, to concentrate exclusively on Lucille's relationship with her mother when looking for clues to her behavior. While Humphreys admits that mother/daughter relationships have been examined more closely since the woman's movement, she says that "all family relationships are uniquely interesting, and they're very mysterious" (796). Therefore, a reader could just as productively look at Lucille's relationship with her father, which is chronicled more fully in the book, or with her sister, both idol and rival, or with her brother-in-law, whom she sees as both mentor and secret lover. Also, Humphreys insists that she is not writing a novel influenced by a particularly female perspective. In a panel discussion with other female writers on whether or not they write as women, Humphreys said that "writing affects my femininity more than femininity affects my writing.... It seems to be constantly modifying my perceptions of myself and of what I am doing" (3). So, it is less that Humphreys writes as a woman than that her writing affects her view of what it means to be a woman. Finally, then, Lucille's relationship with her mother is only one aspect of the novel.

It might be useful to look at the relationship between author and character, rather than one between mother and daughter in the novel. In an interview with Dannye Powell, Humphreys says that "the great talent of children" is that they are driven to "make everything okay in their heads," regardless of their particular circumstances (186). This seems to be a gender-neutral quality for Humphreys, this desire, as she says, to "gloss over the really weird parts" of one's life. In "My Real Invisible Self," Humphreys says that growing up with two sisters and a photographic portrait loving grandmother made her "regard my own childhood with a strange detachment, almost as if it belonged to someone else. I think of it as an interesting story, distinct somehow from my real invisible self." While her "real" self is "lonesome, dark and ornery," she says, the pictures make her life look "bright, charged with possibilities" (9). This discontinuity between appearance and reality, between the photographs and the "real invisible self," is a condition as common to male writers-to-be as to female ones. Humphreys is not talking about the ways in which female subjects are objectified by the male gaze, only about how one might appear to be different on the surface than one's "real invisible self." Her "girl-self" is "lonesome, dark and ornery," much like many boy-selves. In telling her own life story, Humphreys thus can be seen as writing a generic story of development, rather than a particularly female narrative.

Humphreys shares this gender neutrality with her main character, Lucille. Joseph Millichap says that Lucille is "so spunky and dependable that she becomes something of an author surrogate, incisively skewing the foibles of her place and time" (250). As "author surrogate," however, it is Lucille's satirical observations, not her gender, that matter. Indeed, Lucille is frequently sardonic, usually insightful, and nearly always very, very funny in her observations about others, but she understands less about herself. "It stymied me," she says, "that I could fail completely to see my own life, yet have a sixth sense about somebody else's" (15). Like many male protagonists, Lucille is not blessed — or cursed — with emotional intuition.

For example, before her mother abandons them Lucille has a premonition, but she fails to understand the full text of the warning because it involves emotions: Feelings, she says, "were a problem to me at the time. I was prey to them, and yet I could never tell exactly what they meant. They seemed uselessly vague" (1–2). Falling victim to feelings is typical for adolescents; however, finding them "uselessly vague" is more specific to boys than to girls. Being encouraged almost from birth by society to respond to and express feelings, girls are usually more familiar with the nuances and implications of emotions. A "typical" girl would probably have much less trouble figuring out what her feelings *mean* than Lucille does.

Lucille's response to this feeling of vague bewilderment is, not surprisingly (if she were male), to prepare herself for all contingencies. Her main personality trait becomes "vigilance." "Let the world do its worst," she says, "Lucille Odom was ready" (5–6). Like a good Boy Scout, Lucille hopes to prepare herself for whatever is headed her way. She needn't understand something to be *ready* for it, ready to take action, just like boys have for generations been trained to do.

In fact, before her mother is scarcely gone, she rewrites her mother's goodbye letter to make it more palatable (she thinks) to her father. To a letter that is almost cruelly matter of fact, Lucille adds flowery phrases like "dearest," "absolutely adrift," and "emptiness at the heart of things," trying to soften the blow. Acting before fully understanding the emotional complexity of the situation, Lucille does more harm than good with her revision, however. The unnatural tone of the altered letter makes her father believe that her mother didn't leave willingly, and he begins a hopeless quest to find her. Here, Lucille has misunderstood her parents' relationship and her father's reaction, in large part because she acts before she thinks or feels.

Clearly, Lucille is and is not like many adolescent girls — she can be emotional *and* practical; she is hurt by her mother leaving, but she is eager to take action. Combined with her high intelligence, these attributes, not surprisingly, set Lucille apart from her peers. Although she recognizes that her feelings of alienation are typical, she claims their source is unique: a split upper lip that had been repaired in childhood. Lucille's "hardly noticeable" (6) defect causes her to feel, however, as if she is "a member of a third gender or secret species" (7). This feeling aptly describes both Lucille's gender trouble and the acute self-consciousness typical of adolescence; she is both a boy and girl, and perhaps at this point not quite human. When her sister, an acknowledged beauty, criticizes Lucille for her self-consciousness, calling it "vanity," Lucille responds that she is "as tired of self-consciousness as I could be." All she wants is "to never have another thought about myself; never again hear the sound of my own voice, outer or inner; never hear my name spoken" (105). Self-consciousness is a burden, made particularly heavy by the fact that adults are prone to minimize and criticize it, not recognizing, as Lucille does, its involuntary nature.

This heightened self-awareness, combined with her sense of difference, however, can have a positive side effect. It leads Lucille to an intuitive understanding of others, especially other adolescents, who find it difficult to resist temptation. Although Lucille says she "was regarded as an abstainer in every respect," she does feel "the pang now and again" of temptation. "People like me are sometimes hanging onto their so-called goodness by a thread," she says. "I didn't know how I was going to turn out" (14). Clearly, Lucille is on the verge of some kind of action, probably something the former first lady would not approve of, but she is right — just saying no solves only part of the problem, for part of the time, especially if one is "hanging on to their so-called goodness by a thread." Adolescent boys and girls, it seems, are equally tempted and cursed with not knowing how they are "going to turn out."

In some ways, however, Lucille does experience a side of adolescence peculiar to girls. She describes this state as like waiting in a movie theater for something awful to happen. This feeling, she says "manifests itself as a stomachache," and she calls it "girlhood" and hopes "to death that I would one day soon burst out of it" (20). It's not entirely clear whether boys feel "stupid, seventeen, and powerless," too, but "boyhood" does seem different to Lucille. Boys, she thinks "have that extended phase of innocence," which she doesn't think girls have at all. The Adventures of Huckleberry Finn, written by a Becky Thatcher, she says would have been "an altogether different concept. You have something dark" (146).[4] For girls, then, there is an awareness of one's powerlessness and no "extended phase of innocence." Like Bone, in *Bastard out of Carolina*, Lucille jumps from innocent childhood to grown womanhood in a summer, all the while both dreading and anticipating the transformation.

Like many young women, too, much of Lucille's longing and her frustrations center around her stomach. Young people feel a "hunger" for life; powerlessness causes a "stomachache." When she later falls in love with her brother-in-law Billy, Lucille tries to stave off this sense of powerlessness by eating compulsively, wishing for comfort while realizing that what she really needs is "fortification" against the blows of life (127). What Lucille is trying to find, really, fortification against chaos — her parents' separation, her unrequited and inappropriate love for her sister's husband, her sister's depression, and her own movement from childhood to adulthood.

Lucille is also looking for ways to shore up her crumbling identity, damaged by her discovery (at age 10) that she was the other half of a set of twins, one of whom her mother aborted, and undermined further by her mother's desertion, which seems to her at seventeen as a second rejection. It leaves her with a "strange sensation of incompleteness" and "bereavement." It also explains to her why her mother seems "aloof" (51). Being the only remaining twin leaves Lucille feeling bereft, having lost her other half *and* her confidence in her mother's love. Still, Lucille is not quite sure how this information might explain her past or determine her future. Humphreys, as does Tyler and many contemporary women writers, refuses to make too much of her character's childhood traumas. "In the long run," Lucille concludes, " I was alive and well, and I knew some true things about my past. That was all I could say" (51).

Obviously, Lucille is raising profound philosophical questions about identity, about whether individuals are shaped by or shape events, about the conflict between nature and nurture, but a causal relationship between past events and present realities probably doesn't exist. This is not to say that what adults tell children about themselves is unimportant; they are busily forming their identities based in part on these stories, after all. Humphreys says that children "take it to heart [what you tell them]. It sinks in. Children are constantly making their idea of what they are" (187). Finally, however, it seems that being "alive and well" and knowing "some true things" about one's past is as good as it may get.

This practical combination of functioning in the present and accepting the past allows Lucille, at least early in the novel, to cope with the chaos caused by her mother and sister. In fact, she is profoundly skeptical of the power of abstractions, in particular philosophy, to explain anything. For example, she worries about her father's foray into the history of ideas at the bookstore. Philosophy is fine, she thinks, if one is trained in it, but it has the potential to drive people crazy. "Metaphysical truth is beyond the scope of the human brain," she says. " It exists but it can't be known. I respected the limits of cerebral capability. I didn't want Pop to blow his fuses" (91). It is not quite clear if Lucille thinks of herself as an "amateur," even though she does respect "the limits of cerebral capability." She does know that her father may "blow his fuses" with too much abstraction. The human brain, for Lucille, is capable of understanding action, but not motivation; desire but not truth.

Lucille knows she is not going to get answers from thinking, not when there is so much to do. Her mother has left her in charge (she thinks) of a rapidly disintegrating family, and her older sister, in the throes of a difficult and unwanted pregnancy, will turn out to be no help at all. Lucille is "the one saddled with the household worries, of which there were more than I had ever dreamed" (32). At seventeen, she is "unprepared to be the lady of a house" (32). She wants to be "well-organized" because in her family "there was little preparedness, and no rhyme or reason to the daily schedule" (33). Of course, she also wants to be prepared because, as the reader already knows, vigilance is the personal quality she most admires in herself. What she fails to realize is that her family, for various reasons, may prefer the lack of organization.

According to Lucille, "The ragtag nature of the household was due to our mother's nonchalance," an attribute Lucille admired in her mother, until she left (33). This nonchalance carried over into her relationship with her daughter, however, which was not altogether a bad thing: "Mother's interest was downright grandmotherly. Kind, wrathless, dispassionate. She was never upset with me, never dissatisfied, never emotionally entangled" (24). Lucille attributes this in part to her not being wanted, to her escaping the abortion by being a twin, but it could just as easily be attributed to confident mothering. Lucille's attitude about such dispassionate mothering, which could be also seen as creating necessary distance between mother and daughter, changes when her mother leaves. Although she expresses some misgivings about "how events are linked in the world," Lucille says that "a family without a mother is vulnerable. She left us sitting ducks" (24). This is a correct assessment, although Lucille doesn't realize it at the time; the events that follow do show the dangers of such carelessness.

Although her leaving is consistent with her general "nonchalance," Lucille still tries to discover some other origin for her behavior. When she first phones the family, Lucille asks her Mother, "is this something feminist? ... or is it something real?" (26). It isn't quite clear what the distinction between feminist and real is to Lucille, but perhaps it is between making a political and a personal decision, something which feminists have long declared amount to the same thing. According to Shelley Jackson, Lucille asks the question this way because her "desire to maintain the patriarchal family unit demands that she negate something 'feminist' as within the realm of the real" (281). The feminist world view becomes a fantasy, at least until Lucille meets up again with her mother and accepts her changed view of the world. But maybe it doesn't really matter which it is. After all, according to Lucille, philosophically motivated decisions are either insane or best left to the professionals, and emotional motivations are unclear to her at this point in her life. So seen either way, her mother's leaving can make no sense to her.

Her attachment to her mother, finally, is more visceral than emotional or philosophical. When she finally finds her hiding out in an unfinished house near her friend Rhody's and sees her coming up the path, Lucille thinks, "I had forgotten her looks. Her loveliness had slipped out of my mind" (201). Her mother's beauty is a powerful force in her life. It explains to Lucille her father's attachment to her mother, it invests her mother with power, it becomes a sign of successful womanhood, a legacy bequeathed to Rae but withheld (she thinks) from her. Beautiful women, like Rae and her mother, are entitled to be nonchalant about their emotional attachments, she thinks. Unlike Lucille, they cannot be held accountable for their actions; they are forgiven everything, even abandonment.

Later in the evening, when she is spending the night, Lucille thinks about reaching out to her mother emotionally, telling her the troubles she is having. "We could have been the mother and daughter of a true-love ballad," she thinks, "telling what we know" (206). Lucille wants her mother to ask her how she is surviving her disappearance, but her mother remains distant, either out of confidence in her daughter or self-absorption.[5] However, perhaps Lucille must disentangle herself from her mother's loveliness, her nonchalance, and most importantly her silence, in order to grow. She *needs* to be disillusioned. This is not to say that Lucille is not in "grave danger" at this moment, however, but that she has to pass through that danger alone, to move from being unaware of how rich in love she is, to harboring and finally acting on a secret love, to accepting the limitations of those she loves and recognizing the importance of memory, without the help of her mother. With her mother intimately involved in her life, Lucille cannot fully discover the depth and variety of love all around her.

Love — familial, forbidden, romantic, and again familial — organizes this novel, from the early pages, when Lucille foreshadows her later actions by saying she can "imagine ethics outweighed by desire," to the ending, where she discovers her love for her new niece, Phoebe (5). Her early comments on love reflect a child's response to parental love: "I doubt that parents have an inkling how deep a child's love goes," Lucille says. "It is more thorough than adult love. I loved not only my parents: I loved their love" (29). Because of this, it is very difficult for Lucille to accept her mother's disappearance; she can't love her mother separate from her father without mourning the loss of her parents' love for each other. As many children do, she fantasizes about her parents being reunited, trying to prevent her father from seeing his new girlfriend almost to the end of the novel. Still, even with her parents' marriage officially over, the foundation of love they created remains with her: "It had been accumulating silently over the years like equity in a house. I was rich in love, even though no one could see it" (146). She realizes this finally at the end of the novel, when she is able to leave her family home with "almost frightening" ease (260). Lucille no longer needs her parents under the same roof to feel safe; she has created her own network of love.

"Rich in love" does describe Lucille, although it could be read ironically as well. Too much love, especially when it is misdirected, can do more harm than good, like Lucille's attraction for her brother-in-law Billy McQueen. She first becomes aware of her desire when he tells her (innocently at this point in the novel) that she has "a lot of love" in her. Her response is to feel that her real self has been recognized, that she is like an old safe, full of money, just waiting to be opened, either accidentally or on purpose. This is typical of Lucille to question cause and effect, to wonder whether Billy has really identified something in her, whether she has broadcast it, or whether it is entirely an accident. The metaphor is telling, however; Lucille is a safe that has been cracked by her brother-in-law. Still, this right combination remains a "lucky discovery" that she must hide from the outside world.

At first she thinks, naively, that she can keep this secret but comes to realize something different. She starts to see "how a life can divide in two, and the daily, visible portion move further and further away from the secret, invisible part." The problem with such is a secret is that "[l]ike a little fox in the dark, with sharp teeth and claws, the secret life will gnaw and gnaw" (175). Her love for Billy brings her to a point in her development typical for most adolescents. The "unified existence" of childhood is over (although recollected nostalgically), and the adult reality of a divided consciousness — an interior and an exterior life — emerges. Through her love for Billy, Lucille has become a "split personality." The worry, of course, is that her "interior life will get out of hand" and reveal itself to the world.

Although adults reading this novel (who are perhaps more fully aware of the ways in which people can conceal things about themselves) will not be surprised, Lucille is shocked that her preoccupied family fails to notice anything amiss. "It was as if I had deposited a gem in a Swiss bank," she says. " I shared it with no one, paid no taxes" (222). Only an adolescent would be surprised that love can be concealed, that it is both "a little fox in the dark" and "a gem in a Swiss bank," not a vicious beast or time bomb. Only an adolescent (or one who behaves like one) can fail to see that this kind of secret love is a destructive force within the individual and the family.

Once again, however, Lucille's experiences give her an empathy for others, in this case for other teenage girls in the past, like those in Puritan times accused of "witchery." Lucille says she understands how the repression and claustrophobia of those long New England nights in small houses could lead to unpredictable behavior. The important thing, she says, "is to understand that it is an involuntary condition" (228). Several familiar elements are present here in this analogy: the understanding of others' helplessness, the reference to the stomach as locus of emotional strife, the darkness in young girls, and the "involuntary" nature of adolescent action. These factors combine to bring the novel to its crisis point. Not surprisingly, given this previous passage about "witchery," Lucille and Billy's single sexual encounter occurs on Halloween night, and it ends in near tragedy (Rae gives birth in the bathroom and, deeply delusional, fails to acknowledge the birth). Although both mother and baby are rescued, Billy and Lucille are overcome with guilt, and have no further contact with each other, having nearly paid a high price for their indiscretions.

Although Lucille's "witchery" could have led to disaster, the novel resolves itself benignly. Her mother returns to tend to baby (but not to reunite with her father), her father takes up with his hairdresser, Rae recovers, Billy returns to his role as dutiful husband/father, and Lucille makes plans to attend college. Lucille, Ann Henley says, "who originally depended on a specific configuration of walls and roof for her sense of self, has enlarged and remodeled that self so that it fills and accommodates itself to 'all the new places we have settled into'" (86). Like her family house, which has been remodeled by its new owners, Lucille has altered herself to fit the new reality. No longer drifting and ironically detached, she is focused and sincerely determined to impart her hard-won wisdom to the next generation.

Her family, too, is changed but not destroyed: they are "all gravitating back into family lives of one sort or another" following a pattern that "people cannot seem to help, in spite of lessons learned the hard way" (260). People remain drawn to families, Lucille says, to construct and reconstruct them, in spite of previous disasters. They look for the love families give; they refuse to remain alone.

At the end of the novel, though, Lucille is surprised by how little the events of the summer and fall have affected her. She thought that love would "deepen and complicate" her, but it "had in a way not even touched" her. She says she is "unscathed" but asserts that she will not forget what has happened (258). It is clear here that part of Lucille remains an adolescent at the end of the novel, although one quite chastened and cautious. She is "unscathed" it is true, in the way adolescents have of surviving all sorts of stupid choices, but she does have a memory of the near disaster to direct her. She is on the road to adulthood, looking to the future, while reclaiming and learning from the past.

Memory is the key, both for Lucille and for the newest female member of the Odom/McQueen family, Rae and Billy's daughter Phoebe. As Phoebe rides on the back of Lucille's bicycle, Lucille wants to tell this representative of the next generation about "the strength and fragility of things, the love and the luck hidden together in the world." She admits that this will be hard. "We ride father and farther to get a view; we forget more and more what ought to be remembered," Lucille says. "But [Phoebe] is like me, and she will know" (261).

What Lucille has learned in her trying half year are the contradictions in life — strength and fragility, love and luck, honesty and the difficulty of expressing it, remembering and forgetting. What she has retained is the confidence that lessons can be taught, provided one has the necessary humility. Like the young women in Tyler's novels, she has achieved contentment by separating from her mother, like Sam she has found ways to reconcile her past with her future, and like the heroines of the next chapter, Bone and Ellen, she has discovered the power of crossing gender boundaries.[6] On her bicycle as she was in the beginning of the novel, although this time with a passenger, Lucille is imparting her difficult and hard-won wisdom.[7]

"The Hope of the Remade Life": Allison's and Gibbons' Rewritten Girlhoods

> If I could have found what I needed at thirteen, I would not have lost so much of my life chasing vindication or death. Give some child, some thirteen-year-old, the hope of the remade life. Tell the truth [Dorothy Allison, *Skin*, 219].

Younger than the late adolescent girls of the previous chapters, but wiser in the frequently violent and cruel ways of the world, the heroines of Dorothy Allison's *Bastard Out of Carolina* (1992) and Kaye Gibbons' *Ellen Foster* (1987), Bone Boatright and Ellen Foster, are both dependent on and betrayed by their mothers. Bone's mother allows her husband to abuse her daughter, and Ellen's mother commits suicide, leaving her in the hands of her drunken father. Yet these betrayals are seen as complex in motivation and understandable, if not forgivable, and, in spite of their mothers' abandonment, both girls manage to transform their lives into oases of safety and contentment.

Using models from their extended families, which include relations and non-relations, Ellen and Bone change everything about themselves, from their names to their homes, and as their material circumstances improve so do their abilities to imagine tranquil and satisfying adult lives. For these girls, being a foster child or a cast-off bastard represents an *improvement* in their circumstances; for 11-year-old Ellen it provides her with her first experience of a secure (if untraditional) family with food on the table (and in her stomach) and no violence or abuse. For 12-year-old Bone, being cut off from her mother and forced to live with a "maiden" aunt is preferable to a familial connection with a stepfather who beats and rapes her and a mother who allows it to happen.

Unlike the middle-class girls of Tyler, Mason, and Humphreys, these two characters come from the (infrequently) working poor, which necessarily results in them having different needs and ways of meeting those needs. Tyler's adolescents have parents who are high school math teachers and ministers, Humphreys' Lucille has a demolition expert father and housewife mother, and even Mason's Sam, who is most loosely connected to the middle class, has a mother willing — and able — to pay for her college expenses. Ellen's mother is barely able to get out of bed, and her father is usually drunk; Bone's mother waitresses but barely makes enough money to keep her family fed, while her husband's temper keeps him chronically unemployed. Ellen and Bone have to worry about whether they will have enough to eat and remain safe in their homes; they have little time for the more ephemeral concerns of Sam, Lucille, Elizabeth, and Evie. True, each character is developing — learning, growing, changing, but their trajectories are very different.

Renny Christopher aptly describes these class differences in development novels:

> The bourgeois novel is conventionally structured around some
> sort of movement — a quest, a search, a striving for career, for
> love, for fulfillment, for a better address. [Working class] charac-
> ters aren't striving for anything. They're struggling to stay alive,
> but *struggling* isn't the same thing as *striving* (46–47).

The working-class novel, Christopher says, "is created out of a different set of conflicts than the bourgeois novel, which requires not only movement but teleological movement" (47). For novels about girls like Ellen and Bone, there is less a movement toward a final — and fitting — goal than a never-ending struggle to survive. It is true that Ellen has found a "better address," but she hasn't exactly climbed the social ladder when she moves into her foster home, and certainly, while Bone is safe with her aunt at the end of the novel, one wouldn't describe her as having found what she had been looking for throughout the novel. These characters are struggling, not striving, and the movement, when there is movement, is not toward some definite goal, unless that goal is a realistic, or perhaps adult, awareness of their place in the world.

However, while these girls are from working-class environments, they don't fall into the common stereotypes of "white trash"— depraved and lazy or heroic and scrappy. Instead, Allison in particular resists these stereotypes, as Kathleen McDonald points out. Allison's characters "find ways of resisting their appointed roles even as they submit to them," McDonald says. They "contradict preconceived stereotypes and commodified images, thereby creating space for a historical understanding of white-trash identities" (22). Both Alison and Gibbons have created characters who change readers' perceptions about "white trash," transforming the images of poor whites in radical ways.

To add to the complexity, these two novels aren't just about working-class characters struggling to make their way financially and socially; they are also about young girls who are abused, or threatened with abuse by their fathers and stepfathers. Consequently, these girls speak a language and tell stories that seem inappropriate for their age. Renee Curry says that first-person girl narrators in this sort of contemporary fiction "speak with an always already wisdom that profoundly disturbs adult readers because of reader desire for genuine (or, at least, rhetorical) innocence and optimism on the part of girls — regardless of the girls' fiction or lived lives" (98). In other words, readers expect young girls (especially those who are only 11 or 12) not to know very much at all about the adult world, especially about sex and violence. Bone and Ellen resist these expectations and unsettle the reader in the process. Such narrators are already who they will become; they do not grow and change so much as they resist — through their intelligence and will — what seem to be inevitable futures. These kinds of narrators, Curry says, are "deliberate constructions" (102), who "grow into the people they were in their youths" (104), but this is not necessarily an unhappy outcome, as their childhood selves show promise as well as precocity.

It is also important to note that these girls are *Southern* girls, whose fictional incest stories, as Minrose Gwin suggests, reveal "how the father's power in the Southern patriarchal family is produced within and itself reproduces a cultural space that has historically emphasized property ownership and built up an institutionalized system of the containment and usage of women's bodies to that end" (417). Both Bone and Ellen belong to the men heading their family, and their mothers are powerless to defend them; the only solution is to escape the father's (or stepfather's) house. "For the Southern daughter in the patriarchal house," Gwin says, "place and identity become compounded and conflicted because place/identity equal(s) powerlessness" (419). Unless these girls can leave, they cannot develop an individual identity. While these stories cause the reader to question "the ideological constructions of 'home' and its felicity for girls and women when the father is in the house," their conclusions suggest that other homes — particularly without the father present — may prove more felicitous to these girls (437)

So, as poor Southern women, wise for their age, Bone and Ellen refuse to conform to middle-class expectations. Instead of being stupidly resigned to their traditional fates (early motherhood, poverty, violence), they are moving *away* from this prescribed future — at least by the time the novels end— *toward* a certain kind of new life. Like the heroines of previous novels, they struggle to free themselves from the restrictions of their gender and find new connections to replace their lost mothers, but unlike Sam, Lucille, Elizabeth, and Evie, they have to work much, much harder.

Dorothy Allison's Bastard Out of Carolina

> Family is family, but even love can't keep people from eating at each other [*Bastard Out of Carolina*, 10].

In an interview with Carolyn Megan, Dorothy Allison says that for her heroine Bone, "everything was constructed around what these people, who were essentially the aunts and uncles, were giving to this Bone: a sense of who she was in the world — what her possibilities were" (72). These relatives, in particular her Aunt Raylene who shelters her and teaches her independence, are creating for Bone an alternative set of choices for her life, but finally Bone has to do the work herself. As Allison tells Megan:

> Bone is moving toward a kind of truth, and that's real important. She's caught in a network of lies and misrepresentation. ... The

only thing that saves her are the stories, the ones that she needs to make for herself [73].

These stories, where Bone rewrites the abuse as sexual pleasure, are her means of escape, as writing the novel, which is clearly autobiographical, was for her creator. For Allison, and for Bone, the power to tell shocking truths and to re-write trauma brings with it the power to survive.

In *Two or Three Things I Know For Sure*, Allison's memoir of her childhood, she says:

> I know the use of fiction in a world of hard truth, the way fiction can be a harder piece of truth. The story of what happened, or what did not happen but should have — that story can become a curtain drawn shut, a piece of insulation, a disguise, a razor, a tool that changes every time it is used and sometimes becomes something other than we intended [3].

Bastard Out of Carolina becomes all those things for Allison, as do both the sexually explicit stories Bone tells about her beatings and the implicit re-construction of her life that is created by telling her life story. As Leigh Gilmore says, "Allison insists on an alternative construction of the grounds of judgment by relocating truth from the legalistic jurisdiction of autobiography to the expansive borderland between autobiography and fiction. An alternative jurisprudence merges as the bastard daughter rewrites her mother's legacy" (49). By telling her story as a novel, then, Allison is able both to escape the ethical (and perhaps legal) implications of telling the "truth," and to rewrite the narrative.[1]

Much of what Bone (and Allison) has to do in the novel is find a way to explain what her mother's role was — and should have been — in the character's abuse by her stepfather. In *Skin*, Allison's essay collection, she says:

> [T]here was only one story that would haunt me until I understood how to tell it — the complicated, painful story of how my mama had, and had not, saved me as a girl. Writing *Bastard Out of Carolina* became, ultimately, the way to claim my family's pride and tragedy, and the embattled sexuality I had fashioned on a basis of violence and abuse [34].

Her mother "had, and had not" saved her; she failed to protect her from her abusive stepfather *and* she provided her with the resilience and strength of character (or perhaps just a strong will to survive and the stubbornness) to resist and escape. Her mother's legacy is one for both "pride and tragedy," for Allison and her alter-ego, Bone, and it is a large part of the story she is trying to tell.[2] In *Bastard*, Allison wants to explain herself, her mother, and her particular world of impoverished white Southerners, what is known there as "white trash," but she wants to do it in a way that is unconventionally sympathetic.[3]

On the first page of the novel, Ruth Ann "Bone" Boatright, the narrator, introduces herself: "I've been called Bone all my life, but my name's Ruth Anne. I was named for and by my oldest aunt — Aunt Ruth. My mama didn't have much to say about it, since strictly speaking, she wasn't there" (1). Her mother was in a coma after a car accident, but "strictly speaking," her mother isn't fully present for most of Bone's life. Too tired from her job as a waitress and too afraid of losing her husband (Bone's abusive stepfather), she at first fails to notice and then later to acknowledge that his "discipline" has crossed the line into physical and sexual abuse. Bone is named by her aunt, and she is confirmed in her nickname by her attributes — her hardness, her stubbornness, her indestructibility.

In spite of her various kinds of absences, Bone's mother remains important and interesting to her throughout her childhood. Bone is emotionally and physically connected to her mother, demanding that the reader "watch her" working in the diner with almost a lover's eye (14). Here readers are asked to see a woman in control of her environment, refusing "dates, pinches, suggestions" while still making the tips that will feed her family. This is a woman who catches and rejects the gaze of everyone in the diner. Here also is a woman with a "tight stubborn mouth," like her daughter, but also with sunken eyes and lines from work and worry. She represents an ideal of desirable womanhood, a vision of her daughter's future, and the promise of a life from which Bone is desperate to escape (14). In order to survive Bone must emulate her confidence and competence and resist her fatalism and fear.[4]

Before her mother's betrayal, or perhaps more precisely, before her mother chooses her husband's love over her daughter's safety, Bone is willing to "believ[e] anything that Mama said was so" (18). She even accepts unflattering assessments, like her mother's accusation of stubbornness for not cutting her chronically tangled hair: "Mama put both hands on my shoulders and squeezed. She didn't sound angry. I raised my head to look at her. Her brown eyes were enormous close up, with little flecks of light in the pupils. I could almost see myself between the flashes of gold" (29). Bone can "almost see" herself in her mother's eyes. She certainly sees clearly enough how her mother views her, but the reflection also shows "flecks of light" and "flashes of gold." At this point in their relationship, even criticism is tempered by the obvious connections (and love) between them.

This complicated mixture of reactions is consistent with Bone's view of her entire family, including her grandmother and aunts. She knows that in some ways her family isn't exactly *nice,* in a conventional middle-class way, but she loves them, not in spite of their flaws but for their vitality, their earthiness, their hardness and their hardiness. Sitting by her grandmother on the porch, Bone remarks on "the heat of her body through her cotton dress," the way her grandmother "leaned over and spat a stream of brown snuff" and "put my face close to her breast," as well as the smell coming from her of "wet snap beans, tobacco, lemon juice on her neck, a little sharp piss scent, and a little salt" (20–21). Heat and physical affection; tobacco juice and spit; wet beans and piss; Allison doesn't attempt to balance the "positive" with the "negative" here but tries instead to do something much harder — to look backward nostalgically without obscuring the reality, to show how a life that is not exactly neat and tidy could also be comforting and secure.

In spite of the elegiac tone of this passage, though, Bone realizes that her family falls short of ideal, particularly regarding grandmothers. The difference between Granny and the apron-and-cookies model grandmother is clarified by Bone's sister Reese's paternal grandmother, Mrs. Parsons, who looks "like a granny you'd read about or see in a movie" (55). The contrast is stark; Mrs. Parsons dresses the part of a proper grandmother, while Bone's grandmother wears "sleeveless print dresses that showed the sides of her loose white breasts and hitched up on her hips." She also perms her hair and ties it with a string, wears ungrandmotherly red lipstick "that invariably smeared down onto her knobby chin," curses, and spits (55).

The two grandmothers, not surprisingly, are equally different in behavior: Mrs. Parsons speaks "sadly about her lost boys and her distant daughter while shelling peas into a galvanized bucket," while Bone's granny gets mad, throws furniture, moves out of her daughters' houses, and threatens to set fire to them. "I loved Granny," Bone says, "but I imagined Mrs. Parsons might be a better choice for a grandmother, and sometimes when we went to visit I'd pretend she was mine" (55). Sad talk about lost children while shelling peas is appropriate behavior for grandmothers; throwing furniture, cursing, and threatening arson are not. As a way of coping with her embarrassment, Bone pretends her way into a more "normal" family.

The hardest part for Bone is that having only one grandmother — her father abandoned her, and his family doesn't acknowledge his child — allows her no alternative for imagining her future. Granny serves as the only model for Bone's old age, while her sister, whose father died and who is accepted by his parents, "had another family, another side of herself to think about, something more than Mama and me and the Boatwrights." The result of this is that "Reese could choose something different for herself and be someone else altogether" (59). Without more positive models, for either grandmother *or* mother, Bone may be forced to repeat history — becoming pregnant and being abandoned, marrying young and tragically, settling for an abusive husband, and, finally, cursing and spitting through her old age.

One way Bone tries to derail the apparently predetermined course of her life is to change her name (and, she hopes, her identity) after one of her family's frequent moves. She succeeds with surprising (and frightening) ease, "enjoying a brief popularity as someone from a big city who could tell big-city stories" (67). In spite of her success, though, Bone is relieved when her family moves again, and she can go back to her real name. The ease with which she can change her identity scares Bone, but it also gives her a sense of how she might be able to re-invent herself through her stories. Anxiety and confusion about her motives linger, even after the lie no longer matters, but what also remains is her sense that her reality can be altered, maybe for the better. Through fiction, a small-town bastard can become "someone from a big city who could tell big-city stories."

Bone's growing confidence in her ability to rewrite the script of her life leads her to make other, more lasting changes in her circumstances. The most important thing she does is spend more time at her aunts' houses, rather than remaining trapped in her increasingly abusive home. Even though Bone and her sister have to endure repeated washings and chigger bites after getting dirty at the aunts', they "still wan[t] to go visiting at every chance" — anything to escape the dangers and the coldness of their stepfather's house. The aunts' houses are "warm, always humming with voices and laughter and children running around," and visiting them melts the ice that forms at Daddy Glen's (80). Bone chooses warmth and noise over quiet and cold; she chooses her loving, extended family over her small, dysfunctional one.

Staying at her aunts' houses to avoid going home is only a partial solution, however. Another way is to imagine changing her gender, as abuse is more often doled out to women and girls. In fact, Bone notes that men seem to have an easier time in a variety of ways, being treated like "overgrown boys" who were "more to be joked about than worried over." The men in Bone's family always look young (even without their teeth), while all the women seem "old, worn-down, and slow, born to mother, nurse, and clean up after the men." Everything the men do, she says, "no matter how violent or mistaken, [is] viewed with humor and understanding" (23). Bone's response is, of course, to wish she had "been born a boy" (23). Bone, too, wants to be "viewed with humor and under-standing," no matter what she does. Most of all, she wants to avoid becoming "old, worn-down, and slow," taking care of perpetually ado-lescent men for the rest of her life.

However, Bone alternates between wanting to be as childlike as the men in her family and wanting to be a grown-up woman: "I liked being one of the women with my aunts, liked feeling a part of something nasty and strong and separate from my big rough boy-cousins and the whole world of spitting, growling, overbearing males" (91). Because they are truly grown up, the women in Bone's family discuss men (and sex) with a frankness that she finds appealing, and they radiate strength and confidence. In spite of their frank talk, however, they are unable to stand up to the physical abuse these boy-men dish out.

Having a boy's strength would have some advantages, especially in dealing with her stepfather's abuse. As she becomes more and more afraid of Daddy Glen, Bones wishes she was a boy so she could "run faster, stay away more, or even hit him back" (109). Bone thinks that being a boy would protect her from Daddy Glen, and there is some reason to think that his violence toward her has some basis in her gender. Because she is a girl, perhaps, the violence will escalate from slaps to beatings, and finally from beatings to sexual abuse, and eventually to rape.

The sense of Bone's entrapment also increases, pulling the reader, Gwin says, "into the material and cultural spaces of victimization" (433).

Continuing to read "becomes a claustrophobic experience in itself because we as readers are placed in the space of the object. We become Bone" (434). The reader is "inside a textual space that reproduces material female space under patriarchy — a space that will be violated by rape by the end of the novel. A tiny bathroom. Locked door. Sweaty cursing man with belt. Cold porcelain. Slap of the belt. Things can only get worse" (434). And of course they do.

Bone's primary means of escape is one that discomfits the reader; she re-imagines the beatings in a way that is sexually arousing for her. Yet it is possible to see this rewriting as creative and healing, too, another means of resisting the script she has been given. By turning abuse into fantasy, Bone can control the event and minimize the violence and degradation. Although the rape fantasies she contrives are disturbing to readers, they can also be seen as part of a continuing pattern Bone has created to alter the narrative of her life.[5]

Bone has other means of resistance, too; she has the stubbornness bequeathed her at birth and reinforced by her nickname, which reflects and reinforces her strength of will. When Bone reflects on her nickname, she thinks about the bones in her head, "the hard, porous edge of my skull cradling my brain, reassuring me that no matter what happened I could heal up from it eventually. It was the heat in my heart, my hard, gritty center" (111). Bone has internalized the hardness of the outside world, so that even her soft tissue — heart and brain — have become calcified. She has been taught by experience and reminded by her nickname to continually harden her mind and her emotions and find ways to pick herself up after every rejection and calamity.

Bone uses her inner strength in practical — and imaginative — ways. She helps her mother through hard times, allowing her "to lean on my strong, straight back." (118). Because of all the stubborn bone inside her, Bone has more "backbone" than her mother. Her hard mind is also useful, helping her to spin tales of "boys and girls gruesomely raped and murdered, babies cooked in pots of boiling beans, vampires and soldiers and long razor-sharp knives" that make her "very popular as a baby-sitter" and cast a spell over her charges (119). These stories are more than functional, though. They help Bone transform her own helplessness into narratives of empowerment, filled with "gangs of women" who "set fire to people's houses" and witches who "cut off the heads of children and grown-ups" (119). In her stories, Bone is creating a world of powerful (if wicked) women who take action when necessary and take a kind of surrogate vengeance against the Daddy Glens of this world.

Her stories will only take her so far, however. While struggling to resist her stepfather and coping with her mother's increasing disinterest, Bone briefly throws herself into religion as a way of finding some power and control in her life. Her link to that world is Shannon Pearl, a fat, strange albino child whose parents make clothes for gospel singers. Bone first notices Shannon on the school bus, where she is both mocked and shunned by the other students. Watching Shannon, Bone is drawn to something she recognizes in herself, an "impassive, self-sufficient, and stubborn" face and "a deep fire" in her eyes (154). Shannon's "banked and raging" fire matches Bone's stubborn anger, and she defends Shannon against the inevitable cruelties of her fellow schoolchildren, much as she defends herself.

She also uses Shannon and her family's connection to gospel singers to draw some of their power and glamour: "Gospel singers had love and safety and the whole wide world to fall back on — women and church and red clay solid under their feet. All I wanted, I whispered, all I wanted, was a piece, a piece, a little piece of it" (168). Bone wants "a little piece" of what she has never had — "love and safety and the whole wide world to fall back on." Her future as a gospel singer, however, is doomed before it starts because she cannot sing, and her friendship with Shannon is destroyed by an argument. Shannon is eventually incinerated by the family barbeque, a gruesome event so outrageous that it could have been one of Bone's stories, the fire being so obviously (and symbolically) an outward manifestation of the fire burning inside her. Still, her time with Shannon has taught her two things: that a wider world exists out there and that anger turned inward can be explosive.

After Shannon's spontaneous combustion, Bone has to look elsewhere for escape from her increasingly violent and abusive stepfather. She moves in with her Aunt Raylene, a single woman living down by the river. Raylene tells her about running away to join the circus, and Bone is amazed, and jealous, and finally afraid of her exploits. Bone thinks about Raylene's stories "with wistful longing" even while she worries about Raylene's "couple of ugly scars behind one ear." If she decides to follow Raylene's example, she thinks, " I might come back with worse scars, or not come back at all" (179). Raylene presents Bone with another set of possibilities, one that would allow her to act like a boy while remaining a girl. She does recognize, though, that such an escape would come with a price, one Bone is not yet ready to pay.

Although Bone is afraid of what might happen if she follows Raylene's path, she does admire her earthiness, strength, and grace. Raylene, who makes relishes and liquor, smells "a little of alcohol and pepper, chow-chow and home brew, and the woodsmoke tang that clung to her skin all the time." She is "as big around as Aunt Alma but mov[es] as easily and gracefully as a young boy" and loves to dance (180). Raylene embodies both genders — she smells like a man *and* a woman ("chow-chow and home brew"); she is as large as the largest woman and as graceful as a young boy; she moves like a man and dances like a woman. Raylene becomes the model of womanhood that Bone will adopt — a combination of male strength and female grace.[6]

Raylene picks up trash she finds on the river bank and sells it to help support herself, along with the alcohol and relish she makes, and her self-sufficiency provides Bone with further positive models of development. For example, while she is living with Raylene, Bone finds a hook with a lock and chain and finds a way to incorporate the tools into her sexual fantasy life (193). The chain and lock become "magic" in Bone's hands. They are both chastity belt and sexual toy, armor and weapon. Just as she makes fantasies out of abuse, Bone fashions the hard lock and chain into something soft, warm and "tingly," just as, the reader hopes, Bone's hardness will be transformed into survival.

Aunt Raylene's strength and the power of Bone's fantasies are not enough, however, to rescue her from the damage that Daddy Glen's dangerously inappropriate attention has caused. In desperation, Bone wants to change herself into someone she thinks will be more desirable, even to her stepfather. Looking at her "obstinate body, long legs, no hips, and only the slightest swell," Bone wishes she was "pretty." Wanting to be "more like the girls in storybooks, princesses with pale skin and tender hearts," she is, instead, "stubborn-faced, unremarkable, straight up and down, and dark as walnut bark." Bone wants to be feminine, and delicate, so she won't be treated like "peasant stock"; she wants to be rescued, not "worked to death, used up, and thrown away" (206). Bone wants to find something different or "magical" about herself, but all she finds that makes her unique is her "anger, that raw boiling rage in my stomach," which is "bottomless and horrible" (207).

Bone finds justification for Daddy Glen's behavior in what she sees as her repellant appearance. "No part of me was that worshipful, dreamy-eyed storybook girlchild," she thinks. "I could see why Daddy Glen was hateful to me" (208). Bone is convinced that "Love would make me beautiful; a father's love would purify my heart, turn my bitter soul sweet, and lighten my Cherokee eyes"(209). Class, race, and gender converge in these poignant passages. Bone thinks she cannot be loved because she is not delicately pretty, she has dark "Cherokee" eyes, and she is "born to be worked to death," not put on a pedestal and admired. Love, which can purify hearts and sweeten souls, is not available for those who don't fit the profile — small, blond, beautiful, and freed from the need to work.

When she's not wishing for magical transformation into a fairy princess, Bone relies on her "raw boiling rage" to see her through, as when she gets her cousins to play the "mean sisters" game, where they imitate the imaginary sisters of Francis Marion, or Bat Masterson. The mean sisters, she explains, "do everything their brothers do. Only they do it first and fastest and meanest" (212). If they can't be Francis Marion or Bat Masterson (the adventurers and heroes), at least they can be faster and meaner than the boys are.

Around this time, Bone's Aunt Alma has a breakdown, which results in her nearly destroying her house. After the chaos, Bone is "unable to resist the notion that everyone had gone crazy. Women all over Greenville County were going to smash stuff and then sit down to wait for Armageddon or sunrise or something. It sounded like a good idea to me" (268). Given what the women in her family have to put up with from men, Aunt Alma's breakdown makes a kind of sense. Bone surveys the damage and thinks about how delicate and small her aunt had seemed, incapable of doing any damage. She comments, "you just can't tell with women. Might be you can't even tell with girls" (274). That night, she tells her mother that she won't be coming home again, and later she hears her crying. Bone thinks that *she* will never cry again (277). As she has been for quite awhile, Bone is stronger than her mother, free from tears and emotional weakness, the "mean sister" personified. This passage recalls the nighttime scene with Lucille, except in this case the mother, not the daughter, is crying. The lack of connection between them is the same, however.

The final break with her family comes when she returns home briefly, only to be cornered and raped by her stepfather, an event that has seemed inevitable since early in the novel. Her mother arrives and, although she is aware of what he has done, comforts her stepfather, which causes Bone to completely abandon any hope of emotional connection to her. Bone looks at her holding him: "Rage burned in my belly and came up my throat. I'd said I could never hate her, but I hated her now for the way she held him, the way she stood there crying over him. Could she love me and still hold him like that?" (291). The answer to this question is more complicated than it at first seems. Bone's mother *does* love her, just not enough to save her; in their world, sometimes the erotic takes precedence over the maternal.

After this crisis, Bone's mother visits her one last time, before she and her husband leave for Florida, to give her a new copy of her birth certificate (with "illegitimate" removed). Bone looks at her sad mother and wants to "tell her lies" that she trusts and loves her still, but she can't. Still, even though she has lost her mother, Bone doesn't really hold her responsible for Daddy Glen's abuse. "Maybe it wasn't a matter of anybody's fault," she thinks. "Maybe it was like Raylene said, the way the world goes, the way hearts get broken all the time" (306–7). Bone has learned not to blame herself, but perhaps more importantly, to realize that her mother's motivations may be beyond her understanding, that looking for "fault" may be beside the point. Hearts "get broken all the time," and not just the hearts of lovers, but the hearts of mothers and daughters, too.

The final paragraph of the novel is stoic. "I was who I was going to be, someone like her, like Mama, a Boatwright woman," Bone decides. "I wrapped my fingers in Raylene's and watched the night close in around us" (309). This child who would only "be thirteen in a few weeks" is already grown, already who she "was going to be." Her mother has given her one gift that she intends — a statement of her "legitimacy" — but this gift matters more to her mother than to Bone. The unintentional gift from her mother is the sense Bone has that she is going to be a "Boatwright woman," someone like her mother, but not. With Raylene's help she can look forward to her future.[7]

The abuse, then, is not what will be repeated, but the connection between women. Randall Kenan says that by the end of the novel, readers "understand a bit more the strange logic of the heart in the face of such unbelievable cruelty" (3). Through Bone's story, Allison's readers realize the "strange logic of the heart." This logic causes people like Bone's mother to abandon the innocent in favor of a stronger attachment while at the same time leading Bone to make new emotional attachments, as with her Aunt Raylene, no matter how damaging the original ones were. Love, Allison shows her readers, can lead you astray and lead you back to who you are going to be.

Kaye Gibbons' Ellen Foster

> Down the path in the darkness I gather my head and all that is spinning and flying out from me and wonder oh you just have to wonder what the world has come to [Ellen Foster, 45].

> It started with my mother, this writing urge [Kaye Gibbons, "My Mother, Literature and Life Split Nearly Into Two Halves", 52].

Ellen Foster, the eponymous heroine of Kaye Gibbons' novel, is much like Allison's heroine — Southern, working class, undereducated but intelligent, pre-teenaged, abandoned by her mother. Unlike Bone, Ellen has a friend (Starletta) to distract her from her troubles, she is only threatened with sexual abuse (although her drunken father does neglect her), and her suicidal mother is physically, not just ethically, absent. Most importantly, however, both heroines work to change their lives and move from resenting to understanding — if not forgiving — their mothers.

It is important in both novels that the main characters are girls. For Allison, her female narrator presents an alternative version of the typical "white trash" girl; for Gibbons, her novel is an attempt to revise — or expand — the image of Southern womanhood. Veronica Makowsky puts it this way: "Ellen Foster is Gibbons's attempt to rewrite the saga of the American hero by changing "him" to "her" and to rewrite the southern female Bildungsroman by changing its privileged, sheltered, upper-class heroine to a poor, abused outcast" (103). Through her main character, Makowsky says, "Gibbons redefines self-reliance, not as a willed and threatened isolation, but as the maturity that enables an act of faith in others and, in turn, that allows a girl to contribute to, as well as receive from, the female tradition of community and nurturance" (107). Thus Gibbons (as does Allison) changes class and gender in order to rewrite the form.

Similarities exist as well in the reasons the two girls tell their stories. According to Linda Barnes, characters in Gibbons' novels, Ellen in particular, "tell themselves into existence. In the absence of models they must use language of their own to come into being through telling the stories of their own lives" (29). Like Bone, Ellen must tell her story to an imagined sympathetic audience who, unlike her parents, will listen and understand.

Narrative style varies between the two novels, however. The story in *Bastard* is told from the perspective of an adult looking back on childhood, a mature, grammatically correct (although only partially omniscient) narrator who nevertheless is compelled to revisit the painful sites of childhood. The first-person narrator of *Ellen Foster* is the child Ellen, writing shortly after the fact. She speaks as a colloquial and untrained Southerner.[8] Ellen's continuing friendship with African American Starletta further distinguishes Gibbons' novel from Allison's, which has no real interest in cross-racial contacts and whose characters regard their black neighbors with suspicion.[9]

Ellen Foster begins with Ellen excoriating both her parents. Her first words are: "When I was little I would think of ways to kill my daddy. I would figure out this or that way and run it down through my head until it got easy" (1). Her father is clearly worthy of his fate, in whatever form Ellen can imagine, but she is equally critical of her mother's weaknesses. About her, she says, "She could not help getting sick but nobody made her marry him. You see when she was my size she had romantic fever I think it is called and since then she has not had a good heart" (3). Of course the reader knows that Ellen means *rheumatic* fever, but her mother, attached to a drunken and violent man, is just as much a victim of "romantic fever."

When her mother dies, Ellen crawls into the bed with her, tucking herself under her mother's arm, wanting to "crawl in and make room for myself. My heart can be the one that beats" (11).[10] Although it is tragic, Ellen's mother's death, Munafo says, it "sets the girl's quest in motion." Ellen's struggle becomes to "simultaneously reconstruct the figurative and literal dimensions of 'home'" (39). Ellen's mother, although she is often missing from Ellen's life, has, through her own choices, "laid down a path for her daughter to follow in life" (44). She continues: "While Gibbons's attention merely skims the mother's story, it reveals how her choices shape Ellen's life. Ellen inherits from her mother the impulse to transgress restrictive social codes" (44). Ellen's mother has chosen, however foolishly, a man outside her class, and Ellen has chosen a friend outside her race and chooses, eventually, a family outside her biological one.

As Ellen puts it, "I just worked in the trail my mama left" (58). Before she dies, Ellen's mother gives her gardening lessons, instructing her about the right time to pick beans, which becomes a metaphor for knowing when one is ready for a new life (58). Ellen admits that she exaggerates the time she spent with her mother in the garden, but she says "if you tell yourself the same tale over and over again enough times then the tellings become separate stories and you will generally fool yourself into forgetting you only started with one solitary season out of your life" (58–59). The storyteller in Ellen knows that retelling leads to both fixing and expanding the story, so that it becomes more than just "one solitary season out of your life." This garden scene, and others like it, show that "Against the supposed fixity of domestic order," as Munafo says, "Gibbons asserts its fragility and constructedness" (46).

Bored, isolated, neglected at home after her mother's death, Ellen "play[s] catalog" to pass the time, picking out ideal families and all their paraphernalia from department store catalogs (31). Out of the catalog, Ellen is creating an ideal material family, with clothes for every season, camping equipment and even a waffle iron, and out of these goods she can create jobs for her "parents" and happiness (not to be confused with eagerness) for the children. Like Sam in *In Country*, Ellen is using the details of the material world to give substance to family.

The novel alternates between Ellen's past with her parents and other relatives and her present with the foster family she has chosen for herself (and chosen to name herself after), so fairly early in the novel she describes her foster mother. "Of all the ladies in the church," Ellen says, "that could make into a new mama she of all people was the one for me" (68). Ellen watches her "walk straight and square down the steps like she might be a Queen or a lady going to be executed with dignity" (68) and knows that this combination of dignity and straightness makes this women the right mother for her.

Ellen's road to her foster family is treacherous, however. Her father (in a drunken fit) tries to molest her, but she escapes, first to Starletta's family and then to her Aunt Betsy, who thinks she's only staying the weekend and sends Ellen back to her father. When school officials discover a bruise on her arm, she moves in with the art teacher and her husband, two hippies who offer her the first glimpse of a loving family.

However, Ellen is returned to her "real" family by a judge, whose judgment makes no sense to Ellen. "What do you do when the judge talks
about the family society's cornerstone," she says," but you know yours
was never a roman pillar but is and always has been crumbly old brick?"
(66). Ellen's conclusion is that the judge "had us all mixed up with a
different group of folks" (66). The judge, Ellen thinks, must be imagining an ideal family, a "cornerstone" supporting the state, instead of her
"crumbly old brick" family that can't even support its own weight. His
mistaken notion about familial ties causes the judge to send Ellen to her
mother's family.

The first relative Ellen lives with is her maternal grandmother, who
treats her like a field hand and considers her a perpetual reproach to her
mother's memory. Ellen at first hopes her grandmother "might have liked
the idea of having a girl around the house but when she saw my actual
self ... she changed her mind." "You cannot blame her," Ellen says. "I
am not exactly a vision. But Lord I have good intentions that count"
(72). Unfortunately, these good intentions count for very little in her
grandmother's home. Like Bone, Ellen blames her ordinary looks for her
family not adequately loving (and protecting) her.

To teach her some sort of lesson that is neither clear nor humane,
her grandmother puts Ellen to work in the cotton fields. "By July I was
like a boy," Ellen says. "When I started out both my hands were a red
blister but then I toughened up good" (77). Becoming "like a boy" is a
goal for both Ellen and Bone; in their worlds "toughe[ning] up good" is
a necessary protection.

As much as she would like to be male, Ellen is finally nothing like
her father, although she worries that her grandmother's desire to see her
prejudices confirmed will make her into the spitting image of her father
(80). Ellen knows that her grandmother wants her to resemble her father
to justify her ill treatment. Still, Ellen is worried that she can be wished
into becoming something other than she is. Whether or not this is case,
Ellen is shaken in her confidence in her identity by the malevolent wishes
of her grandmother.

However, it is clear that Ellen is in the process of creating a new
and productive identity, which the alternating narrative structure shows.
As Ellen struggles with her grandmother, the following chapter has her
at home with her "new mama" in the foster family. It also shows her
assumption of a new name, Ellen Foster, which she mistakenly assumes

is the last name of the family she wants to — and will — join. A school psychologist tries to reason her out of her choice, telling her "it is not uncommon for a child to pretend he is somebody else. He doesn't necessarily have to know that other person. Just so he does not feel the pain anymore is all that matters" (102).

When he finds out why she has chosen this particular name he "laugh[s] like I had said a joke." He explains her "mistake" to her, and Ellen thinks about coming up with a new name, until he tells her that "The problem is not in the name. The problem is WHY you feel you need a new identity" (103). Ellen's response is "Not identity. Just a new name. I wanted to write that big across the sky so he would understand and the picking into my head would stop" (103). She tells him he is the one confused and that she doesn't "plan to discuss chickenshit" with him again (104). Like Freud's Dora, she leaves the psychologist who repeatedly fails to hear what she is saying. At their last meeting, she informs him: "I might be confused sometimes in my head but it is not something you need to talk about. Before you can talk you have to line it all up in order and I had rather just let it swirl around until I am too tired to think" (104). What Ellen is trying to tell the psychologist is that her re-naming is not a sign of any pathology but a creative re-writing of her past. Like Bone, who gave herself a name more indicative of her personality and tried on new identities, and like Elizabeth (Gillespie) who found that a new name changed her sense of herself, Ellen is adopting a name that suits her new life and her future.

At this point, the narrative turns back to Ellen at her grandmother's house. When her grandmother dies, Ellen is farmed out to her Aunt Nadine, who clearly prefers her own daughter to her niece. Nevertheless, Nadine does take her shopping for a new dress, which is a turning point in Ellen's life. Ellen says, "It is a dress you catch somebody's eye with. It is like nothing you have ever seen especially when I put it on and gazed in the store mirror I said Lord I could fall in love with my own self" (114). This is a dress "that decorates you in the front and the back both. Even when I am walking off I thought while I watched myself turning in that dress somebody could look at me and smile." The new dress, she says, "was the first sign my luck was changing;" she could "pass for a princess in that dress" (114). Ellen even believes the dress leads her to her foster mother, and she thanks God for it (114).[11] God, in whose benevolence Ellen is not sure she believes, has intervened to bring her, through the agency of the dress, to a new family. This beautiful dress has made Ellen "fall in love with [her] own self," which is crucial if anyone else is going to love her. Like Elizabeth's remaking of herself through her unconventional clothing, Lucille's discovering freedom in a Halloween costume, and Sam's resisting gender expectations by *not* buying a dress, Ellen has discovered that external appearance has the power to transform internal reality.

Eventually, Ellen leaves her Aunt's house on Christmas Day and arrives at her foster family's door. They take her in, and the simple pleasures of having enough to eat and a room of one's own, and a caring group of people around her astonishes Ellen.[12] Most importantly, she is able to invite Starletta to spend the night; a family of such mixed origins isn't bothered by interracial friendships. As Munafo says, "At once a family and not a family, Ellen's foster home provides many of the elements she deems necessary to an acceptable home, yet it allows for reconstruction, revision, and experimentation" (53). Having Starletta in her new home causes Ellen to reevaluate her situation, and the novel ends with Ellen concluding that even though she "came a long way to get here" that Starletta "came even farther." This revelation, she says, "will always amaze me" (146). Because someone has finally decided to care about her, Ellen is now able to empathize with someone else; she can finally be "amazed" by another person's struggle. Pearl Bell sums up the ending nicely: "Ellen's story is horrifying," she says, "but it ends in quiet triumph because she is determined to outwit her predestined fate" (40). "She is telling us that she has learned something important from ugly experience, and we believe her" (41).[13]

"Ugly experience" is all that Ellen and Bone have out of which to make a life. Lacking loving (or living) parents, avoiding (or surviving) abuse, having to make do with the cast offs and refuse of others, they nevertheless fashion — out of refuse and stubbornness — safe and satisfying worlds for themselves. Extending the notion of family far beyond middle-class norms, they create — from aunts and strangers at church — a place to belong and the ground for the beginnings of their adult identities. Being girls has made them more vulnerable — to sexual stereotyping and sexual abuse — but finally it has neither hindered nor enabled their struggle towards adulthood. Kaye Gibbons and Dorothy Allison show their readers that working-class Southern girls are limited less by their gender or their poverty than by the richness of their imagination.

SEVEN

"Claim What Is Yours": Tina McElroy Ansa's Spiritual Journey

> "Crazy ain't all bad, child. Sometimes it's the only thing that protects you. This world you living in can be so mixed up, so backwards, that not fitting into it, being what some folks call crazy is a blessing. And you, Lena, you got the power to do something with your craziness" [*Baby of the Family*, 262–63].

Tina McElroy Ansa's 1989 novel *Baby of the Family* explores the growth and development of Lena McPherson, an African American girl living in rural (and imaginary) Mulberry, Georgia, who has the power to see — and talk to — ghosts. Named one of the Notable Books for 1989 by *The New York Times*, the novel is described as "likeable from beginning to end. The story has a "nubby, homespun texture that is unpretentious and engaging"(6), and it is populated with genial living characters as well as somber visitors from the spirit world. While it is possible to see such phrases as "nubby," "homespun," and "unpretentious" as condescending, especially from the *New York Times*, the novel *is* truly "engaging," a loving and complex portrait of one girl's progress toward independence. Along the way from childhood to adulthood, Lena McPherson struggles with the mixed blessing of her supernatural gifts and finds support from her extended family, both living *and* dead.

As is frequently the case with coming-of-age novels, the story seems to be largely autobiographical, although Ansa has told interviewer Barbara Smith Henderson that she and Lena "share some common history and characteristics, but I am me, and she is Lena" (63–64). Still, clear parallels do exist. Based on Ansa's own community in a suburb of Macon, Mulberry is, according to Joyce Cherry, "a cozy community typical of many African American enclaves in the South" (1). While one might question the "cozy" nature of the fictional (as well as the actual) "enclave," Mulberry does resemble the primarily African American community in which Ansa was raised. Nellie and Jonah McPherson, Lena's parents, are loosely based on Ansa's (the mothers share the same first name and the fathers the same occupation), and Lena McPherson's life has been drawn from young Tina McElroy's experiences — and her stories. Baby of the family herself *and* born with a caul, Tina quickly discovered "Storytelling was something you got attention for.... I knew that if I could tell an interesting story, I could hold court" (Ansa in Carroll 18). With *Baby of the Family*, she has succeeded in telling an interesting story that resonates with all readers who have struggled through adolescence.

Other than just being able to "hold court," Ansa had two goals for the novel: to celebrate the power of African folk lore and call attention to women's issues. She tells interviewer Carroll that she wants to "snatch back our culture; to snatch back the part of our culture that really comes from Africanisms that tell us to respect and make reference to our ancestors, to make a connection between those who are living and those who have passed on" (22). The ghosts in *Baby of the Family* thus serve to make a connection between the past and the present; they "snatch back" a culture Ansa feels is slipping away from contemporary African Americans. Lena serves as the link between those two worlds, sometimes at her peril, and she also makes the novel, as Ansa puts it "woman-focused." The things that really interest her, she says, are "gossip, stories, the kitchen, gardening, sitting around the hearth, and most of all, getting inside of things; what does family mean, what does community mean, what does freedom mean to a black woman?" (Ansa in Carroll 25). By concentrating on Lena, her mother, her grandmother, and various other female role models in Lena's life, Ansa manages to focus the reader's attention on both black life and women's lives.

Although *Baby of the Family* fulfills both of Ansa's goals — to "snatch back" aspects of African culture and keep the book "woman-focused," it still reaches across race and gender lines and tells a story of development that resembles, with its determined main character's ability to incorporate the personalities surrounding her without losing her sense of self, the stories of Gibbons, Allison and the other novels discussed in this book. Perhaps more self-consciously woman centered than Tyler, Mason, or Humphreys's heroines, and certainly more racially aware than any of the other characters except perhaps Gibbons' Ellen or Taylor's Cassie, Lena has the introspection of Sam or Lucille combined with the stubbornness of Bone or Evie.

Ansa's attention to African American literary and cultural heritage and community, however, sets her novel apart from all the others in this study, although it links her to 20th century African American women writers, several of whom she considers her most profound literary influences.[1] She especially admires Toni Morrison for her "craftswomanship" and ability to make the supernatural not "so much natural as it is real" (24); Gloria Naylor, who, in *Mama Day* "created the most gorgeous Sea Island, so real, and so right" (24); and Zora Neale Hurston, who "captured everyday, common, working-class people ... and then gave them such a wonderful, strong inner life" (Ansa in Carroll 25). Ansa continues this proud literary tradition with *Baby of the Family,* which celebrates a working-class family, brings Mulberry to life, and fills its readers with a strong sense of the supernatural. She extends the tradition, however, by concentrating on the life of a girl who is younger than Naylor's heroine, less troubled than Pecola Breedlove in *The Bluest Eye,* and less philosophical than Janie in *Their Eyes Were Watching God.* In many ways, Lena is more normal, more familiar, than her fictional predecessors, in spite of her special gifts.[2] Ansa provides readers with a picture of development that most of them would recognize, at least in part.

The novel takes Lena from birth to sixteen, and unlike the other girls in this study, her challenges are often as metaphysical as they are emotional. Born with a caul (the membrane enclosing the fetus) still surrounding her body, she has the power to see ghosts. Her mother, in a desire to be modern and hence not superstitious, refuses to engage in the proper rituals (such as having the infant drink a tea made from the dried and then boiled caul) when instructed in them by midwife Nurse Bloom. By not correctly caring for the caul, Nellie handicaps Lena for life, as drinking the caul tea would have protected Lena from fear of and danger from the ghosts she will see. By failing to do this, Nellie creates a childhood for Lena punctuated by misery and terror, and, more importantly, she cuts her daughter off from her birthright. As Nurse Bloom tells Nellie in the hospital, "you're overlooking the real thing that this child's caul is a sign of. It's a sure sign that this child is special. That caul is a gift from God, that's what it is. This little girl has been chosen by God as a special person on this earth. She can't hardly help but do something great in this life because God has touched her in the womb" (16–17). From the moment of her birth, Lena is "special"— marked by God to be visionary and by her mother to be tormented by those visions. Lena has the power to see things others can't (or won't) see, but her special tasks in growing up amount to learning how not to be frightened of what she sees and how to use the ghostly information to her psychological advantage.[3]

As well as being accompanied by ghosts throughout the novel, Lena is surrounded by biological and extended family members who offer advice, interfere in her business, and generally annoy and protect her. From her parents to the hangers-on at their bar and restaurant, Lena has people watching out for her and making her feel part of the community. As the reviewer for the *New York Times* puts it, Lena's family "envelops her," and this sense of envelopment — and entitlement — is something Ansa cultivates (6). For example, in an essay on first novels for the *Library Journal*, Ansa talks about the importance of her home town, Macon, which is in the geographic center of Georgia. Macon's location made her feel "surrounded, protected, centered," and it explains why she remains connected and "enveloped" by the South. In *Baby of the Family*, she says, "the South and home are strong elements in most characters. In my novel, the images of home are not always comforting and safe, but ever-present, surrounding the characters like the state" (52).

Interestingly, Ansa also uses the word "enveloped" to describe her experience of her home town; for Ansa, clearly, one is surrounded and protected by one's environment, not restricted or smothered. Indeed, this feeling of belonging is typical for almost all the girls in this study; their town or region defines and supports them. (The only exception might be Mason's Sam, who has an ambivalent relationship with Hopewell.) What is equally interesting is that Ansa claims a particularly Southern heritage for her characters, linking her to the regional orientation of most of the writers in this study. Her characters feel themselves to be Southerners as well as African Americans, just as Ansa claims Macon as the center of her universe. As Ansa told an interviewer, being African American, Southern, and female "should all be given equal billing. If you took away any one of them I would be a different person on this earth. I am a story teller because I come from the South" (Henderson 62).

Although Lena fits smoothly into her world for the most part, her supernatural abilities work to try to alienate her from it. The first incident concerns a picture of Lena's infant aunt in her grandmother's bedroom. When the baby comes to life for three-year-old Lena and tries to draw her into her world, Lena screams, bringing her family into the room and causing the little girl in the picture to release her. However, when Lena attempts to tell her family about the picture, she goes into convulsions, and refuses to sleep in her grandmother's room. This leaves her grandmother "stung to the quick," and she "reluctantly took the treasured picture down and stored it in the attic" (41). Although her fear diminishes after a few weeks, Lena "always remembered the sickness, the vomiting, the fits that had struck her when she told her family about the ghost," and she comes to realize the large gap her visions have created between herself and her family (41). Although she is quite young, Lena learns to keep her ghostly world separate from her ordinary one, and the result is that even her grandmother's bed — and by extension her family home — is no longer safe.

Another example of her separation from the world view of her family consists of Lena's early discovery that she is "real." Looking into the mirror, she sees that she is "this living, breathing, exciting person" (55), and this revelation, familiar yet somehow strange for having been spoken, has a disturbing effect on her more "normal" brothers, making them worry about whether or not they, too, were real (57). Lena's "crazy" ideas have a dual effect: they help define how she differs from those around her, and they pass on a little bit of her strangeness to others. Her family never quite completes the empathetic connection nor shares Lena's unique perspective on the world, however. After another incident where Lena has made her family uncomfortable with her supernatural gifts, she resigns herself to their nervousness. It doesn't even hurt her feelings; she just assumes "that their reactions were part of the way life was, like her seeing ghosts and knowing not to tell anyone about it" (61). What is "part of the way life was" for Lena is that her family will never understand nor be comfortable with her gifts; she has no choice but to accept this estrangement.

Still, this is not so different from any novel of development with either male or female protagonists; the main character, in order to engage the interest of the readers, needs somehow to be set apart from the characters who surround her. By concentrating so explicitly on the metaphysical aspects of identity, passages like these also help Ansa foreground ontological questions in a novel written in the third person. Obviously, every *Bildungsroman* must at some point take up issues of identity formation, and a novel not employing a self-reflective first-person voice has to find other ways to highlight this issue. *Baby of the Family* does it by contrasting Lena's heightened sensitivity to the unseen world with the more ordinary insights and experiences of her family.

Aside from her ghostly visitors, Lena at this point hasn't ventured outside her immediate family. She remains mostly inside her house, which is "a community unto itself with a mind of its own," watched by her brothers, who are beaten if they fail to protect her from harm, and protected by the stern guidance and often peevish love of her mother and grandmother (63). Fortunately, however, a new girl moves in across the street to draw her out of the protective cocoon of her family home. She first notices Sarah as "a little girl with dark glassy eyes" standing under a tree "with a piece of fruit resembling a big red jeweled brooch in her hand" (71). With her pomegranate and her mysterious appearance, the little girl reminds Lena of the ghosts she has seen, and she worries "that with no one here to protect her, this other child could very easily rise from the dusty ground where she stood and soar into the treetops." Even though she is only "going on six," Lena knows that ghosts "could appear at any time they wanted to appear" (71).

Sarah, whose hair "formed a roll like a diadem around her face," has torn, dirty clothes and ashy skin, and her disarray is irresistible to the pressed and polished Lena. She asks the girl if she is real, and Sarah says, "What you mean, am I real? I'm as real as you is. Here, feel my hand. What's that feel like to you?," and she offers her some of the pomegranate, although unlike Pluto, she warns Lena not to eat the seeds (72). Sarah may be "real," but she is also not quite of Lena's world, offering Lena a glimpse of a forbidden and hence tantalizing underworld in Mulberry.

Lena finds her friend Sarah "magic" (76), and Sarah, whose clothes come from the charity box and who doesn't know what breakfast is, thinks Lena's house is "like something in her dreams," or something that "didn't seem real" (85). Although she has no problem with Lena's questions about identity, she finds a comfortable, orderly home nearly impossible to imagine. After their first encounter, the girls are inseparable, and their favorite game is "Let's Pretend." Their friendship comes to an abrupt halt, however, when Lena and Sarah pretend to be married. Sarah, whose less organized household has allowed her a glimpse of adult sexuality, is more experienced in these matters and leads Lena in a game of simulated sex. Lena's first sexual experience is brought to an abrupt halt by Sarah's mother, who resents Lena with her "little red dresses and [her] hair ribbons and [her] big house" (97). She tells Lena that she is "just another dirty little girl, trying to do nasty when you think ain't nobody looking" (97). Judging rightly that Lena's family would think the game was entirely Sarah's doing, she doesn't tell Lena's parents, and then Sarah and her family move from the house next door. Lena is devastated by Sarah's leaving and mystified about why she never sees Sarah in Mulberry.

Sarah, who appeared to Lena first as a ghost with a magical piece of fruit, disappears as completely and mysteriously from her life as if she had really been a spiritual and not an earthly being. Sarah is Lena's first experience with friendship, sexuality, and a world very different from her orderly and secure one. It is also her first experience with the arbitrary cruelty of adults, and a necessary part of her development, convincing her that the natural world can be as dangerous and as strange as the supernatural one.

Lena's next step outside the world of her immediate family is to The Place, the liquor store/café her father owns and her mother manages. Interacting with her parents at work and with the people who frequent The Place complicates Lena's vision of herself, by allowing her to see her parents in a new light and to see herself reflected in the eyes of others. "There was hardly anywhere on earth that Lena enjoyed more than The Place," the narrator says, "[a]nd The Place seemed to love Lena as much as she loved it" (121). Lena is enveloped by The Place, and the neighborhood around The Place is equally hospitable. Everyone from "whores" to "hard-working women from the box factory" treat Lena "like a precious commodity" (123). Being treated "like a precious commodity" gives Lena the confidence, eventually, to face her fears, both mundane and metaphysical. Commenting on the parallels in her own life, Ansa says that her parents gave her "a real strong sense that people were people no matter what, that there were no classes of people, especially since we made our living on people drinking our liquor" (Ansa in Carroll 24–25).

In addition to making her feel connected to a larger world of adults who adore her, Lena, like Ansa, is able to respect the fundamental similarities in all people. This sense of a common humanity will give Lena a sympathy for the weaker and more vulnerable around her and enrich her sense of self. It will also serve as a counter to the mysterious vindictiveness of adults like Sarah's mother.[4]

Along with interacting with people at The Place, Lena arrives at a more complex sense of identity from watching her mother, whose confident persona behind the bar or office desk bears little resemblance to the mother "who had given Lena life and went around the house with a whine or a roar in her voice all the time" (117). Lena's mother at work is radically different from the mother she knows at home, and this picture of a competent contented working woman provides the model for working life that Lena will follow as an adult. Nellie McPherson at work is selling, filling, writing, and tearing, while at home she merely complains or criticizes. From watching her mother, Lena learns the therapeutic value of work — and the often debilitating responsibilities home life places on women. Like the other young women in this book, Lena has a complicated relationship with her mother; while she admires and emulates her, she also at times fears and despises her.

Having mixed feelings about her mother is useful, however — the negative emotions provide the emotional distance necessary for psychological growth, and the positive ones nurture Lena's confidence.[5] Much more contented at work than she is at home and failing her daughter at a crucial moment after her birth, Nellie gives Lena a complex legacy. Like Bone struggling with her weak and negligent mother, Jenny with her abusive one, and Bone, Ellen, Sam, and Lucille with their dead or absent ones, Lena must cope with a mother that is most herself when she is *not* mothering. Just as she takes over The Place in *The Hand I Fan With* in honor of her father, Lena chooses not to have children herself in part because of her memory of her mother's ambivalent mothering.[6]

Also like the young women in previously discussed novels, Lena finds female role models other than her mother, although Lena seems more to *add* maternal figures to her mother's foundation, while several of the girls — Bone, Ellen, and Sam, in particular — seem bent on replacing their mothers with various surrogates. For Lena, too, the maternal figures don't have to be found in the world of the living. One of the women Lena discovers is Rachel, the ghost of an African American slave, whom she meets on a family vacation to the Atlantic coast. Lena's grandmother has complained about the vacation, saying that black people are out of place on the beach. Rachel assures her that, contrary to her grandmother's opinions, "Black folk belong here. You belong here. Don't believe black folks don't belong on the beach. Don't never believe black folks don't belong nowhere. Don't be afraid, Lena. Claim what is yours. I died to be here on this beach, Lena. Don't never forget that. You belong anywhere on this earth you want to" (168). The gift Rachel gives Lena is a sense of belonging, both to the coast and to the country. She also teaches Lena about her history, the history of African Americans who died in order to claim what they believed was theirs.

This pride in her troubled racial heritage also sets Lena off from most of the other girls in this study, who may wonder how they fit into the adult world, but fail to consider how they fit into a world divided by race. However, Lena's racial awareness connects her, at least indirectly, to Bone and Ellen, who feel excluded from the financial and emotional security of middle-class life by their marginal social status. On the other hand, most of Lena's experiences *do* resemble the other girls' development; she has to struggle, as they do, to identify who she is — and where she belongs. Her meeting Rachel just extends her sense of entitlement outside of Mulberry.

Ansa herself strongly identifies with the Sea Islands and has made her home on Georgia's St. Simons Island. Until coming there, she says, "home to me was a dry, dusty town in the middle of the state.... In my ten years here, everything on St. Simons Island has told me the same thing: This place is yours" ("Sea Island Daughter" 49). So, for Ansa as for Lena, the ocean and the Georgia Sea Islands have become an extension of her home in the middle of the state. Interestingly, a *New York Times* reviewer who disliked the supernatural scenes in the novel called the one with Rachel "especially disappointing." Rachel's message, the reviewer said, "is profoundly moving, but off-key" (6). Perhaps the reviewer has underestimated the power and freedom (and pathos) of the Atlantic coast for landlocked descendants of African slaves. The water that carried them to slavery in central Georgia now provides Lena — and Ansa — with a way to incorporate that troubled history.

After Rachel, Lena's next role model is Mamie, the new girl at the beauty parlor, who is an attractive, strong, and sympathetic figure. About 20 years old, Mamie is "tall and sturdy looking, not heavy but robust," and she seems able to "take care of herself." Mamie "wears her size proudly like a suit of armor," looking to Lena "like a warrior, with her broad hands and strong-looking arms and legs" (179). Lena is drawn to Mamie's "warrior" strength, and from Mamie (who has a knack for asking the right questions) Lena learns how to find out things about people. Because of her exposure to Mamie, Lena comes to accept her own ample body and her physical strength, and she discovers the importance of listening and the power of knowledge. Mamie, with her attention to storytelling, is clearly the heart of the novel. In fact, Ansa has said that *Baby of the Family* "started as a short story about a little black girl in a small southern town who goes up the dusty street to get her hair done at the beauty shop" (Ansa in Carroll 19). Learning how to listen both to others and herself will also be at the center of Lena's growth. Eventually Mamie leaves, but when she does, Lena takes a piece of her, "the questioning part. Around her own house she gingerly began investigations about events, family, neighbors, situations that interested her" (188). Mamie, Rachel, and her mother help Lena to grow into herself; from them she has learned about the importance of place, the need for purpose, and the value of listening to other people.

Lena is less easy with her peers, especially the girls in her class, who were "beginning to get giggly and flirty with the same boys they had ignored the year before" (211). Unlike her classmates, Lena is unable to be "truly swept up in passing love notes and writing boys' names on notebooks" (211). This puts Lena in the same camp as Lucille Odom, who feels profoundly alienated from her silly classmates, and Sam Malone, who finds her best friend's early pregnancy and desire to get married puzzling and vaguely frightening. Lena's discomfort continues throughout her adolescence, and she irrevocably alienates herself from her female classmates when she inadvertently tells on one of classmates' mothers. (A ghostly voice takes over and speaks the truth to school authorities.) The incident makes Lena afraid — perhaps with some justification — that because of her gift that she will never fit in. This event, combined with a particularly scary sleepwalking episode, precipitates the crisis of the novel — Lena's dark night of the soul. During this troubling time, Lena tries to reassure herself by remembering what Rachel told her about belonging, with little effect, and she comes to the conclusion that she "can't trust anything" (238).

In order to get past this difficult spot in her life, Lena realizes that she has to reconnect with her mother and her grandmother. By looking in the mirror once again, she discovers that her body resembles her mother's, with the same "big low butt [and] long waist," as well as similar "slender legs and fragile-looking ankles," and "beautiful breasts"(239). If she resembles her mother on the outside, it is very possible she has inherited her mother's confidence and skill, too. Her developing body, with breasts that don't weigh her down and figure that is a "perfect counterpoint," may be signs of a psychological balance and potential lightness of spirit within.

Lena's grandmother also has some very matter-of-fact advice for her, although it is from the grave. When Lena sorrowfully asks to go back with her grandmother's ghost, she refuses. "Hell, no, baby, you just starting out," she says. "You got a whole lot to do before you over on this side. That's what you was made for. That's why you had that veil over your face when you was born. That was a sign of the things you can do, things you can be" (263). Lena says she just wants to be normal, and her grandmother just laughs and tells her, "Normal? Baby, you ain' never gon' be normal" (262). Then, she reminds Lena what the other women in the story have been telling her all along, from Nurse Bloom to Rachel: "Baby, you can't run away from what you are. You was born a special child. Now you got to claim what is yours" (264). Lena has to accept who she is; for better or worse, the visions and voices are going to be as much a part of her adolescence as emotions and acne. Like Bone, she has to accept what she is — and isn't — and move on with her life.

Her grandmother can only help her so far, though. When Lena asks her what's going to become of her, her grandmother says: "Shit, baby, I'm just dead. I ain't no fortune teller. But you, you can do more than me and four other like me put together if you let yourself" (261). In *Baby of the Family,* the dead can offer advice (and swear, apparently), but they can't predict the future. Lena's future is in her own hands.

In spite of Lena's rocky road, behind and ahead, the final image of the novel is one of security combined with apprehension, the perfect twin emotions of adolescence. Not surprisingly, Lena is having trouble sleeping after her talk with her grandmother, especially since she has returned to her grandmother's room, where she saw her first ghost in the picture. For the final time in the novel, she looks in the mirror, so long that "her pupils began to dilate." Then she shuts off the light, goes back to bed, and pulls "the quilt her grandmother had made for her up around her waist and sat up in bed the rest of the night" (265). Covered in her grandmother's quilt but still afraid of ghosts, staring at her familiar face and figure but looking too closely for comfort, cozy but unable to sleep, Lena is on her way toward adulthood. Fortunately she is as armed with her grandmother's insights as she is warmed by her quilt, as sure of her mother's love as she is worried about turning into her, and as afraid of ghosts as she is resigned to them. No wonder she "sat up in the bed the rest of the night." Like Lucille on her way to college, Sam on her enigmatic journey to the Vietnam Memorial, and Bone looking out over the river with her aunt, Lena is moving toward her future with some trepidation but with the support of her family and its complicated legacy.

EIGHT

"Odd How Things Are and Then They Aren't": Janisse Ray's Identity of Loss

> If bios is "the course of a life, a lifetime," and if it is already spent and past, then how is it going to be made present again, how is it ever going to be recaptured, how is that which is no longer living going to be restored to life? [James Olney, "Some Versions of Memory/Some Versions of Bios," 237].

Throughout Janisse Ray's 1999 moving autobiography *Ecology of a Cracker Childhood* the author mourns both the loss of the longleaf pine from her rural South Georgia home and the consequent loss of the ecosystem surrounding the pine forests: animals, plants, and insects that are now extinct, severely diminished in number, or that have simply moved elsewhere. Like every autobiographer, though, she also mourns the loss of her childhood, spent with her fundamentalist parents and two siblings in a junkyard near Baxley, Georgia. Her autobiography thus has a dual purpose, which is both ecological and archeological: to make an ardent claim for the resurrection of the longleaf pine and to reconstruct her present in light of her past. Ray wants to create a consistent narrative stream between past and present, to make it seem, as she says about the South Georgia landscape, that "everything that comes you see coming" (4).

Through her careful reconstruction she can make the current circum-stances of her life and her land predictable. By linking her story with the story of the natural world, Ray is also trying to stop what she sees com-ing ahead, what appears at this point to be inevitable: the loss of the Southern Georgia pine ecosystem and the end of the particular human life of her region.

Although she is writing an autobiography (at least in part), much of Ray's work resembles the fictionalized narratives of the other girls in this study. Like Dorothy Allison and Kaye Gibbons, she is detailing and celebrating the world of "white trash" Southerners, while at the same time revealing the violence and tragedy that underlies a subsistence lifestyle. Like Tina Ansa, she invests the natural world with supernatural force, and like the narrator of Josephine Humphreys's novel, Ray sees the connection between the loss of natural habitat and Southern identity. Like Mason and Tyler's heroines, she suffers loss and emerges stronger for it, and like *all* the young women discussed here, she struggles — and succeeds — in establishing an identity both separate from and respectful of her past.[1]

In her introduction, Ray says that the memory of the virgin long-leaf pine forest "is scrawled on my bones, so that I carry the landscape inside like an ache. The story of who I am cannot be severed from the story of the flatwoods," and, indeed, the structure of her narrative, which alternates between stories from her childhood and stories of the pine barrens, insists on this connection (4). This dual narrative structure presented logistical and practical problems for Ray, however. According to reviewers Anne Raver and Jingle Davis, various presses refused to pub-lish the book unless she removed all the natural history. Finally, though, Milkweed Press, a small Minnesota publisher devoted to environmental issues, accepted the book and suggested that she alternate chapters of the story of her life with chapters on the endangered Southeastern Georgia ecology.

Not surprisingly given publishers' reactions to her hybrid work, Ray's reviewers have had very mixed responses to her juxtaposition of natural and personal history. This is not to say that it hasn't been well received in some quarters, however. Michael Paulson from the *Georgia Review* speaks of the text's "expressive synthesis of ecology and history" (178), and *Publisher's Weekly* says that "[w]hat remains most memorable are the sections where Ray describes, and attempts to prevent, her own disconnection from the Georgia landscape" (1). Both of these critics recognize Ray's attempt to link life history with natural history, to make the stories of the woods metaphors for the stories of her childhood.

On the other hand, Jan Z. Grover from the *Women's Review of Books* regrets that Ray "separates the history of her family and the ecological history of the place so emphatically" (10). According to Grover, Ray is at her best when describing her childhood; the natural history chapters are too short and so stuffed with information "that they can feel a bit like a thin filling surrounded by sumptuous bread' (10). *Orion* magazine is even harsher, and, reversing the food metaphor from the *Women's Review,* says that Ray "lards her narrative with mini-essays on south Georgia's natural history that interrupt the autobiographical narrative with the suddenness of clearings in the woods..." (75). The reviewer for this journal (which, surprisingly, claims it is dedicated to "reconnect[ing] human culture with the natural world") says that the movement between autobiography and natural history leaves the reader feeling "a little whiplashed" and that the personal narrative "puts the bland, elegiac tones of the chapters on the woods to shame" (175). The objections in both the *Orion* and *Women's Review* seem to stem from a belief that human narratives are inherently richer, more sustaining, than natural history. Whether it is thin filling or lard, Ray's story of the pine forests leaves certain of her reviewers unsatisfied.

Tony Horwitz, reviewing *Ecology* in the *New York Times,* offers what is perhaps the harshest criticism. "Ray's paeans to pokeweed and yellow pine become repetitive," he says, "and too often read like protracted public radio commentaries, ending with bromides that tell us what to think" (2). Horwitz continues: "This is painfully and powerfully told, but Ray's insistence on alternating chapters — one on family the next on nature — dilutes the impact of her memoir and makes it as choppy as a clear-cut forest." Ray, he says, "remains a shadowy figure at the heart of her own story" (2). Horowitz's dismissive references to "paeans to pokeweed" and "clear-cut forest[s]," however, reveal more about his lack of understanding of the link between the Southern landscape and the Southern psyche than they offer any meaningful criticism of the book.

More than just regional insensitivity and sentimental subjectivity, the reasons for these negative responses are complex, and may be relying on Rousseauesque notions of autobiography and of the self: that it is possible to fully describe an individual life, to make the internal external and the external representative. In this Romantic scenario, the form of the autobiography would follow the function — a unified, consistent, and connected narrative of identity — and certainly would not "whiplash" between pines and personality.

However, as noted theorist James Olney says in "Autobiography and the Cultural Moment," autobiography is "the most elusive of literary documents" (3). When thinking about autobiography, he says, "there is a great and present danger that the subject will slip away altogether." It is impossible "to bring autobiography to heel as a literary genre with its own proper form, terminology, and observances." (4). In other words, there is no "proper form" for autobiography in an era of subject positions that threaten to "slip away altogether." Thus Ray's linkage of the forest (clear-cut or otherwise) to her childhood can be seen as her strategy to keep her narrative (and her self) from vanishing "into thinnest air."

Other contemporary theorists of autobiography concur. Ray's deliberate blending of narrative forms represents one way to solve the dilemma articulated by theorist Leigh Gilmore, who says that the path to achieving a narrative of identity "is strewn with obstacles. To navigate it, some writers move away from recognizably autobiographical forms even as they engage autobiography's central questions" (7). Ray's mixing of genres helps her navigate this treacherous path. The obstacles to which Gilmore refer arise in part from a postmodern conception of the self. Sidonie Smith agrees, saying that

> Postmodern incursions on the old "self" of humanism and its
> privileges of autonomy, epistemological certainty, authorial
> intentionality, and imperial self-presence have unloosed all the
> ties to a convenient and secure anchorage of "selfhood" and an
> unproblematized "experience." (39)

No longer able to claim the "privileges of autonomy," contemporary writers of autobiography must find other ways to establish identity.

Perhaps the most interesting contemporary theorist of autobiography, Paul John Eaken, puts it this way: Even though "there is a legitimate sense in which autobiographies testify to the individual's experience of selfhood, that testimony is necessarily mediated by available cultural modes of identity and the discourses in which they are expressed" (4). Recent theorists of identity, Eaken says, "agree that any attempt to remodel our concepts of the subject, self, or consciousness (as they variously term the subjectivity they study) requires a return to the body, undoing the original Cartesian exclusionary move" (9). This "return to the body" as a way of undermining the link between consciousness and identity resembles Ray's return to the visceral reality of the land. For Ray, the natural world embodies and metaphorizes her individual identity and the identity of her region.

Ray's emphasis on the evolutionary adaptation of the natural world is also similar to Eakin's theory of the developing autobiographical self. Using neural biologist Gerald M. Edelman's concept of "neural Darwinism," which asserts that the brain adapts and evolves based on the experiences of a lifetime, Eaken formulates a concept of autobiographical development that claims that "we are all becoming different persons all the time, we are not what we were; self and memory are emergent, in process, constantly evolving, and both are grounded in the body and the body image." As a result, we come to depend upon a "notion of identity as continuous over time and the use of autobiographical discourse to record its history" (20). Seen in this light, Ray's autobiography, and all other contemporary autobiographies for that matter, can be seen as recording the "constantly evolving" sense of self. Interestingly, though, the autobiography creates as it records, contributing to a "notion of identity as continuous over time."

This idea of adaptive identity pertains whether the subject is male or female, which is especially relevant for women's autobiographies. Of course, it also refutes recent essentialist notions of the differences between genders, which Eaken calls "an unfortunate polarization by gender of the categories we use to define self and self-experience" into binaries such as "the individual as opposed to the collective, the autonomous as opposed to the relational, and ... narrative as opposed to non-linear, discontinuous, nonteleological forms" (48). These very binaries have been elaborated by social theorists like Mary Pipher and Carol Gilligan and by critics of male-oriented definitions of autobiography like Mary Mason, Lucinda H. MacKethan, and Jo Malin. However, Eakin says that recent research by psychologists and neural biologists suggests that "[a]ll selfhood ... is relational despite differences that fall out along gender lines" (50). Contemporary autobiographies, he says, show us, repeatedly, "that the self is dynamic, changing, and plural" (98). This relational, dynamic, changing, and plural self is fully present in *Ecology of a Cracker Childhood*.

Perhaps most significant for those who write — or read — autobiographies like *Ecology* is that identity narratives may actually contribute
to the *creating*, not just the recording, of the self. Eaken comments that
in autobiography "narrative and identity are so intimately linked that
each constantly and properly gravitates into the conceptual field of the
other" (100). The bottom line is that "the writing of autobiography is
properly understood as an integral part of a lifelong process of identity
formation in which acts of self-narration play a major part" (101). Thus,
Janisse Ray's act of telling her story may also be the act of creating her
sense of self, and her linkage of that created self to the natural world serves
as a commentary on identity, creation, and restoration of self and landscape.

From the very beginning of *Ecology of a Cracker Childhood,* Ray's
awareness of herself as a girl, as a daughter, as a Southerner, and as a nat-
uralist are all linked to her sense of place. Here development is inextri-
cable from the development and destruction of the natural environment.
In fact, from the moment of her birth, she is linked to the Southeast Georgia landscape by family stories. Early in the book, Ray describes the family legend of her mythic birth in a palmetto palm: "Pine needles cradled
a long-limbed new-born child with a duff of dark hair, its face red and
puckered. And that was me, his [her father Frank Ray's] second-born. I
came into their lives easy as finding a dark-faced merino with legs yet
too wobbly to stand" (6). In this fantastic version of events, Ray enters
the world as "red and puckered" fruit of the palmetto palm, as much a
part of the vegetation as pine cones or magnolia seed pods. She is also
born as easily as a "dark-faced merino" sheep — no tortuous or emotional
human labor involved. From the moment she began absorbing her birth
narrative as a child, Ray was creating a self aligned with nature, a heroic
creature who is nevertheless as commonplace as the palmetto.

In spite of her almost mythic connection to the natural world, Ray
will soon turn out to be all too human. As a young child, she struggles with her limited physical form, listening for a signal telling her to
"leap toward the sky, hoping finally for wings, for feathers to tear
loose from my shoulders and catch against sweeps of air" (9). Intimately
connected to the natural world around her, and yet earthbound and
human, Ray struggles to reconcile the freedom of her imagination with
the confines of her body. Although she feels more animal than human,
more lamb or bird than girl child, part of her growing up will involve

accepting her human limitations. Unlike the characters in Ovid's *Meta-morphosis*, the only place Ray will fly or hide inside palm fronds is in her narrative.

Along with her passionate engagement with the natural world around her, the manmade location of her birth and childhood — a junk-yard in the rural South — emphasizes her separateness from the world of other human beings. In one particularly poignant example, her life in the junkyard alienates her from the world of her fellow college students. The first boyfriend from college she brought home is shocked by where she lives, barely leaves his room, leaves early, and breaks off the rela-tionship. Ray is convinced her botanist boyfriend could accept that she "come[s] from scavengers" (32). Rejected for living in a junkyard, Ray stubbornly chooses to assert her right to both the world of the botanist (the plants and animals of her region) and the world of the junkyard (her family and her heritage).

She insists on the connection between the two by linking them metaphorically in her autobiography. She makes us, as one reviewer says, "privy to the wonders of junk" (Paulson 178) and insists that both the junkyard and the forest "are devotees of decay," filled with "random order, the odd occurrence and juxtaposition of miscellany, backed by a sem-blance of method" (268–69). This combination of "method" and "decay" in both junkyard and nature is reminiscent of the first planned wilder-ness in Judeo-Christian tradition, the Garden of Eden, and one critic has remarked that "[l]ike all childhood paradises, this one was invaded by the asp of Shame" (Grover 10). For Ray, both the junkyard and the pine forest are gardens corrupted by both shame and carelessness. Her auto-biography attempts to address this corruption and through it perhaps find a way to return to paradise.

Like the junkyard, which got her ditched by the botanist, Ray's Southern heritage sets her apart from the sophisticated intellectual world she wants to join as an adult. She has to relearn pride in her home land, to "whip the shame" and "own the bad blood." The important thing, she says, is "[w]hat I come from has made me who I am" (32–33). What Ray "comes from" is (at least) dual: she hails from the rural Southern junk-yard and the pine forests. Her task in life, and in writing, is to reclaim that past, to "whip the shame." As James Olney puts it, "to redeem the time is one of the autobiographer's prime motives, perhaps *the* prime motive — perhaps, indeed, the only real motive of the autobiographer"

("Some Versions" 240). Ray wants to undo the rejection of the botanist
and other Northern intellectuals by embracing her Southern natural and
social heritage and junkyard childhood; she wants to "own the bad
blood."

The junkyard and the Southern way of life are a troubled legacy,
however. Unlike Ray, most of her "people" have no time for, or appre-
ciation of, the land. "Nature wasn't ill regarded," she says, "it was
superfluous. Nature got in the way" (128). The poverty of the rural
South is perhaps most to blame for her people's disregard for and disre-
spect of nature (165). Ray is not able to ignore the land, nor to use it for
her own purposes, at least unreflectively. Somehow she has managed to
learn to see the land the rest of her neighbors and family cannot, and
much of *Ecology* is devoted to explaining how she came to that important insight.

It was not an easy road, however. Her family, who might have taught
her about the natural history of her area, were too constrained by the
need to make a living, overcome by fear, burdened by psychological
demons, or distracted by domestic concerns to help her appreciate the
wonders of nature. Neither her grandfather, her father, nor her mother
were able to pass on a love and respect for the environment.

Her grandfather, who was quite adept in the ways of the wilderness,
was too far in the grips of madness to be able to share his knowledge
with his granddaughter. Still, she says, he did manage, albeit inadvertently, to show her some of nature's beauty — and bounty, as when he
shows her "his secret copse of huckleberries." Unfortunately, though,
"[w]hat is left of this mythic terra incognita is a map I cannot follow."
Still, Ray says, she has "not stopped trying to go back" (64). *Ecology
of a Cracker Childhood* is Ray's way to find her grandfather's "secret
copse of huckleberries," to "go back" and learn the lessons of the
woods her grandfather was unable to teach her. Although she cannot
find it, although it remains "terra incognita" and a "map [she] cannot follow," Ray keeps trying to find those huckleberries. In fact, her autobiography is the account of her search, and may be, in the end, her treasure
map.

Changing the metaphor from visual to aural, Ray longs to hear the
music that her grandfather heard but couldn't sing for her, music that
"must have resounded for hundreds of miles in a single note of rise and
fall, lift and wane, and stirred the red-cockaded woodpeckers nesting in

the hearts of these pines" Unfortunately, the music "falters, a great tongue chopped in pieces" (68). Although the music is like "a great tongue chopped in pieces," the song can still resonate. Just as not having a map doesn't necessarily prevent successful return to a long-lost paradise, so a mutilated tongue is not necessarily silent.

Changing metaphors one last time to a tactile one, Ray shows how the natural world can still refresh. She says she "drink[s] old-growth forest in like water" and "walk[s] shoulder to shoulder with history — my history"(69). On a parched spirit, the natural world is "like water." Her family may have left her mapless and voiceless, but Ray has found her way back to her "history." She has also discovered immortality. In the pine forest, she can see her "place as human in a natural order more grand, whole, and functional than I've ever witnessed." She is not afraid but "humbled" and "comforted." Ray feels "as if a round table springs up in the cathedral of pines and God graciously pulls out a chair for me, and I no longer have to worry about what happens to souls" (69). Surrounded by the Southern Georgia pine forests, Ray both sees her place in the natural cycle of life and death and is assured of her immortality. She may not have found her way back to the original garden but has found in the "cathedral of pines" a chair reserved for her in heaven.

Still the forests are threatened, as is Ray's personal and collective identity. "More than anything else," she says, "what happened to the long-leaf country speaks for us. These are my people; our legacy is ruination" (87). Immortality and ruination — in her autobiography Ray rehearses the ancient parable of the exile from Eden. In the Biblical story, of course, this dialectic between paradise and corruption implies a future redemption, and one exists in Ray's world as well. The longleaf pine, which Ray calls "the pine that fire built" for its ability to adapt and flourish after fire, becomes her symbol for this cycle of destruction and regeneration (38). Her family may not have been able to lead her back into the garden, but the longleaf pine will.

Continuing the family tradition of neglecting the woods, Ray's father fails to teach her what she needs to know about the natural world. Worse, *his* father has bred in him a fear of the wilderness, which is exacerbated by his manic depression. What her grandfather "planted in [her] father was a crazy fear and mistrust of being lost in a wilderness alone. If there ever was a wilderness misunderstood, insanity is it" (97). Her father and grandfather have their wilderness inside them; consequently, they are unable to share a love or understanding of the outside with their daughter and granddaughter.

Perhaps toughened, like the pine, in the fire of her father and grandfather's madness, however, Ray looks at nature differently than they do. She looks for "vital knowledge of the land that my father could not teach me, as he was not taught, and guidance to know and honor it, as he was not guided…" (97). Just as it offers her a glimpse of immortality, Ray hopes the natural world will keep *her* from the "errancies of the mind," from the "dark territory" of mental illness, forging a personal ontology and metaphysics while keeping the demons at bay.

Her father, on the other hand, turns to religion for solace and identity. "God had put us here and given us the Bible as a field guide," Ray says, "and my father would serve him" (105). Like living in a junkyard and being a rural Southerner, the fundamentalist religion of her father set her apart from her neighbors, as the only child who doesn't watch TV, go to football games, or hunt Easter eggs. The fact that their town was small made their separation "absolute," she says (118) Because of her family's religion, Ray and her siblings were excluded from the sacred rituals of small-town life: Friday night football and holiday celebrations. Outcasts among outcasts, fundamentalists in the small-town South are "absolute" in their isolation.

However, this exclusion didn't prevent her from feeling loved. Ray and her siblings are "constantly reminded of our blessings: health, enough food, a place to live, parents who loved us beyond reason" (115). Her parents loved her "beyond reason," but their isolation from the "normal" world led, Ray surmises, to a more profound isolation from the natural world. The transcendent beauty of the pine forests, she says, "was subverted by the world of the soul, the promise of a future after death" (120). For Ray, "the chance to be simply a young mammal roaming the woods did not exist" (121). The supernatural has laid its claim on the natural.[2]

As a way to become "a young mammal roaming the woods," Ray began to look for answers in the plant and animal world around her. In the pitcher plant, for example, she "was looking for a *manera de ser,* a way of being — no, not for a way of being but of being able to be," searching "for a patch of ground that supported the survival of rare, precious, and endangered biota within [her] own heart" (128). The pitcher plant, along with the longleaf pine, becomes a symbol of the "rare, precious, and endangered" nature of her own life. In *Ecology* the "biota" has been merged with "bios" discussed by Olney — natural history becomes life story.

Ray's mother might have provided a counter to her father and grand-father's obsessions, but her self-sacrificing nature made her less of this world and more of the next. She is "angelic, simple, kind," but as Ray matures she becomes "impatient with my mother's refusal to assert her-self," and only later could she come to "appreciate her wisdom, her stead-fastness." Her mother's life, Ray says, "is one long gift to those she bore and loves. One long backbreaking gift" (196–97). As angel, her mother offers Ray little insight into either the natural or the emerging political world. Although her mother is wise, kind, and giving, Ray cannot learn from her experience, except by rejecting it, or taking advantage of her sacrifice. Her mother's "backbreaking gift" means that Ray could escape, and her life provides the model of future to be avoided. Her mother, who was "Superwoman disguised as a chaste Cracker housewife with four children and a husband who smelled often as not like car grease," sacrificed her life for the life of her husband and children (199). Ray has chosen not to follow her mother's model, although in her passionate plea to save the pine forest ecosystem, she takes on her shoulders an even larger burden, sacrificing herself to protect the environment instead of just her family.

Still, like many of the other girls in this study, Ray has a compli-cated relationship with her mother. As a child she thinks her mother is beautiful and "love[s] her desperately, but she doesn't want to emulate her self-sacrificing nature. Still, Ray admits that her mother is "the most steadfast, generous, and honorable person I have ever know, wise in her unassuming way, and because of this, she approached sainthood" (203–4). However, although she loves and admires her mother, Ray does not want to *be* her, to be a saint at such a price.[3] In Ray's economy, to be a saint means to be a martyr to a husband's wishes and manias. Ray has chosen to look outside of husband and children (although she does have a child herself) for meaning in her life. Having no desire to be a "saint" on her mother's terms, Ray seeks instead to entwine *her* identity with her strug-gle for the preservation of the pine forests.

Ray ends the story of her life and of the endangered South Georgia ecosystem in a manner that echoes another Southerner, Martin Luther

King, Jr., who also dreamed of a paradise on earth. Ray wants to "bring back the longleaf pine forests, along with the sandhills and the savannas, [and] all the herbs and trees and wild animals, the ones not irretrievably lost, which deserve an existence apart from slavery to our own" (270). Ray's dream envisions the restoration of spoiled landscape, rather than a world of equality and justice, but like King, she dreams of a world that may never be recovered, one that is in the realm of nostalgia even as she speaks about it.

Finally, she is not just concerned with a loss of the natural world, but a loss of Southern uniqueness, and her final paragraphs link her cultural identity to the eroded landscape. "Culture springs from the actions of people in a landscape," she says, and what Southerners "are watching is a daily erosion of unique folkways as our native ecosystem and all their inhabitants disappear" (271). As the forests are disappearing so is the distinctively Southern way of life, and so is Ray's connection to that life. As one critic says, Ray's sense of self is "suffused with the same history-haunted sense of loss that imprints so much of the South and its literature" (Horwitz 1).

What happens is that Southerners like Ray can no longer find *themselves* in the world around them. As their landscape and its creatures are destroyed, Southerners wonder: "Where do we turn? To what then do we look for meaning and consolation and hope?" (271). Like many of the other young women in this study, Ray is wondering where to look "for meaning and consolation and hope," and like them she is struggling to create an identity in a South that is rapidly losing its regional identity, its unique traditions, and even its distinctive landscape. She is also, as are many of these girls, struggling with a complex and often burdensome legacy of poverty, defeat, and racism.

In *Ecology of a Cracker Childhood*, Janisse Ray has turned to ecology, to restoration, to preservation, and to memory for "consolation and hope." She has turned her autobiography into a story not only of her life, but the life of her region — the life of the trees, the plants, the animals, and even the insects. Attempting to preserve them, she is preserving herself, her family, and her past. In her autobiography, Ray has given us the story of her own loss of innocence, as well as her region's fall from grace, both historically and ecologically. Her story is a contemporary one as well, as it raises questions about identity and the representation of identity as surely as it shows us the intangible and delicate nature of our surroundings. Ray's junkyard is the "foul rag and bone shop of the heart," and it is the lost paradise of childhood; Ray's endangered pine forest is also the fragile security of adulthood.

NINE

"A Whole World of Possibilities": Jill McCorkle's Troubled and Tenacious Adolescent Girls

The fraught but stimulating combination of unlimited possibility and emotional intensity associated with adolescence intrigues North Carolina writer Jill McCorkle, who says she concentrates on young women because adolescence is when "the emotions are working in their purest, simplest form" (Bloom 296). As she has said several times, "by thirteen your emotional bags have all been packed and then you spend the rest of your life unpacking" (McCord 108). In her novels and short stories, McCorkle seems unable to resist chronicling both the packing *and* the unpacking. Although the challenges facing women of all ages are the focus of much of her work, McCorkle's novels *The Cheer Leader* (1984) and *Ferris Beach* (1990) deal most extensively with adolescent girls and their re-evaluations of their relationships with mothers, lovers, friends, and their futures. McCorkle's novels, as Barbara Bennett says, "are rife with ... awakenings as characters face truths which change their perceptions of themselves and others forever" ("Reality" 107). These truths, however life altering, are necessary to their growth into self-reliant adults.

Along with adolescence, McCorkle is particularly interested in young *Southern* women. Originally from Lumberton, North Carolina, McCorkle says that she "love[s] the South and feel a great pride for where I come from" (Lesser 61). She is not interested in caricatures or Southern gothic, however, telling an interviewer that she thinks that there is "a tendency to overdo some of the southern southernness these days...." "I don't want to write the *Beverly Hillbillies*;" she says, "I don't want my characters to be targets of ridicule" (61). Instead, McCorkle's inspiration comes from writers like Harper Lee, Katherine Anne Porter, Carson McCullers, Flannery O'Connor, and Lee Smith, Southern women who take their subjects (and their region) seriously, and write about "everyday life and small town life" (McCord 104).[1]

Like her contemporaries Bobbie Ann Mason and Kaye Gibbons, however, McCorkle is writing about the "New South," where regional attitudes, values, and behaviors are being homogenized into a more generic American culture. She is writing about "the newness of any small area that at one time seemed remote, and then suddenly you have chain stores and malls, [and this appearance of being like any other place" (McCord 106). Of course, becoming "like any other place" can be seen as a loss, but can also be a liberation for its young female inhabitants, who no longer have to live under the restrictions and expectations of the past. As Todd Pierce says, McCorkle's fiction "accepts the task of trying to find a new system to replace the old code." Her novels, he says, "throw new ideas out into the void, hoping that they might produce the rarest of fruits, a sense of satisfaction" (22). This enthusiasm for "throwing new ideas out into the void" is what marks McCorkle's Southern adolescent characters and what makes their progress such interesting and valuable reading.

The Cheer Leader

In her first novel, *The Cheer Leader*, McCorkle tells the story of anorexic, manic-depressive, and relentlessly busy cheerleader and prom queen Jo Spencer. The first-person narrative, which takes Jo from her earliest memories (even including snapshots from before she was born) through her turbulent teens, to a relatively tranquil early adulthood.[2] As Jenifer Elmore puts it, the novel, which is "sometimes cited as a warm-up Bildungsroman for the more mature *Ferris Beach* ..., is the story of the emotional breakdown of the most popular girl in a small southern town" (601). Yet, eventually, in this as in many McCorkle novels, "actions — often rebellious, daring or otherwise unconventional — lead to insights that alter the characters' interpretations of their own histories, allowing them to take control of their own lives and connect with the lives of other simultaneously" (Elmore 603).[3] Learning how to take control of one's life while still making connections to others presents Jo's biggest challenge.

She won't accomplish it without considerable struggle. In *The Cheer Leader*, Barbara Bennett says, "the danger lies in not getting beyond adolescence, in letting the temporary fears and pressures of the age become permanently debilitating" (*Understanding* 14). It looks for much of the novel as if Jo may never get "beyond adolescence" and remain trapped in the anxieties and disappointments of her teens. While Bennett calls McCorkle's first novel "*The Bell Jar* for the last part of the twentieth century," she adds that the hope in the novel comes from "the tentative progress [Jo] continues to make in developing an identity that is real, rather than one that is based on external labels…" (*Understanding* 31). Jo may be as troubled (and possibly suicidal) as the heroine of *The Bell Jar*, but her future is filled with qualified hope, and McCorkle (who was a cheerleader herself) seems to be telling her readers that it is possible to escape even the most consuming obsessions of adolescence.[4]

The novel begins with Jo thinking about the emotional distance between her mother and herself, a situation that has appeared in many of the novels in this study, although Jo's need for her mother's attention seems even more excessive and unrealistic. Looking at family photos, for example, Jo finds it "wrong" that her mother had "no knowledge of me behind those familiar eyes" (1). Even before she was born, Jo seems to be saying, her mother should have known she was coming; she should *always* have been the focus of her mother's attention. She also organizes the family photos by marking the ones that precede her "B.J.," which stands for "Before Jo" (2). By doing this, Bennett says, Jo "creat[es] a history for herself, a connection, and an identity transcending chronological time. She also minimizes the existence of life Before Jo, thereby increasing her importance" ("Reality" 108). Clearly, Jo is engaged in the narcissism of early childhood, but she is also trying, even at this stage, to form a coherent narrative of self.

This self-centeredness is fairly typical for children; what is not characteristic is Jo's other response to the family album. Looking at another picture, Jo feels panicked that she is "unable to control what is about to happen" in a particular photo (5). This compulsion to control everything in her environment will have disastrous consequences when Jo is on her own in college and able to control, ruthlessly, all aspects of her life. Yet while this need for control can be seen as pathological, it also represents a situation common to young Southern women trying to break out of traditional patterns and take control of their own lives, a struggle that is not without its psychic cost, primarily the awareness of a loss a security and familiarity.

Her fear of losing control causes Jo to keep many aspects of her personality secret. In fact, keeping secrets comes to define Jo, who describes herself as "discreet, tactful, mysterious and sneaky" (24). "Lying becomes a way for Jo to control her life," Bennett says, "replacing what is real with the illusions she *wants* to be real" ("Reality" 110). Clearly, Jo will lose track of what is real and what she "*wants* to be real," with disastrous consequences, but it also possible to see lying as the first step in a strategy to remake her life, which she will eventually accomplish. Like Ellen, who lies to her psychologist, Jo lies to protect herself and to imagine what an alternative future might be like.

Indeed, Jo has other more pressing problems than lying. For her, childhood is the last time when "guilt was not associated with pleasure" (5) and when she is "protected by [her] ignorance of things" (42). Jo comes to link guilt with *every* pleasure (especially sex and food) and consequently is unable to enjoy much of her life. She also becomes aware of the human vulnerability. By ninth grade, for example, she has come to believe that people "were all like trees, flexible youths, saplings, who grow up heavy and stiff, spread seeds and get chopped down and turned into notebook paper" (46). Even though she is only 14, she has come to believe that growing up inevitably leads to first rigidity and finally to destruction. As a result of her feelings of guilt and vulnerability, she is "spinning, spinning like a top" (54), losing the control that has meant so much to her.

At this point Jo becomes involved, first romantically and later sexually, with Red Williams and, typically but unfortunately, puts all her energy into the relationship, deciding that "all of the things that I had wanted and looked forward to were not important in comparison with Red" (108). She begins to fantasize about married life with Red, seeing herself as "a glamorous wife and mother who nonchalantly is always nominated and elected to various titles and positions, but who reserves herself and time for her husband and home" (100). Jo imagines that she will continue to be "popular" as a adult, even though she will turn down the invitations of her admiring fans, much as she has ignored her friends while in the grip of her infatuation. She imagines a traditional role — the Junior League, PTA, country-club lifestyle of a typical upper-middle-class Southern matron. To achieve this dubious goal, she will have to devote all her attention (and imagination) to Red. She thinks that her work for Red and her neglect of her friends will "pay off" when Red asks her to marry him.

Not surprisingly, she soon becomes disillusioned with Red and his (typically male) obsession with sex and disinterest in romance (as well as his disinclination to offer proposals of marriage). One night, after a particularly dismaying sexual experience, she thinks that "[h]is heart and his brain and all the really important organs are concentrated between his legs," and the only "future promise" she will ever get is "a thick white puddle on my stomach" (112). Red's heart and brain are located in his penis, while Jo's are in their normal places, and Red isn't able to satisfy either of them. The "future promise" that Red offers is merely the residue of disappointing sex.

Experiences like these lead Jo to the realization that her romance with Red was really just a brief fling, but Jo isn't able yet to learn from such experiences and move toward a more mature (if somewhat jaded) understanding of young love. Instead, the breakup with Red initiates her descent into obsession, as she sees her loss of Red as one in an increasing series of losses of control, including an attempted suicide by a childhood friend and her growing sense that she is trying to straddle two worlds — the proper cheerleader and the party girl. Her obsession with losing control leads to anorexia: Jo starts thinking that "there is simply too much" (148) of her and that she "must get thin, stay small, stay very little so that people can't see" her (161). For Jo, guilt is now firmly associated with the pleasure of food, and she decides to deny herself in order to avoid the other problems in her life. Her reaction to leaving high school sums up her state of mind: As she leaves the school building for the last time, Jo feels that "something had crumbled up inside of [her]" (158). She spends the rest of the novel trying to find a way to build back the broken edifice of self.

Jo's shattered self image becomes most obvious when she goes to college. Here, the narrative shifts from the first to the third person, clearly demonstrating Jo's alienation from herself. At college she continues to starve herself, barely passes her courses, and deceives her roommate into thinking she is fine. Having finally achieved what she set out to do in high school, Jo becomes "so small that she can hardly be seen. She can live without others seeing" (179). Now invisible to others and to herself, Jo doesn't have to face her troubles. As if this is not bad enough, Jo is also plagued by insomnia, brought on by bad dreams and obsessive/compulsive rituals designed to give her some semblance of control over her increasingly distressed psychological condition. Lying about her weight, her grades, and even her sleep habits has come to dominate her life.

Interestingly, though, when things looks most dire (Jo's roommate calls her parents when Jo passes out in the room and can't be roused), Jo begins her slow return to sanity, fueled in large part by her remembrance of things past, her connection to home and family. When she is struggling to sleep, Jo longs for the "Saturday night squeaky clean" feeling she had watching T.V. with her father and dog, dressed in a warm robe and pyjamas, when "every fear of the day dissolve[d] into the gray, into the hum and the lullaby will hum in the warm bed where only nice dreams are allowed" (170). Jo remembers that her "jammies" and "big dog Jaspar," combined with the security of her "Daddy's knee" and the "knotty pine paneling," make her feel safe and loved. These details, while not physically available to her any more (she a college student, after all, and too old for pyjama parties with her dad), are nevertheless present as a *memory* of peace and security that is comforting and sustaining.

These memories of home may be the imaginative mechanism of her psychological transformation. If Jo can tap into the memories of childhood, she in a sense start over, making a new plan for her adult life. As she continues to think about her current situation, Jo re-considers her past and her family, hoping it will be possible for her to return to a life of church and Sunday dinners (216). Not surprisingly, her memories involve typically Southern comfort foods like fried chicken and pecan pie. In thinking about eating these foods, Jo gets back in touch with her culinary roots and with her family. Thus, much of Jo's recovery will involve giving herself the right to eat again, to feel pleasure untainted by guilt and to reconnect with the South of her childhood.

Soon after her breakdown, Jo begins to meet with a psychiatrist, who asks her what she is "good at." She answers, still speaking about herself in the third person, saying that she could dive, play tennis, do ballet, write poetry, and teach the dog tricks (243). These are mostly childhood accomplishments — ballet and swimming and playing with the dog. In her obsessive state, Jo has been unable to turn these into anything like an adult career (or even avocation). Jo has, essentially, been stuck in childhood. In order to create a coherent adult self, her psychiatrist knows, Jo will have to build her self esteem and her memory of accomplishments, but she will also need to move beyond childhood. One way to do this may be to think about what makes her happy, but once again all Jo can come up with is *childhood* happiness: watching T.V., saying her prayers, picking up pecans in second grade (244). These will be a reservoir of happy memories for Jo, but she will need to incorporate more adult pleasures into the mix.

However, one adult realization that Jo has, even during her breakdown, is that "[t]o know pleasure and truly appreciate it, you must know pain, the opposite, to be happy you must know sadness" (230). In an almost Wordsworthian sense, Jo has come to realize that one appreciates the memories of childhood more completely when one realizes that they are fleeting, that life is transitory, that pain and sadness increase the value of pleasure. Jo may be stalled in childhood, but she has this one element, at least, of adult awareness.

In the coda to the novel that takes up Jo's life after her breakdown and recovery, the narrative returns to the first person from the disembodied third person. In her rediscovered voice, Jo reflects on life, thinking that "life is like a cardiogram where you must always be moving up and down, back and forth, past and future, briefly touching down in the present, coming some distance before a pattern emerges." With such an inherently dynamic structure, life demands that you keep moving, or "you are a dead duck " (261). For Jo, life is no longer like the trees that start out flexible, grow rigid and then are mulched, but more like the ebb and flow of the cardiogram, moving in waves from low to high. This is clearly an adult pattern of development (back and forth movement), rather than the downward progress from birth to death envisioned by the child Jo.

As well as seeing life as an ebb and flow, Jo also realizes that she will have periods of emotional instability again and that those periods are necessary and probably even productive (266). Evoking Yeats's "Among School Children," Jo asserts that the key to life is to keep moving, to keep dancing, to, as she says in the last lines of the novel, "begin to begin the whole process again and again and again"(267). She has also discovered the double meaning of the word "crazy," which can be either miserably insane or wildly pleasurable, and decided that she wants to be "crazy." Jo has, as Pierce puts it, "fought her way into grace, and the final hint of grace appears especially true and deserved after years of strife" (23). Still, though, this is a qualified "grace"; Jo is only "probably" sure that these things will come to pass.

Although with her compulsive dieting and her other-directed self, Jo Spencer resembles the traumatized adolescents of *Reviving Ophelia*, she emerges at the end of her ordeal stronger for having gone through the oscillating processes of life. By connecting with her Southern family, while at the same time rewriting the rules under which they defined her, she has both found — and created — herself. Jo doesn't necessarily have control over her life, nor has she completely learned how to feel pleasure without guilt, but she has learned how to "peruse [her] dance" (266).

Ferris Beach

In her fourth novel *Ferris Beach*, McCorkle once more calls attention to the psychological, social, and sexual struggles of a Southern adolescent heroine. This time, she gives her readers a realistic and moving portrayal of Kate Burns' progress toward adulthood that is less harrowing than Jo's in *The Cheer Leader* but nevertheless difficult, and just as transformative. *Ferris Beach*, Bennett says, "follows Kate's psychological journey as she discovers the many variations of love, shattering most of her childish and romantic definitions" (115). Kate, like Lucille in *Rich in Love*, comes to understand the complex varieties of love. She moves, as Lynn Bloom says, "from innocence through experience to understanding — of themselves, their Southern world, and human nature — within the context of one's family and without" (297). Although all of McCorkle's main characters learn "from an unpredictable combination of the bitter, the sweet, and the horrifying," Bloom says, "the novels' prevailing mood is of resolute, sometimes utterly comic, good cheer" (297). "Comic good cheer" in the face of "the bitter, the sweet, and the horrifying" aptly describes *Ferris Beach* in particular, which deftly combines horrible events (that happen primarily to others this time) with unlikely optimism.

McCorkle's novel takes Kate from nine to sixteen and explores her initial confusions and eventual insights about her family, her friendships, her sexuality, and her morality. In this first-person narrative, Kate (also like Lucille) feels burdened by a large and visible birthmark, worried about her place in the community, annoyed at her mother's emotional distance, and drawn to disabled heroes like Helen Keller, and like Lucille she does not seem particularly resentful or morbid. Following a model that has traditionally been the province of boys' development narratives, McCorkle moves Kate from questions about her origins, though various emotional crises, to a hopeful vision of the future. As Todd Pierce says: "McCorkle's fiction, in its most serious and original moments, accepts the task of trying to find a new system to replace the old code. Her novels and her characters throw new ideas out into the void, hoping that they might produce the rarest of fruits, a sense of satisfaction" (22). McCorkle is clearly having Kate search for that "new system" among the scattered pieces of the traditional Southern landscape as well as the troubled terrain of contemporary adolescence.

Her approach for developing this new system includes a female revision of the traditional quest novel, which has the male protagonist searching for his lost father (Bennett 189). Here Kate is looking for a new mother to replace the one who embarrasses and disappoints her. Kate is dissatisfied with her mother Cleva, whose grey hair and severe hairstyle "made her look older than she was,"(3) and works through a number of apparently attractive candidates in a search for the ideal mother. Bennett correctly points out that while Jo Spencer "finds support and identity through her family, Kate rejects her mother and the identity she represents" (*Understanding* 79). However, there is an important similarity between the two young women. Both Jo and Kate want unrealistic emotional connections with their mothers. Jo wants her mother to know her, even before she is born, and Kate wants *her* mother, the practical and stoic Boston native, to be more impulsive and effusive than her nature and upbringing will allow. And although Kate initially rejects her mother, she finally returns to the mother with which she began, as does Jo.

On the first leg of her search for a new and improved mother, Kate begins to fantasize about her cousin Angela (whose complicated past could easily have accommodated an unplanned pregnancy). Kate attaches to Angela "everything beautiful, lively and good"(7) when she remembers a trip she makes at five with her father to see Angela at Ferris Beach.

Angela is "the easy flow of words and music, the waves crashing of Ferris Beach as I spun around and around"; Angela is the "energy, the eternal movement of the world, the blood in my veins" (7). When she first sees Angela, it is "almost like seeing a movie in slow-motion, seeing every step of her long bare legs, her feet sinking into the hot loose sand" (19). Angela's physical attractiveness, her warm and impulsive nature, as well as her insistence that she "remember[s] that day well" (69) when Kate was born, makes Kate long to have her as her biological mother. She comes to believe that Angela had left her with her mother and "that's why we weren't close." This thought makes her feel "both guilty and exhilarated" (80). After Angela visits them, Kate's mother tells her that Angela was staying with them when Kate was born, and Kate wonders "what if it was all true, everything that I had imagined," that she was a "love child" of Angela's (89).

Her fantasies prove to be unfounded, and when she concocts an elaborate plan to see her birth certificate, saying she needs it for a school report, her mother responds sincerely, "What a wonderful idea that is," and quickly produces the document (96). "I can tell you so much about that day," her mother says. "From the moment I opened my eyes until the moment you were born" (96). Although her neighbor and best friend Misty insists that it is "possible" that her mother might have made a fake birth certificate, Kate is reluctantly convinced by the facts. She is also disappointed by Angela's unreliability and lack of concern for the feelings of others, in particular her mother's, and decides to abandon her as a mother surrogate.

As Kate tries to sort out her feelings about Angela, she also begins to wish that she could be adopted by Mo Rhodes, Misty's unconventional mother (54). Mo, with her "thick dark hair ... pulled back in a ponytail as she stood there barefooted in cropped jeans, her toenails painted pale pink" (10), seems the perky, youthful alternative to her older, reserved mother, and she is more immediately available and (apparently) more domestic than Angela. When Kate first meets Mo she is "in complete awe of this woman whose purple wooden earrings swung back and forth as she talked" (10). Kate's mother looks "so plain and somber compared to Mo Rhodes and her loud-colored pillows and sparkly wall hangings in Oriental designs" (14). Mo is "the youngest mother I had ever known, and the only one who ever would have let us eat all the s'mores we wanted" (35). Kate is attracted to Mo's indulgence as well as her energy. Unfortunately, Mo is a little *too* youthful and self-indulgent: She impulsively runs away with a neighbor with whom she is having an affair and is later killed in a car accident. After Mo's desertion, Kate (like Lucille when her mother leaves) feels "vulnerable, exposed, as if someone was out there hidden in the darkness, hidden and waiting" (105). Mo's selfish insistence on her sexual nature has made the rapidly maturing Kate (who is starting to notice boys herself) feel at risk.

The disaster with Mo and her disappointment with Angela causes Kate to turn her attention to Perry Loomis, the lovely and tragic working-class girl whom Kate admires, mostly from a distance. Perry is more like Bone in *Bastard Out of Carolina* or Ellen in *Ellen Foster* than she is like Kate, but Perry is finally incapable of taking charge of her fate in the ways that Bone and Ellen do. Still, Kate is unable to stop looking at her "thick blond hair that hung past her shoulders and dark brown eyes" (137), and she feels "almost like having a crush, so taken with this person's appearance, so much wishing I could claim it as my own" (141). In fact, Kate sees Perry "in the same way I saw Angela, the way I had seen Mo, glittering and shining, rare like a jewel" (141), and Perry joins the line of briefly-adored surrogate mothers.

Perry has unexpected lessons for Kate, however, the first one concerning social class. When Kate clumsily (but inadvertently) makes it clear that she is wearing Kate's hand-me-down coat. Perry defensively responds, "Who needs a stupid new coat. All of ya'll come in here like a fashion show" (148). Shocked by Perry's reaction, Kate is "not prepared for the twang of her voice, the rusty flatness that went against every smooth line of her face," and she finds the sound of it "coarse and grainy" (148), in part as a result of her embarrassment. Seen through Perry's eyes, Kate becomes "one of them... one of the enemy," (148) who show off their new clothes and talk about girls like Perry; there is no chance — if there ever was — that they will become friends. Kate has Romanticized Perry's perfection as she has Romanticized Mo's youthfulness and Angela's mystique, but in this case the reality of their class differences creates an unbridgeable gap between them. Kate is repelled by Perry's coarseness, and Perry resents Kate's condescension.

As well as the difficult lesson about social class, Perry will also teach Kate about her vulnerability as a woman. Shortly after the confrontation over the coat, Kate, hiding in a tree and spying on her love interest Merle, accidentally witnesses Perry being gang raped by Merle's brother and his friends. Shocked into silence, Kate is unable to call out or run away: "I knew something was about to hit; I knew it. It was like seeing the head-lights round the curve or hearing the load roar of a freight train in the split second before a tornado touches down and inhales a portion of the world" (214–5). Merle tries to stop his brother Dexter and fails, while Kate stays in the tree, afraid the boys would catch her: "I could feel the cold silver blade of the knife daring me to cry for help, daring me to do anything other than give in to their gropes and slobbers" (218). Paralyzed by their violence, Kate is unable to act.

After these incidents, Kate no longer sees Perry as a goddess, but as a fragile human being whose breasts are "just those of a young girl, pale blue veins underlining the pale white skin, breast bone as fragile as that of a chicken ripped and torn apart" (219). As she tries to block out the images of helplessness and violation, Kate links Perry's vulnerability to the vulnerability of the other people in her life. She thinks about Mo Rhodes at the moment of her death, Merle as he tried to stop his brother from raping Perry, and Misty as she grieves for her lost mother (219). Like Jo Spencer in *The Cheer Leader*, a necessary but painful part of Kate's development is an awareness of her own (and others) impotence in the face of catastrophe. Unlike Jo, though, Kate also realizes her own moral weaknesses, and she avoids telling anyone about the rape, fearing that they will ask her why she did nothing.

Their shared trauma, however, links Kate and Merle, and Merle becomes her next teacher. On Christmas Day, he asks to meet her in the cemetery to talk about what happened, suspicious, as is Perry, about her motives and her class-conscious friends. When he realizes that her spy-ing was not out of prurient interest in the working class but romantic attraction, and that she has no intention of spreading rumors about Perry, Merle kisses her. This is not the end of the encounter, though. Merle insists on making a connection between Kate and Perry, telling her that Perry is "not that kind of girl any more than *you* are" (228). He asks her: "How would you feel if they had done that to *you*," (228) reminding her that she cannot hold herself apart from what happened. Through this conversation, Kate comes to realize that she isn't that different from Perry Loomis, just a young girl, after all, although slightly less vulnerable because of her family's social status and her good luck in picking the bet-ter of the two brothers.

Following her epiphany, Kate is ready to leave her childhood, and her first sexual experience becomes part of this process. When Merle (now her boyfriend) asks Kate to meet him behind the stage in the school auditorium, she decides to do it, believing that in some way her actions are inevitable. She also decides "to pretend that there was no day other than this one, no world beyond those trees; there was no future, no guarantee that I would turn sixteen, this was it" (281). Although this sounds like a rather fatalistic capitulation, Kate appears to be strengthened and not distressed by her experience. It may be true, as Elinor Walker says, that Kate "loses her notions of romanticism along with her virginity, and she approaches adulthood with few of her prior ideas about femininity intact" (90), but this can be seen as a gain rather than a loss. Unlike Jo, for whom sex is another demonstration of the pointlessness of her life, Kate uses her experience to discard her worries about social appearance (the person "spying from some window") and her uncertain future (whether she would even "turn sixteen"). Learning how to live in the moment, or at least learning how to "pretend" to do so, is part of Kate's growth.

Disappointed in her search for a perfect mother, and seasoned by her experiences with Perry and Merle, Kate returns to her friend Misty, who, in her reaction to the loss of her mother, provides Kate with an effective model for dealing with the crises of life. Kate says she is amazed by Misty's confidence that things would improve. "In spite of her toughness, or maybe because of it," Kate, says, "Misty's optimism was stronger than ever; she was determined that she was going to win, believed that she *had* to win" (135). By watching Misty's confident approach to life, in spite of her personal sorrows, Kate learns that "toughness" is a necessary part of "optimism." In ways that her mothers — either real or imagined — or her romantic attachments cannot, Misty has taught Kate about the power of faith and determination. Struggling with the loss of her mother and a new stepmother, along with the other more minor traumas of adolescence, Misty shows Kate how to accept her losses with grace and hope. In this way, Misty becomes — in spite of her age and obvious immaturity — Kate's next role model for her emerging adult sensibilities.

This pose of confidence in the face of uncertainty continues through the rest of the novel, and in keeping with its positive spirit, Misty provides the final commentary. After a drive with her mother, Kate returns home and sees her neighborhood (and neighbors) with new eyes. She sees

Misty practicing her baton twirling and Sally Jean, Misty's stepmother, "proudly watching this high-stepping girl she had grown to love; she was an answer to a prayer, a second chance." Misty throws the baton up, and as Kate watches it fall "neatly into her outstretched hand," she sees "a whole world of possibilities spinning around her" (342–3). At the end of the novel, Kate has moved from uncertainty through various crises to a "whole world of possibilities spinning around her." She realizes that she lives a world of death and betrayals large and small, where in spite of them, people's prayers are answered and second chances are given.

It is significant here that Kate is riding in the car with her mother, the cool and detached Cleva. Kate's final move is to return to an acceptance of her not completely desirable but nevertheless dependable mother. As Bennett says, "Kate watches all three [Angela, Mo, and Perry] topple off the unsteady pedestals she has constructed for them, leaving her to replace them with the more stable and real mother she initially rejects' (Folks 189). Kate is left with a mother, who, she says, "never gave a person exactly what he or she wanted, she always held out just a little, enough to get a beg, or maybe just enough to maintain control over a situation, or maybe it just never occurred to her" (129). Like Lucille, Kate is forced to accept a mother who is much less warm and connected than she would like, but she has learned to appreciate what she has. A living, present mother is after all much better than none at all.

In *Ferris Beach,* then, McCorkle shows the reader the familiar world of adolescence, a world of childish idealism combined with teenaged insecurity, but the novel's strength lies in replacing that idealism (although not all of the insecurity) with "the belief in people, in possibilities, and in self-direction" (*Understanding* 94). At the end of *Ferris Beach,* Kate "stands at the shore of an earned adulthood, ready and willing to launch herself into a world of possibilities where she wants to make her choices with her eyes open" (Loewinsohn 10). Kate has earned her hopefulness; her eyes are wide open, but her confidence is strong.[5]

The main characters in Jill McCorkle's two novels that focus on adolescent girls have a hard time of it: They lose their minds, their lovers, their family, and their friends. They learn of fatal car accidents and suicides; they witness rapes and nearly diet themselves to death; they deal with insensitive boyfriends and indifferent (or powerless) parents. In spite of all of this, Jo and Kate come to love the pulsating, spinning qualities of life; they grow into young women who are battle scarred but optimistic nevertheless. In *Ferris Beach* and *The Cheer Leader*, Jill McCorkle has given her readers a new picture of Southern girlhood — one still tied to home and family but not strangled by it, a little dizzy with choices but not sick with fear. McCorkle adds her strong young women to the growing list created by the other women in this study — Jo and Kate join hands with Bone and Ellen, Sam and Lucille, Janisse and Lena, Evie, Elizabeth and Jenny, while reaching back to their earlier counterparts created by Welty, Spencer, and Lee. These girls are not perfect nor perfectly happy, but they are funny, self aware, and able to see beyond the world of adolescence to a future filled with possibility.

TEN

"Keep on Asking Questions": Tough Girls in Young Adult Fiction

When asked to discuss iconoclasm in children's literature, author Madeline L'Engle has said that those people "who dare disturb the universe" have a lot in common: like resisting bullies, not accepting falsehoods, not settling for easy answers. Most importantly, though, "They keep on asking questions — of themselves, of the world, of the universe — long after it is clear the people want answers, not questions; bread and circuses, not justice" (215). Of course, L'Engle was referring in part to the well-known protagonist of Robert Cormier's *The Chocolate War,* Jerry Renault, who keeps a poster with Eliot's famous line in his locker, but she could also be writing about female main characters in young adult novels since the 1970s. These girls/young women never "settle for the easy answer" about what their roles in society will be; they "keep on asking questions" and resting gender stereotyping. Characters like Gilly Hopkins in Katherine Paterson's *The Great Gilly Hopkins* (1978) and Sara Louise Bradshaw in *Jacob Have I Loved* (1980), Cassie Logan in Mildred D. Taylor's *Roll of Thunder, Hear My Cry* (1976), *Will the Circle Be Unbroken* (1981), and *The Road to Memphis* (1990), and Dicey Tillerman in Cynthia Voigt's *Homecoming* (1980) and *Dicey's Song* (1991) see it as their job in life to raise questions about what their families and their societies expect of them as girls and women. In the process of their development, they redefine what being female, and Southern, will mean for them.

"Hope Rooted in Reality":
Katherine Paterson's Gutsy Girls

In *The Invisible Child*, young adult novelist Katherine Paterson says that children "do not go to novels looking for role models":

> They may go for adventure, for escape, for laughter, or for more serious concerns — to understand themselves, to understand others, to rehearse the experiences that someday they may live out in the flesh.... When they go to a serious novel, they expect to find truth, and everyone knows that role models are ideals not reality. They want hope rooted in reality, not wishful thinking [139–40].

With all of her characters, but especially with her two most memorable adolescent female characters — Gilly Hopkins from *The Great Gilly Hopkins*, and Sara Louise Bradshaw in *Jacob Have I Loved*— Paterson gives her readers "hope rooted in reality" for a self-determined life. Although not without controversy (especially *Jacob Have I Loved*), Paterson's novels feature young women who struggle to make the best out of bad situations, who strike out on their own but return to home or traditional families, who are funny and smart but full of vices (like jealousy, prejudice, pride, and anger) that make them appealingly human (if not always sympathetic).

Like many of the heroines described previously in this study, Paterson's characters have to construct their lives without much help from their parents. Paterson makes the point that a writer "can't have too much of a story without adventure and conflict, and good parents are always getting the way of both, especially when there are two of them around to back each other up" (*A Sense of Wonder* 201–2). Gilly is a foster child abandoned by her teenaged mother who refuses to accept any permanent placement; Sara Louise's parents are "good," but her father is fishing all day, her mother is kind but strangely remote, and her grandmother is mean spirited and growing increasingly senile. Not surprisingly, though, both girls find surrogate parents in unexpected places and eventually discover their true homes where they never imagined them to be.

Perhaps more important than their lack of parental support, however, is the impact of Southern settings on the lives of these young female characters. According to Paterson, setting "is not a background against which a story is played out, but the very stuff with which the story will be woven. The characters will not determine the setting, but the setting to a great degree will determine both what they will be like and how they will act" (*A Sense of Wonder* 95). Sara Louise's Rass Island in the Chesapeake Bay defines both the limitations and the possibilities of her life and determines what she "will be like." Gilly's somewhat eccentric home with her Southern foster mother, Mrs. Trotter, comes to shape her personality in profound ways as well.

Also, the endings to the girls' stories are a direct result of the settings in which they live. Gilly would have been unable to accept her final home with her biological grandmother had she not had the love and security of Trotter's home first, and Sara Louise would never have found the courage to leave Rass Island if it had not already molded her determined character. This is not to say that the girls are comfortable in their environments; in fact, they are as often as not reacting in anger and frustration to the limitations and disappointments of their surroundings. As Paterson says, Sara Louise "could be molded by her adaptation to her environment or by her rebellion against it. Either way, the place is of vital significance to the person she is and will become" (*The Invisible Child* 163). This applies equally to both girls: Just as Gilly must abandon her role as foster child from hell and her unrealistic dreams about her mother in order to come to rest in her biological family, so Sara Louise must lose her island self and her jealousy of her sister in order find the courage to leave.[1]

Another way to understand the importance of setting for Paterson — and the influence it has on her characters' personalities and actions — is to consider the ways in which Southern culture shaped both Paterson's storytelling skills and her complex portrayal of self-determination and grace. Paterson scholar Gary Schmidt says Paterson's "childhood and formative years were spent in the South, which, she suggests, has a tradition of fine storytelling. And reading the Bible through all these years also contributed [to her sense of story]" (3). Paterson admits that her knowledge of the Christian Bible has influenced her narrative structures and her representation of fate. Quoting Eudora Welty, Paterson says that Southerners have inherited "a narrative sense of human destiny," which "is closely related to that time line on the blackboard, a biblical time line that begins with 'creation' and ends with 'eschaton.'" The South is known as the Bible Belt, she says, because Southerners are raised on "this book that has a beginning, a middle and an end — a coherent plot, with wonderful, richly human characters, a vivid setting and a powerful theme" (*Worlds of Childhood* 161).

In the two novels under discussion here, readers can clearly see the "coherent plot," "richly human characters," "vivid setting," and "powerful theme," but more importantly, they find an almost eschatological inevitability about the endings to these girls' stories. Gilly *will* find a place to settle down, although not with the family she thinks she wants; Sara Louise *will* find a way to escape her island prison. This inevitability doesn't preclude moments of grace, however, as when Gilly finds the strength to leave Trotter or when Sara Louise discovers that she is no longer jealous of her sister. Thus, while their plots may move toward their destined conclusions, the characters' emotions are subject to the mysteries of grace.

Another influence of Paterson's Southern background on her novels is her sympathy for lost causes. She says that "since 1865 we white Southerners have been suckers for a losing cause. Struggle dashed to defeat by inexorable might is somehow more glorious than mere success" (*The Invisible Child* 201). Although Sara Louise and Gilly are not exactly "losing cause[s]," at least by the end of their stories, they do struggle with the "inexorable might" of sexism, abandonment, and insecurity. Gilly is nearly undone by the abysmal foster care system and kept afloat only by her pugnaciousness; Sara Louise is almost paralyzed by what she perceives as the privileges given her sister by her family and friends. However much Paterson might admire "struggle dashed to defeat," though, she refuses to give up on her characters.

Some readers, however, are convinced that she *does* give up on them. They think that Paterson's girls, particularly Sara Louise, find themselves in a "losing cause" against patriarchal society. What bothers feminist critics is 1) Sara Louise chooses to become a nurse midwife, when her dreams of becoming a doctor are dismissed by her(male) college advisor and 2) she leaves Rass Island's patriarchal culture only to arrive in an isolated Appalachian mountain community and "settle" for marriage and children. The assumption is that Sara Louise has sacrificed her dreams and replicated the limited life of her mother.[2]

Although Sara Louise is not a doctor, she might as well be, and she is a wife and mother as well. Gilly, too, has to learn to work with her particular circumstances: her mother doesn't want her, but her grandmother does, so she chooses to be satisfied there. Both young women are not role models for young readers (nor does Paterson intend them to be), but they do show ways in which female characters can adapt, accept, and eventually grow strong. As Anita Tarr puts it, Paterson's "books do not offer a haven from storms, but rather a way to live through them" (262).

The Great Gilly Hopkins opens in the middle of just such a storm. Galadriel "Gilly" Hopkins starts her story sounding brash and self confident. Gilly tells us she is "not nice" but "brilliant[,] famous across this entire country [and] too clever and too hard to manage" (3). This is already the voice of an imaginative, forceful girl. Her actual life, however, is considerably bleaker and more uncertain than her self portrait. Gilly is a foster child who has been abandoned by her teenaged mother and who, because of her rude behavior (and ruder mouth), has been shuffled from foster to home to foster home, convinced that any day her perfect mother will come for her. Like Ellen in *Ellen Foster,* Gilly is suspicious of adults, sarcastic, and often very funny.

She is secretly vulnerable, though, as are many children abandoned by their parents. Thoughts about her mother "trigger something deep in her stomach," what Gilly calls the "danger signal" that will start her "dissolving like hot Jell-O" (9). At an emotional level at least, Gilly misses her mother and knows that she won't be coming for her. "Why did it have to be so hard?" she wonders. "Other kids could be with their mothers all the time. Dumb, stupid kids who didn't even like their mothers much" (29). Gilly's abandonment has made her jealous of even "dumb, stupid kids" and causes her to feel inferior to them. She hides these feelings with her tough exterior.

As the novel begins, Gilly is on her way to the home of Mamie Trotter, an immensely fat woman (she looks like the "Before" picture in a diet ad, Gilly comments) who will be her new foster mother. In her run-down house, Trotter is also fostering a probably retarded child, W.E. Although she is miserable at first, Gilly will learn about the importance of love and the ties of home. When Gilly tries to run away, W.E. pleads for her to come home, and Gilly feels like "the ice in her frozen brain rumbled and cracked" (92). It is more likely the ice in her *heart* that is rumbling and cracking, as Gilly learns to care for her unlikely family. She also comes to realize that the fairy tale she has been telling herself of her mother "sweeping in like a goddess queen, reclaiming the long-lost princess" is not going to come true (115).

Before she comes to this realization, however, she writes a letter to her mother, hoping that she will come to her rescue. Instead, she attracts the attention of her maternal grandmother, and like "Bluebeard's wife, she'd opened the forbidden door and someday she would have to look inside" (115). At this point Gilly has decided that she wants to stay with Trotter and is horrified when her grandmother arrives to take her "home." This forces her to think about what she really wants, which is "to be real without any quotation marks. To belong and to possess. To be herself, to be the swan, to be the ugly duckling no longer" (124). Unlike the young Lena in *Baby of the Family*, who realizes that she is "real" when she is quite young, Gilly, without the security of family from which to form an identity, is still unclear at eleven.

She also isn't at all sure where she belongs — at Trotter's or her grandmother's house. All she really wants is to have her unlikely fairy tale come to an end, to come to "the end of road" (130). When she finally meets her mother, she is disappointed in her "flower child gone to seed" appearance, and by the fact that her mother doesn't intend to stay or to take Gilly with her. Gilly makes a desperate phone call to Trotter, telling her that "nothing turned out the way it's supposed to." Trotter responds, "How you mean supposed to? Life ain't supposed to be nothing 'cept maybe tough. [A]ll that stuff about happy endings is lies" (147). Then Gilly asks her, "If life is so bad, how come you're so happy?", and Trotter responds, "Did I say bad? I said it was tough. Nothing to make you happy like doing good on a tough job, now is there?" (148). The message here seems to be that happiness comes from hard work on a "tough job," not from the passive realization of some dream.

In the last paragraph, Gilly tells her grandmother that she's "ready to go home now" (148). Gruesome Gilly has given up her hard exterior and (more difficult) her secret illusions and is now ready to accept a real home, a real life, a real ending. Gilly starts out "gruesome" and unlovable; she finds a surrogate family and reluctantly comes to love them, only to be separated from them by her own fantasies about her mother. Finally, she has to accept that her home will not quite be what she expected, but it will be home. Once wild and alone, she has tamed herself in order to be allowed inside.[3]

The problem for Sara Louise in *Jacob Have I Loved* is equally difficult: how she can become a contented adult in a world that denies her the kinds of emotional and creative outlets she needs. Also, in order for

Sara Louise to begin her quest toward this kind of life, she must first overcome her jealousy of her talented, beautiful and (apparently) privileged
twin sister Caroline.

For the reader, Sara Louise's difficulties may be harder to unravel
than Gilly's as *Jacob* is Paterson's first use of the first-person narrator,
and, as Gray Schmidt, points out, her first unreliable narrator (77). Paterson says that she doesn't really like the first-person narrative style, which
she sees as "an arrogant and limiting point of view," but she found to her
"unhappiness that the book was refusing to be told in any voice but
Louise's" (*Worlds of Childhood* 168). In order to get inside Sara Louise's
feelings of jealousy and inadequacy, the story had to be told in her voice.
As Paterson says, "jealousy can only speak in the first person. I can't imagine another point of view" (168). Although Gilly may be in some ways
harder to like that Sara Louise, it is easier for the reader in *Jacob* to con-
fuse Sara Louise's position with the position of the novel because of the
narrative style.[4]

When the story opens, Sara Louise describes herself as "tall and large
boned, with delusions of beauty and romance" (4).[5] One of her struggles in the novel will be to give up many of those "delusions." More
importantly, she must learn to curb her jealousy of her sister, Caroline.
Sara Louise s jealousy poisons her relationship with her sister (of course)
but also distances her from her parents and friends. It diminishes her self
confidence and limits her self determination as well. Believing herself to
have been abandoned at birth for her more delicate sister, Sara Louise
remains in her shadow. Sara Louise says that in an early picture Caroline "is tiny and exquisite, her blonde curls framing a face that is glow-
ing with laughter, her arms outstretched to whoever is taking the picture,"
while Sara Louis is "hunched there like a fat dark shadow, my eyes cut
sideways toward Caroline, thumb in mouth, the pudgy hand covering
most of my face" (16–17). This is how Sara Louise will remain for most
of the novel "a fat dark shadow" in the light of her sister her face and her
light dimmed by her sister's brilliance.

Having Caroline as her twin is like the very mixed blessing of having God with you, Sara Louise says. Caroline is "so sure, so present, so
easy, so light and gold, while I was all gray and shadow." Sara almost
wishes she were "ugly or monstrous" so she could "command attention,
if only for [her] freakishness," from her parents (33). Unlike Lucille in
Rich in Love and Kate in *Ferris Beach*, Sara Louise doesn't have a physical

deformity to set her off from her sister, to make her special, if only for her "freakishness." There is no outward sign of her inner strangeness. Like many of the heroines in this study, however, she realizes that "life begins to turn upside down at thirteen," even though at the time she blames her sister, the rest of her family, and even the war for her troubles. She longs for her parents "to notice me, give me all the attention and concern that was my due" (34).

The title of the novel is obviously connected to this issue of sibling rivalry. Throughout her life, Sara Louise has seen herself as Esau, the hated twin in the Biblical story of Jacob and Esau. At one point, her spiteful grandmother quotes the relevant verse to taunt Sara Louise, who comes to believe that she is cursed by God to be inferior to her lovely and talented twin. Although she says that Sara Louise was obviously supposed to be Esau, not Jacob, Paterson makes an important point about the dichotomy between light and dark:

> [D]eep inside ourselves exists the image of the twins — two parts of one whole. The light and the dark. Jacob looks into a darkened mirror and sees Esau. Sara Louise looks into a bright mirror and sees Caroline. In order to be whole, Jacob must make peace with Esau, Sara Louise must make peace with Caroline [*A Sense of Wonder* 152].

Sara Louise may be Esau, or believe that she is, but she nevertheless must come to terms with Jacob, who is both her sister and the goodness and generosity inside herself. Without conquering her jealousy, she will never be able to create her own independent life.

To make things even more difficult, Sara Louise realizes that she will not be able live an adult life on Rass Island, that there is "no future" for her there. The culture will not allow her to be a waterman, and she cannot be a waterman's wife, facing "a lifetime of passive waiting"(37). She doesn't want to turn into mother, passively waiting for her husband to come home, or, worse, into her grandmother, fearful of the water's destruction, and resentful of anyone who has had more opportunities than she has.

As she tries to discover her role in life, Sara Louise toys with the ideas of becoming a spinster like Aunt Trudy Braxton, having a romantic relationship with the much older Captain, marrying her best friend Call, or living as a waterman. None of these dreams can be realized, but they each help prepare her for her future. For example, the one-sided romance with the Captain, who is in his 70s, leaves her feeling that she was "going crazy" (116) and out of control, but it paves the way for later emotional and physical relationships with adult men. Her season on her father's boat leaves her exhausted but feeling "for the first time in my life, deeply content with what life was giving me" (164). In fact, during that time she describes herself as a good oyster, closed and protected. "Not even the presence at Christmastime of a radiant, grown-up Caroline," she says, "could get under my shell" (166). Even though her father (and the rest of the fishermen) will not let her continue on the boat, she has learned their lessons of perseverance and stoicism.

She also decides, after passing her college entrance exams, that she was "stupid" to think she might have to live a life like Auntie Braxton's. "I was young and able, as my exams had proved," she says. "Without God, or a man, I could still conquer a small corner of the world — if I wanted to" (173). She won't be another Auntie Braxton, her father won't let her stay on the boat, Call decides to marry Caroline, and, finally, Sara Louise accepts that she must leave the island. The Captain tells her that she was "never meant to be woman on this island. A man, perhaps. Never a woman" (192). This comment, which has been read by some critics as evidence of Paterson's capitulation to traditional values, actually can be seen as a wake-up call for Sara Louise. The emphasis should be placed on "this island," not on "woman" or "man." Elsewhere, the Captain knows, Sara Louise will be able to make a useful and satisfying life.

After an epiphantic conversation with her mother, where she discovers that she is as much — if not more — loved as her sister, Sara Louise realizes that she is free to leave, able "at last to leave the island and begin to build myself as a soul, separate from the long, long shadow of my twin" (201). She starts out for college "Shiny as a new crab pot. All set to capture the world" (209). Sara Louise has traded her "good oyster," closed and resistant to life, for a "new crab pot," which is ready to embrace new challenges.

However, she has forgotten "that life, like a crab pot, catches a lot of trash you haven't bargained for" (209), and Sara Louise has some "trash" yet to get rid of. At college, her faculty advisor tells her to become a nurse, not a doctor, and, after some anger and disappointment, she does, becoming a nurse midwife in the Appalachian mountains. There she meets

Joseph Wojtkiewicz and marries him because "when he smiled, he looked like the kind of man who would sing to oysters" [as her father does] (209). Sara Louise may not have ended up where she planned to be, but she has arrived in a place where she can be satisfied.

In *Jacob Have I Loved*, Sara Louise's main job is to find her way home, both to the place she will able live comfortably and productively as an adult and to reconcile herself to her family, especially her sister.[6] The last scene in the novel is of Sara Louise as an adult, bringing twins into the world, making sure to pay attention to the larger, healthier one, too. Nursing the littler one herself, she thinks of Caroline and her beautiful singing voice. She experiences a moment of grace, where she is able to forgive her sister and accept her life. Paterson says that the "overarching theme" of her novels is "the biblical theme of divine good will." However, "[l]ike God, good will can't be divined. We are always reduced to simile, to metaphor, to once-upon-a-time" (*Worlds of Childhood* 171). Sara Louise and Gilly become the way in which Paterson metaphorizes grace, forgiveness, and acceptance. These girls are not passive, nor do they accept their fate stoically; instead, they embrace their futures willingly and with a kind of joy. "No clouds of glory" (148), as Gilly says, but lightly and (somewhat) happily they come home. In *The Great Gilly Hopkins* and *Jacob Have I Loved*, Paterson shows the ways in which girls get, not exactly what they wished for, but what they really need.

"They Do Anything to You?": Cassie Logan and the "Miseries of Ladyhood."

In the eight novels Mildred Taylor has published chronicling the Logan family, Cassie Logan plays a role in six, and she is scheduled to be featured as an adult in an upcoming novel. Taylor's three longest and best-known novels, *Roll of Thunder, Hear My Cry*, *Let the Circle Be Unbroken* and *The Road to Memphis*, show Cassie growing from an innocent (but stubborn) nine to a wiser (if not completely adult) seventeen. Throughout the trilogy, Cassie struggles with issues of identity, racism, friendship, and family loyalty, as well as from the political and social turmoil surrounding African Americans in Mississippi in the 1930s and '40s. Most importantly, though, Cassie consistently resists the gender expectations of her family and time, railing against what she calls the "miseries of ladyhood": the restrictive clothing, and the even more restrictive movements and career expectations for a young African American woman. At the same time, however, she comes to appreciate herself as an attractive young woman and potential romantic partner. Taylor effectively balances Cassie's developing identity as a woman and as a potential lawyer with the forces that are trying to keep her subservient, both to white racism and to her family's traditional expectations. Cassie main challenge in the three novels will be to negotiate among these conflicting visions of her future.

Taylor's clear sense of the opposing forces in Cassie's life comes in part from her complex relationship with the South into which she was born. Although part of her family still lives and owns land in Mississippi, Taylor and her parents and sister moved to Toledo after her father had a violent encounter with his white boss. Taylor was only an infant when she moved North, but she retains strong connections, both emotional and creative, to her relatives in Mississippi. For example, in her introduction to *Roll of Thunder, Hear My Cry,* Taylor tells how she got started as a writer around the fireside of her family home, where she "learned a history not then written in books but one passed from generation to generation ... a history of great-grandparents and of slavery and of the days following slavery; of those who lived still not free, yet who would not let their spirits be enslaved" (1–2). As with many of the writers in this book, Taylor's Southern family was the source both of the content of her stories and the style of her storytelling.

Her attitudes about her Southern roots, however, are more complicated than merely fond memories of stories around the fire. As an African American girl, she was frequently exposed to the terrors of the racist South, even as she remained emotionally connected to the region. Chris Crowe, in the only full-length study of Taylor, says that on their frequent trips South, Taylor and her sister "fell in love with the beauty of the place, with the memories, and with their family and friends." However, they soon realized the effects of racism and segregation and "learned to fear and hate that situation" (7). From this description, one can see the ambivalent feelings Taylor justifiably must have had toward the South. For example, although Taylor says in her Newbery Award acceptance speech [for *Roll of Thunder*] that as a small child she "loved the South" (401), at some point, things changed. Taylor is not sure exactly when "the adventure [was] no longer an adventure," but she knows that one summer she "felt a climbing nausea as we crossed the Ohio River into Kentucky" (402). Taylor's nausea, her anger at being silenced, at being restricted even in bodily functions, pervades Cassie Logan's story.

Also prevalent is Cassie's sense that as an African American *girl*, she is even more restricted than her male counterparts. The widespread belief in the racist South that African American women's sexuality belonged to any white male wanting to exploit it causes Cassie's family (and eventually Cassie herself) to police her behavior rigorously. Throughout her three novels, and most especially in *Road to Memphis*, Cassie will be harassed by white men, interrogated by her family about possible assaults, and limited in her behavior and actions by their fear.[7]

Another related conflict in the trilogy arises particularly from Cassie's relationship with her family. While, as Crowe says, nearly all of Taylor's books might be categorized as *Bildungsromanen* because the main characters "move away from childhood notions of how people should and do act and learn often painful lessons of the real world," (122) the stories of Cassie Logan have an extra dimension — the difficulties a young woman faces as she tries both to move away from her family and also keep them close.[8]

In spite of all these problems, Taylor manages to infuse both humor and hope into her portrayal of Cassie. She begins the trilogy with the young Cassie, whom she describes her as "a spunky eight-year-old, innocent, untouched by discrimination, full of pride and greatly love" ("Newbery" 405) and ends with 17-year-old Cassie, who is planning to be a lawyer and to put off marriage and children (if not love) until she has achieved her goals. Throughout various trials, Taylor also shows Cassie surrounded (if sometimes smothered) by the love and care of her family. As Mary Turner Harper says, "[I]n the midst of such negatives, where her characters are daily victimized, Taylor presents a positive picture of togetherness where warmth, love, and humor abound" (77). In all three novels, Cassie is able to triumph over the twin adversaries of racism and sexism as she tells her story.

Roll of Thunder, Hear My Cry and *Let the Circle Be Unbroken* are of less interest in this study than *A Road to Memphis*, as in those novels Cassie has not quite begun the process of adolescent development. Nevertheless, she shows many of the same basic characteristics of the Cassie in *Road to Memphis*. In what will become a typical move for her, Cassie begins *Roll of Thunder* complaining about the Sunday dress she has to wear for the first day of school, saying, "there's little I could do in a dress" (5). Right away, she also shows her determined side. Within the first five minutes of the first day of school, Cassie is in trouble for not responding to the teacher's question with the rest of the class. ("I never did approve of group responses," she says [20].) Then she gets into further trouble by challenging the poor quality of the textbooks given to the African American children by the school board. Never one to capitulate either to the group or to injustices of any sort, Cassie shows herself early on to be a fighter.

This introduction prepares readers for a Cassie who will plan an elaborate revenge against a condescending white girl and who will carry out an even more dramatic retaliation against the white school children and bus driver for splashing the Logans on the way to school. She also challenges a white shopkeeper and cries at the injustice that causes young T.J. to be arrested for a murder committed by his white partners. Although she is innocent of the pervasive racism in her community at the beginning of this novel, Cassie comes to learn that things are not the same for her family as they are for the white families. Still, she grows stronger and never loses her voice, her confidence, nor her willingness to stand up for injustice.

In *Let the Circle Be Unbroken,* Cassie is somewhat older and wiser, but still stubborn, opinionated, and reluctant to be silenced, although there are hints in this novel of the particular restrictions that will be placed on Cassie when she matures. A local girl has gotten pregnant by a white boy, to the shame of her family, and her parents use this as an example for Cassie. Her father tells her, "I don't want you walking them roads by yourself," and although Cassie doesn't yet understand why, she senses the seriousness behind the command. Later, her father reprimands her for keeping a picture of their white friend Jeremy Simms, telling her that one day "there's going to be white boys looking at you too — for no good, but they'll be looking. I don't want you looking back" (154). Already, Cassie is getting the message that she is in part responsible for the interest she generates in white males, and that even the most innocent encounter can have disastrous consequences.

In this novel, however, Cassie is still relatively free from the "miseries of ladyhood" that will bedevil her in *The Road to Memphis.* She plays marbles even though her father has forbidden it, she helps Mrs.

Lee Annie prepare for her voting exam, she and her brothers attend T.J.'s trial against their parents' express commands, she confronts her half-white cousin Suzella about her desire to pass as white, she braves talking to the strange Wordell, and, although she is quiet when her older brother Stacy hushes her, she refuses to resign herself to his "so-called authority" (77).[9] Still, the novel seems about the need for all the children to keep close to home. The last third of the text is taken up with the family's search for Stacey, who has run away to work in the cane fields. He is nearly killed during his escapade, and when he returns declares that home is "the very best place to be" (339). The last words of the novel are Cassie's agreement with this sentiment, suggesting that dangers wait for those children brave — or foolish — enough to venture outside the safety of the family.

Although Donnarae McCann says that *Let the Circle* is "more compelling" (97) than *The Road to Memphis*, and that Cassie is "less plausible" (97) than she was in the earlier novels, it is in *Road* that Cassie finally comes into her own. Critics seem to agree that *Road* is Taylor's "harshest" (Crowe 86) or her "angriest" novel (Smith 255), and that the focus is much more on racism than on family and home (Crowe 111), but it is this novel that brings Cassie to center stage. For the purposes of this study, it is also the more typical female *Bildungsroman*, which takes Cassie out of the house and puts her on the road. Finally, It is the novel in which her role as an African American young *woman* is most fully developed.[10]

The novel begins in a familiar way, with Cassie once again complaining about having to wear a skirt, this time as she waits for Stacey to return home from a job in Jackson. A breeze blows up the skirt, and Cassie angrily slaps it down, wishing she could have worn pants. As in the previous books, her mother and grandmother have forbidden her to wear pants, saying they aren't "ladylike." Cassie responds: "[N]othing much I did these days was ladylike, now that I was seventeen. I sighed at the miseries of ladyhood"(6). Cassie is clearly unhappy about the ways in which the "miseries of ladyhood" restrict her movements and distract her attention from attractions like Stacey's new car, for example. Things don't get any better when Cassie gets home; she wants to admire Stacey's car with the other boys, but she is forced inside to work on dinner.

Later, she wants to go hunting with the boys, which precipitates a long discussion of her lack of femininity between Papa, Mama, and in particular Big Ma, who clearly disapproves of Cassie acting like the boys (46–7). Papa reminds her that she hunted in her time and even was a "mighty fine shot," (47) but although Big Ma is proud of her accomplishment, she declares that she *had* to hunt because the men were away. To deflect the argument, she says that Cassie spends too much time with the boys and that she should start "taking on womanly ways" (48). Cassie responds that she *is* womanly, that she cooks and washes dishes, and Big Ma responds "Girl, don't you get smart with me! You knows what I mean!" (48).

It isn't quite clear what Big Ma means by "womanly ways," but her disapproval of Cassie is quite clear. Big Ma and Mama want Cassie to wear a skirt while hunting, so she puts on an old skirt with pants underneath hurries out. "I was eager for the hunt," she says (60). Once in the woods, Cassie takes off her skirt and "r[uns] to catch up with the boys" (62). The adventure ends in disaster, however, when racist whites Leon and Statler Ames, hunting with their cousin Jeremy Simms, come across Cassie and a friend, Harris, and consider chasing him — or her — like a "coon." Leon says that "maybe it be more enjoyable it was Cassie there the coon. Sure would be delightful we was to get her cornered" (68). The ever-loyal Jeremy Simms distracts his cousins from this plan, and they finally settle on chasing Harris up a tree. Unfortunately, Jeremy doesn't stop the chase, and Harris falls and breaks his leg.

Cassie runs back to her brother and their friends and tells them about Harris. Stacey asks "They do anything to you?" (71) This will become a refrain throughout the novel, with male characters asking Cassie if "anything" has happened to her; i.e. whether she has been sexually assaulted by white men. The message here seems to be that it is dangerous for a maturing Cassie to be out in the woods with the boys because it may put her in the vicinity of white boys as well. In fact, throughout the novel, Cassie's sexuality will cause a variety of problems, both for herself and others.

Interspersed with the scenes of sexual threat, though, are ones of the *pleasures* of ladyhood. Before the hunting trip, Cassie is planning her outfit for church the next day, and like Lena in *Baby of the Family*, she looks in the mirror, finding similarities between herself and her mother (55). She says likes the way she looks but doesn't "think about it much" (58). Instead, she plans on getting her education before she gets seriously involved with a man. She tells her mother that she wants to do what her mother did and secure a career before she gets married (56).

Like her mother, Cassie is attractive, but also like her, Cassie will postpone marriage and family until she has accomplished her other goals. The difference is that she will not settle for teaching in a small rural school; she has plans for law school. As Lena does in *Baby of the Family*, Cassie is aware of the ways she is like (and unlike) her mother.

The novel suggests, though, that her plan may be unrealistic, given her situation as a young African American woman in the Jim Crow South. Throughout the novel, the narrative will alternate between affirmations of Cassie's femininity and demonstrations of her vulnerability. Repeatedly, Cassie will realize her attractiveness, take a chance and violate the norms of "ladyhood," and then pay the consequences of unwanted attention of white men. For example, shortly after the hunting incident, Cassie is getting ready for the Reverend Gabson's funeral. She admires her new clothes, especially her coat, which fits her "almost like a dress, snuggly around the bodice and waist and flared nicely around my hips and legs" (81–2).

Cassie is pleased with her looks, but her "snuggly" coat and dress shoes will prove to be a dangerous liability when she leaves the safety of Great Faith Church and ventures down the road to visit Sissy, a friend and neighbor: Statler and his other cousins see her on the road and start to flirt with her, with sinister implications. Cassie responds haughtily and then realizes her mistake: "I was a fool to use a smart mouth. These were young white men standing here. They could take offense to my words or be encouraged by them. Either way, I couldn't win" (102). Cassie plans her escape and worries she can't outrun them in her "Sunday pumps" (102), but her father shows up and discourages the boys, asking her, once again, if they "ain't touched you none" (103). Like Stacey, her father immediately assumes that the young white men have somehow compromised her. He explains his intervention: "Got no laws t' protect our girls from the likes of him, but I ain't gonna stand for him forcing his attentions on you" (104). Although he is unable to use the law to keep Statler away from his daughter, Papa can use his imposing figure and age to intimidate the boys. Telling Cassie he worries more about her because she's a girl, and implying that she needs more protection, he warns, "Don't get so smart, Daughter, you don't use your head" (105). This is hard advice for a girl who wants to go to college and then law school. The implication seems to be that if she becomes too smart — or too reckless — she will put herself (and others) in danger.

In fact, the main conflict in the novel, family friend Moe's attack on the Ames brothers and his subsequent flight to Memphis, is at least indirectly caused by Cassie. On what starts out as an ordinary trip to Strawberry, the closest town, Moe holds up as well as can be expected under the familiar humiliation of the Ames brothers (they are "rubbing" his head for luck), but then Statler says that maybe he can "get lucky with Cassie"(123). The disparaging reference to Cassie causes Moe to explode: "Suddenly the anger in Moe burst forth like a thunderstorm. He knocked Statler's arm away with the tire iron, then smashed it full force into Statler's side" (123). The result of this violent encounter is that Moe must flee Mississippi to avoid lynching, so Jeremy hides Moe and spirits him out of town while Stacey, Clarence, Cassie drive to Jackson to rendezvous with Moe, take him by car to Memphis (hence the title of the novel), and put him on a train for Chicago. Although this incident is necessary to propel the action (and initiate the road trip so common to young adult novels) the message appears to be that Cassie's sexuality causes violence and destruction to those around her.

Following its pattern of alternating positive and dangerous sexuality, the novel has Cassie first see Solomon Bradley, a handsome former lawyer turned newspaper publisher, right after the incident with Moe. She notices that he is "a very attractive man" with "an intriguing face" and fascinating eyes, which, Cassie says, "gave his face such appeal and made me keep my eyes on him longer than I should have" (143). Not surprisingly, Bradley will become Cassie's romantic interest for the rest of the novel. He will also become her mentor, guiding her in her reading and her career. Bradley is the king of mixed messages, however. He admires her ambition — and her looks — but teases her about how "some young man could possibly come along and change your mind" about her goals, saying that her determination to postpone marriage means that she hasn't "been in love so far" (146). While it may be possible to see Bradley as a harmless distraction on the way to Cassie's future, the novel never seems to question the romance or Bradley's condescending attitude toward Cassie.[11]

Solomon disappears while the young people are on the road, and during the trip there is a final incident that highlights the interconnected issues of race and sexuality. At a gas station where they stop in the middle of the night, Cassie thinks about using the whites-only restroom: she tries to sneak in, but a white woman sees her and calls for the attendant. When the men turn on her, and the gas station attendant says that Cassie was thinking about "putting your black butt where white ladies got to sit" (178), the woman becomes uncomfortable. Cassie says she thinks she "felt my fear," and she tries to withdraw the complaint. However, the woman walks away "leaving me in the hands of the men," who insult Cassie. She tries to run, but once again, she is handicapped by her shoes, skirt, and stockings. She says the attendant's "shoe struck me sharply, but that's not what wounded me. It was my pride that suffered. I was stunned by the humiliation" (179). Again, Stacey worries that someone has touched her (180), and Cassie keeps the incident secret, sensing that she is some way responsible, and tries to ignore her fear and humiliation.

However, the fear recurs when she tries to sleep later that night. Cassie can't stop shaking; she is nauseous, and she keeps re-living the incident (187–88). She tries to think of home, but the comforting images don't last, and the memories come back: "I was in the mud, and angry, foul-talking men were kicking at me. I felt the humiliation and the fear again, and they were more than I could bear" (189). Cassie screams and vomits all over her new clothes.[12] Once again, Cassie's overconfidence has led to her putting herself and "everyone in the car" in danger. She can't tell anyone because she believes (after years of being told) that she is somehow responsible for what happened.

Later, after they arrive in Jackson and reconnect with Solomon Bradley, Cassie starts to confess to him, when he interrupts and asks her, like her father and brother before him, "Just what happened out on that road, Cassie?" (232). She has a hard time telling him, however, as she feels responsible for the attack, and thus her explanation is halting and hints at things unsaid. After hearing her story, Solomon, as do the other men in the novel, asks her if "anything else" happened, assuming that the violation was sexual as well as emotional and physical. In spite of her shame and reluctance, however, recounting her mistreatment seems to comfort Cassie.

In what should be by now a familiar pattern, at this point the narrative veers from the miseries into one of the joys of ladyhood — romance. Telling Cassie that he likes the way her mind works, "among other things," Solomon Bradley, against his better judgment, kisses her. Cassie says that she "was Cinderella and he was my Memphis Prince" (248). What follows is the stuff of romantic daydreams:

> I swirled in a daze.
> I was a princess.
> And he was a prince.
> The world was at war.
> Moe was in trouble.
> But for the moment none of that mattered. Solomon Bradley had me in his arms [251–52].

The result of all this kissing is that Cassie's "head was in a cloud and all [her] thinking was blurred" (252). For a girl so recently making plans to attend law school and put off romantic relationships, Cassie seems awfully easy to cloud and blur. Perhaps Taylor wanted Cassie to have a positive romantic experience to (literally) remove the bad taste left by the encounter at the gas station, but the reader wonders whether Bradley might be right about the ease with which Cassie might give up her dreams if she met the right man.

Indeed, much of the conflict concerning Cassie's future is unresolved by the end of the novel, although this is fairly typical for young adult novels, especially those in a series. Moe escapes to Chicago, but Jeremy Simms, now disowned by his racist father, disappears into the military never to be seen again, and Stacey plans to follow him soon. Cassie thinks that many people she loves are leaving, and she is "fearful of what was to come" (288). Chris Crowe says that Taylor is planning another novel that brings Cassie to adulthood (64), but for now the novel leaves readers with many unanswered questions. She clearly intends to go to law school, but she is easily distracted by handsome men, although not those, like Moe, of a lower social class; she is proud of her good looks but now (justifiably) wary of the dangers they cause and will continue to cause for her; she remains in the bosom of her family, but she is looking outward toward the future. Of all the novels in this section, the future for this protagonist is the least clear. Paterson's girls may have to have accepted a more traditional role than one they had planned, but they appear to be contented, even happy, with their choices, and Dicey Tillerman, discussed in the next segment, finds a way to reconfigure home into a place that fits her needs. Cassie Logan, perhaps because she comes from the strongest home, may have the most work to do to free herself from it. She also has to balance a sense of hope with the reality of racism.[13]

"Money and a Map": Dicey Tillerman's Search for Home and Identity

In the first novel in Cynthia Voigt's Tillerman series, *Homecoming*, 13-year-old Dicey Tillerman is abandoned (with her three younger siblings) by their troubled mother. After the "sad moon-face[d]" woman leaves them in a mall parking lot with instructions to find an unmet aunt, Dicey decides to walk to Bridgeport, Connecticut, with the children in tow. Dicey, who always "looks for the worst" because, as she says, she "likes to be ready," (8) knows that she will have to be the one to get the other children to their aunt's house safely, find food and money on their trip, and deal with whatever (as yet unimagined) circumstances await them when they arrive. Along the way, Dicey will grow and change, as the journey demands a premature adulthood of her, and she will refine her definitions of gender, family, and home in the process.

As Virginia Wolf puts it, the novel "celebrates 'coming' as much, if not more than, 'home'," (43) and it is true that the story is centered on Dicey's growth and development as she makes her way first toward her aunt's and eventually toward her grandmother's house. This growth also has a feminist trajectory, as Dicey comes to redefine her sense of gender. Like the heroines in Paterson and Taylor's novels (as well as the other girls discussed in this study), Dicey will manipulate traditional ideas and create entirely new configurations that, while they may *resemble* conventional models, actually offer profound challenges to those conventions. In the first book-length study of Voigt, Suzanne Reid says that Voigt's "protagonists begin as obedient and uncritical, silent or inarticulate about their own reactions to life and people around them. A major step toward growth is their realization that they can express opinions and ideas that are different from the expectations or conventions of the context in which they live" (52). Of course, this could apply to her male characters as well, but the movement from "obedient and uncritical" to expressing unconventional opinions is especially relevant to young women, who are more often expected to remain silent and docile.

Another important issue in *Homecoming* (and the second novel in the series, *Dicey's Song*) is how Dicey comes to reconsider her conception of family. From the first page of the novel, for example, motherhood is called into question — and redefined. Dorothy Clark says that while "the institution of motherhood — conceptions of motherhood as functions of patriarchy — does not work ... the experience of mothering, of caring and nurturing, permeates it" (198). The children are abandoned by their mother, but Dicey immediately takes on that role. Throughout the novel all the children are "mothered" by various unconventional surrogate parents they encounter on their journey, from circus performers to male college students. Finally, their grandmother, who — with her bare feet and prickly manner — radically redefines the role of mother, assumes the job.[14]

Along with her redefinition of gender, and mothering, Voigt also modifies the mythic structure of the *Bildungsroman*. Several critics have mentioned the ways in which Voigt modifies fairy tales, the orphan story, and the myth of Odysseus. Consistent with Lissa Paul's position that child protagonists have more possibilities because they are not yet restricted by the rules of the adult world, Betty Greenway says that "Voigt's novels are reassuring in the same way fairy tales are. The small and powerless child can and does succeed through cleverness, resourcefulness, and active innocence" (127–8). Clearly, "cleverness, resourcefulness, and active innocence" are the hallmarks of Dicey's character, although one must add determination and stubborn persistence to the list. In fact, by the time Dicey gets to the second novel of the series, *Dicey's Song*, she will have to learn how to relinquish some of the control she is trying to maintain over her siblings' lives.[15]

From the beginning of *Homecoming*, Dicey shows her determination. Dicey, who "read the maps," has been put in charge of the others: ten-year-old intellectual James, nine-year-old lovely but probably dyslexic Maybeth, and pugnacious six-year-old Sammy. Almost immediately, Dicey realizes that she will have to get them to Bridgeport, with only a little money and some paper sacks of food and clothing, and she decides that, in spite of her situation, there is no point worrying. All there is, Dicey thinks, is "Just going ahead. People might give them food. She might be able to earn food or money, somehow. She couldn't think how they'd manage it. But they would have to manage it, somehow" (27). Although she decides not to worry, thinking about what to do to keep her family together is what distinguishes Dicey from other children, and even from her mother, who abandoned them when she could no longer cope. James comments that it is "lucky for us" that Dicey isn't their mother, as *she* would never "go off and leave us" (38). It quickly becomes Dicey's job to be the solid foundation for her family; throughout the trip she will have very little time to indulge her emotions or imagination, but she will have to use her good sense.

For example, when Dicey thinks about hard it must have been for their mother to *want* to take care of her children when she was unable to do so, she quickly decides that "imagination doesn't do any good" and begins to plan a new strategy for getting money and food. Or, after they recover emotionally from one of many setbacks, Dicey consoles herself that they "had money and a map, their stomachs were full — it wasn't a bad way to begin" the rest of the journey (85). What is most important is that they are "runaways to, not just runaways" (49). The kids have a destination, which means that they are moving *toward* their future, not running away from their past. Dicey, too, has goals: to keep her family together and find them a permanent home.

Along the way, though, Dicey will change her mind about what kind of home she really wants. A recurring motif in the novel is introduced by an epitaph Dicey sees, which reads: "Home is the hunter, home from the hill, and the sailor home from the sea" (85). At first, Dicey is chilled by this stoic commentary on life and home, but she decides that "she wouldn't mind having this poem on her tombstone, now that she thought about it. She was the hunter and the sailor, and she guessed dead people did lie quietly in their graves" (85–6). This acceptance of the inevitable will change as she moves through her journey, however, and she eventually abandons the notion of home as merely a final resting place.

After their difficult trip, the children eventually get to Bridgeport, at what they think is their Aunt Cilla's house. Their aunt has died, however, and the house, which isn't as grand nor as near the ocean as Dicey had imagined, is now occupied by Cousin Eunice, who thinks of the children as an unwelcome but necessary Christian burden. Not surprisingly, Dicey soon decides that this sterile and unwelcoming place cannot be their permanent home. Something in Aunt Cilla's house "make[s] Dicey's brain slow down," perhaps because of "the routine of every day," or simply fatigue, or "maybe it was that nothing seemed to happen, except the same thing happening over and over again" (134). Two things jolt Dicey out of the lethargy that has overwhelmed her at Cousin Eunice's:

her (very legitimate) fear that the family will be split up and her new job washing windows. As is always the case for Dicey, "having money made a difference." It "woke her up" and makes her "feel like her old self again" (141). For Dicey, fear is her driving force, and money is her fuel.

After Dicey has accumulated enough cash, the children decide to leave Cousin Eunice's and head south toward the home of their newly-discovered grandmother in Crisfield, Maryland. Dicey muses about home once again, thinking that perhaps "there could be no home for the Tillermans." If they were looking for a place to be "home free," then Cousin Eunice's clearly wasn't the place. It was "expensive," Dicey says. "The price ways always remembering to be grateful" (168). Dicey's expectations about home have been lowered by the disappointment of Cousin Eunice's house. Now she "wanted only a place where the Tillermans could be themselves and do what was good for them" (168).

She discovers on the way to Crisfield that perhaps they don't need to find a home: maybe they could "sail along, deeming, not caring where they were going or when they would get there or what they would do there" (199). In fact, she comes to believe, after their single encounter with a truly malevolent adult, that "[e]very house was a secret place, a fortress, within which anything might be going on. Every house was perhaps a trap" (226). Instead of falling into a trap, Dicey thinks that she might prefer the life of perpetual travel. After a brief respite in a traveling circus, for example, Dicey feels peaceful: "Contentment was too small a word for what Dicey was feeling. They had food and a warm place to sleep, and Dicey had money in her pocket. They were traveling and had purpose and destination, but no conclusion. Dicey had nothing to worry about" (235). Although she may prefer "purpose and destination, but no conclusion," Dicey is driven to complete her journey and find her family a home.

Finding a home with their grandmother proves complicated, though, as their grandmother has her own troubles and doesn't want to take on those of the rest of the Tillermans. Still, Dicey stubbornly insists: "Here was the place, a farm with plenty of room and plenty of work for them to do, and the bay just beyond the marshes, and a sailboat in the barn. She wasn't about to let this grandmother keep them from it" (261). Her grandmother, while stubborn herself, doesn't know "the kind of thinking and planning Dicey could do" (262). Although Dicey is worried briefly about whether or not she can give her siblings a home and keep their spirits strong, she comes to believe that they are at home with their grandmother and notices "a warm feeling in her stomach, as if she had swallowed sunshine" (299). When her grandmother asks her at the end of the novel is she is ready to go home, Dicey says "ready" (312). In much the same way as Gilly accepts the home she hadn't expected, so Dicey is ready, at last, to settle down.

Like Tyler, who has always maintained that she is more interested in what happens after the happily ever after, Voigt is not content to end Dicey's story with her homecoming. *Dicey's Song* begins with what Voigt has called a "killer first line" (Reid 7), which she fought to keep in the novel:

> And they lived happily ever after.
>   Not the Tillermans. Dicey thought. That wasn't the way things went for the Tillermans, ever [1].

Still, Dicey isn't going to let that "get her down," since "that was what happened to Momma" (1). Even though her family may not live happily every after, Dicey is determined to be positive, or at least stoic. This doesn't mean that it will be easy sailing, though. Throughout this novel, Dicey, who is settled with the kids on Gram's farm, struggles with letting go of her responsibilities.

Although Gram tells her that she's "not the only one responsible," Dicey finds it difficult trying to "take a rest" (21). She worries that her family is "turning away from her" (73), but she realizes that "holding on was time consuming," especially if one is trying to hold onto things that are pulling in different directions. In her short life, Dicey has gone from child, to adult, to parent, having to deal first with the responsibility of children and then with the burden of their increasing independence, all before she learns to drive.

Not surprisingly, the home/harbor motif recurs, although subtly changed. Dicey now feels as if she is "sitting at anchor." Still, although it is "good to come to rest," Dicey recognizes that "a boat at anchor wasn't like a boat at seat" (202). Dicey knows that she has the best of both worlds: she has the freedom of the boat and the security of the anchor. The possibility for change is always there, too. "Furled sails were just waiting to be raised, when the sailor chose to head out again," she thinks, speculating that maybe nothing was as permanent as it might seem (202).

At the end of the novel, Dicey revises her definition of home, family, and identity even further. Confused about whether or not she should contact her mother's brother to fill in the missing pieces about her history, Dicey realizes that she has to accept a certain amount of uncertainty in her life. This new confusion, she says is "like a windy storm," but she decides (like Jo in *The Cheer Leader*) that she might as well get used to it, even come to enjoy it, since it isn't going to go away (210–11). Dicey has gone from a feeling lost without a home port, to not wanting a permanent home, to finding one that offers both freedom and stability, to discovering that confusion, those story seas, is probably a "permanent condition." As Dorothy Clark puts it, "Dicey expands upon the epitaph *Home is the Sailor,* transforming it from a reference to permanence and death to one of change and life" (196).

In all of her seven novels about the Tillermans, "Voigt describes how characters escape from damaged relationships by *reaching out* beyond themselves, *holding on* to the nature strengths of familial bonds, and finally *letting go* of ties that imprison" (Reid 31). In the novels that feature her, particularly *Homecoming* and *Dicey's Song,* Dicey grows to a young woman who has perhaps matured before her time, but who has, through the help of family, friends, and her own determined character, gotten everyone, including herself, into safe harbor.

Notes

Introduction

1. Actually, it appears that social theorists may have now turned their attention to boys. Recent books such as those by Michael Gurian, James Garbarino, Daniel Kindlon and Michael Thompson, Michael Porter, and William Pollack suggest that the new "crisis" may be one of boys' confidence and success. Writing in *Salon* magazine, Amy Benfer carefully outlines the recent paradigm shift.

2. Much of this debate was fueled by a 1992 report by the Association of American University Women, "How Schools Shortchange Girls." This study claimed that "girls do not receive equitable amounts of teacher attention, are less apt than boys to see themselves reflected in the materials they study, and are often not expected or encouraged to pursue higher level math and science" (6). The consequences of being thus shortchanged, the study found, include higher rates of eating disorders, suicide and depression than boys; decreased self-esteem; and lower enrollment in university math and science majors.

3. There have been some challenges to the rhetoric of female adolescent crisis, in particular from Christine Hoff Sommers,

who in her recent book *The War Against Boys* argues strenuously that girls are *not* on the wrong side of the educational gender gap. Other critics of the AAUW report, like historian Diane Ravitch and psychologist Judith Kleinfeld, however, may be more interested in promoting a conservative political agenda than they are in changing the way society views girls — and boys.

Chapter One

1. Joan Brumberg's 1997 book *The Body Project* provides a more recent formulation of the same problem. For an additional elaboration of this position, see Orenstein xii.

2. Criticism has been leveled at Gilligan's assertions in recent years, primarily from sociologists and historians, although not enough to seriously undermine her position in both feminist criticism and popular culture. The most common objection is the one raised by Phyllis Grosskurth in her 1991 *The New York Review of Books* essay, which says that Gilligan's book "seems saturated with sentimentality" (30). Another approach questions Gilligan's sample, in particular her nearly

exclusive attention to upper-class white girls in private schools (Stacey 540–43).

3. Perhaps the most familiar of these maternal linguists is Julia Kristeva, who extends the power of the maternal bond beyond psychological development to language development. Kristeva establishes a linguistic model that has influenced all subsequent discussions of the relationship between the mother and language ("Women's Time" 196). For the ways in which Kristeva's notions about language can be applied to literature, as well as to personal psychology see Hunter 98–99. For a discussion of the ways in which the resulting separation anxiety is reflected in the ways in which female writers create characters, see Homans 25. See Brownstein for a discussion of the ways in which the novel is an inherently female form.

4. Alice Jardine offers just such a caution to maternalistic readings in *Gynesis* (101). Feminism must be seen, Jardine says, as part of the larger, male culture it attacks, with all of its complexities and oppositions. As far as language and literary studies are concerned, then, feminist critics must remain aware of the ways in which their language *is* the language of Western culture, and their oppositions within the framework of that culture. Jardine's position is aligned with Betsy Erkkila's concerns about defining poetic language (42). Toril Moi also calls for skepticism, in her case concerning the dominance of patriarchal structures and the need for feminism to acknowledge complexities in the relationship between the dominant male world view and the female (64, 124).

5. Diana Fuss' attention to context is similar to Butler's concentration on the cultural nature of identity.

6. Jane Gallop aptly describes reader's frustrations with and attractions to psychoanalytic readings of texts, in particular novels of development (*Thinking Through the Body* 138). For a formalist alternative to both traditional and feminist psychoanalytic readings, see Peter Brooks.

7. It is true that many novels written before 1970 *have* followed the pattern described by Rosowski. For a study of novels for female adolescents written between 1960 and 1984, see DeMarr and Bakerman.

8. Much recent criticism of contemporary novels of development has relied on psychoanalytic (and hence apolitical) definitions of family and/or on reification of mother/child relationships as well. See, for example, Roni Natov's reading of *Annie John* by Jamaica Kincaid.

9. In a similar study, Michelle Fine and Pat Macpherson interviewed a number of young women and discovered that while they rejected traditional feminism, they actively redefined their notions of the feminine in ways that gave them the agency and freedom typically associated with boys.

10. Useful discussions of gender and modernism in Glasgow's novels can be found in Raper 153–58 and Wagner-Martin 199.

11. For the relationship between McCullers and the South see Presley 100, 105, and for discussions of gender see Spivak 133 and Westling 157. Issues of gender in Welty are discussed in Costello 90, Hankins 399, and Harrison 57.

12. The only extended treatment of Lee's novel can be found in Johnson. See particularly pages 56, 65, 101. For a discussion of Spencer's relationship to the South, see Evoy 571–77.

Chapter Two

1. Nancy Parrish connects Smith to the "new southern regionalist movement," which includes Tyler, McCorkle, and Gibbons (575), but she says that Smith is the "most intellectually independent" (578). For an extended treatment of Smith's connections to past and present Southern women writers see Hill 121–135.

2. Regional identity may also not be the most important factor in creating personality. Smith insists to Virginia Smith that the real division between people is not "between the North and South but

between urban and rural," as Bobbie Ann Mason, Dorothy Allison, and Janisse Ray also recognize (75). Still, Smith says that there is a distinctively Southern narrative style that involves "transmitting information in the form of anecdote" (McCord 172).

3. Rebecca Smith says that Smith's novels preserve the past while foregrounding her particular time (5), while Linda Tate says that Smith uses her storytelling to keep live "a sense of history as a collaborative, dynamic enterprise" (93). For Michael Kreyling, the question Smith's novels raise is what the connection is between "lived (southern) experience, contemporary or historical, and varieties available for replication" (113).

4. Sexuality is another important part of this equation. Much of her work, Smith says, is "bound up in the body" (Smith 69), and critic Anne Jones agrees. Smith's characters, she says "find a kind of health in assertions centered in the self, in the body" (121). For other formulations of Smith's redefinition of gender roles, see Hill and Kearns.

5. See Parrish 577, Prajznerova 31, and Hill 24 for critical discussions of the ending.

6. Rebecca Smith (29), Hill (31), and Buchanan (328) disagree about the level of hopefulness at the end of this novel.

7. See also Kalb 24 and Kearns 183.

8. Prajznerova s (90–91), MacKethan (8), and Buchanan (332) compare Crystal and Agnes.

9. For further discussions of the relationships between Crystal and later Smith characters see Byrd-Cook 218, Rebecca Smith 47, 58, and Hill 51.

10. See Rebecca Smith 122, Hill 107–09, and Bennett 76, 94 for various interpretations of the ending of *Fair and Tender Ladies*.

11. For discussions of the various meanings of "grace" as both name and idea see Parrish 578 and Byrd-Cook 98.

12. Joan Wylie Hall says that "In finally returning to her early homeplace, Florida Grace also returns to the mother whose life

she recovers and whose garden she explores anew" (92).

Chapter Three

1. For discussions about personal development in Tyler, see Gullette 100.

2. For further analysis of the conflict between change and continuity see Evans 53, Gibson 166, and Shelton 176.

3. Theresa Kanoza outlines this process well (29).

4. According to Evans, "Evie must learn about the world of women from the radio, and from the ads and articles in magazines like *Good Housekeeping* and *Family Circle*" (93).

5. Rose Quiello says that Evie is a "young woman who has literally engraved her desire as well as her anger on her forehead for everyone to see" (52). See also 54.

6. See Clifton Fadiman's interview with Tyler, which highlights Tyler's apparently cavalier approach to life.

7. This is consistent with her character. Earlier in the novel, Evie briefly becomes a minor celebrity at a local revival, where her name is brought up as an example of the dangerous excesses caused by rock and roll. When they decide to visit the church as another publicity stunt, Evie hears the minister saying she has ruined her life. "You're speaking libel. Slander," she says. "I did not ruin my life, it was not for nothing. How can you say such a thing?" (180). She continues in her resolute defense of her actions to Drum, when he asks her why she no longer wears bangs (to cover up her scars). "I don't wear bangs." she says, "because I don't back down on things I have done" (188).

8. Alice Hall Petry discusses the feminist slant of the novel (67–68). See also Nesanovich 32.

9. For more discussion about childbirth, marriage, and identity see Betts 2, Evans 111, Gullette 100, Quiello 57, and Volker 47.

10. Still, like many Tyler characters, Elizabeth is participating, according to

Gullette, in "the apprenticeship necessary before a woman is ready to accept family life" (102). In fact, she "serves an actual apprenticeship to the Emerson family's possessions — by becoming their handyman — before she marries into the clan and becomes the caretaker of them all" (102).

11. According to Ruth Saxton, female dress, and femininity itself in Tyler's novels can be read as "constructed." Whether they dress in jeans and moccasins, or twin sets and high heels, her female characters' various styles "hint at self-creating and suggest the possibility of a whimsical distance from the constructions of the feminine, a space within which to celebrate with playfulness and exuberance the carnival of everyday life" (76).

12. Volker says that Elizabeth's rebirth as Gillespie represents "a culmination of the efforts she has shown throughout the book to evade specificity, including that of gender. It is a sane avoidance of the consequences of Mrs. Emerson's femininity" (64). However, it may be possible to see both female characters as Bennett does, saying they, like Lucille in *Rich in Love*, "learn to abandon the traditional, patriarchal order in which they have lived all their lives — with its ticking clocks and its specified roles for women — and instead discover the freedom and power in a life that includes flexibility, risk, and individual growth" (48).

13. See Shelton on the end of *The Clock Winder* (117). Others have entered into the debate about the ending of the novel, in particular Kanoza (32).

14. Shelton sees the conclusion as bleak and Jenny's pronouncements about luck as deluded (182). For more positive interpretations of Jenny's development and the end of the novel, see Volker 126–36, Petry 197, and Evans 116.

Chapter Four

1. Reviews of *In Country*, while for the most part positive (although not as positive as those of her short stories), do share an awareness of the difficulty Mason sets for herself when she writes about people very different from her own highly educated, intellectually sophisticated readers. See Molarsky 58, Conarroe 7, and Johnson 15–16.

2. The detective story has been a favorite of Bobbie Ann Mason's since childhood. She has even written a critical analysis of the genre called *The Girl Sleuth: A Feminist Guide*. In it she says that the trappings of the mystery genre are used to "glamorize the trespass into adulthood" (6). Mystery novels, she says, are the best vehicle for "thrilling girls safely — teasing their desire for adventure without threatening the comfortable advantages of femininity. By solving mysteries girls could confront the unknown with ease" (15).

3. Weighing in on the novel's traditional focus, Thomas Myers says it is "a small town *Bildungsroman*, reassuringly traditional in mode, style, and tone, a quilt of pop culture references and symbolic details wrapping a warm affirmation of old-fashioned ideals" (423). Sandra Bonilla Durham says that "Sam's quests are for the knowledge and strength to choose her role and her place" (48). For other discussions of the *Bildungsroman* motif in *In Country* see Pollack 101, Dwyer 72, and Krasteva 80.

4. Joanna Price notes that for Sam, "the acquisition of adult femininity entails a coming to terms with bodily identity within a culture which both denies and exploits the female body" (182). See also Pollack 97, Bennett 29, Blais 107, and Price 184.

5. Robert H. Brinkmeyer, Jr., while calling the novel "Mason's most significant and forceful statement of personal growth through the challenge of history" (28), says that unlike earlier generations of Southerners, Mason's characters "possess much more individual freedom," but they substitute "self-fulfillment" for "moral vision" (22). For Mason on the South, see Wilhelm 37. See also Tate 147 and Krasteva 78 for further discussions of Mason's attitude toward the contemporary South.

6. Leslie White puts it this way: "Complacent but restless, inarticulate about their frustrations, they are grotesques in a way, products of a culture that asks nothing of them and rewards their compliance" (72). However, White says, "Mason writes also to find out what brand of popular art destroys naïveté, which kinds are threatening, which are powerful or seductive enough in themselves to demean a life, or enrich it" (73). It isn't quite clear how this is accomplished, but "Mason shows how popular art, especially popular music, can be a means of continuity and communication" (79). In other words, *M*A*S*H* doesn't trivialize her father's death, it allows Sam a context in which to understand it.

7. Critics are divided about the final scene. Matthew C. Stewart finds it unrealistic and sentimental, even "optimistic to the point of sanguinity" (176). The final simile, he says, is "jarring in its departure from the simple language that has heretofore been inseparable from *In Country's* style and its goals as a realistic work" (175). Other critics have been more positive about the ending. See Blais 117, Krasteva 81, 89, and Price 186.

reenacted past, the tourist pageant that the modern South has become [and she] is not paralyzed when she confronts the absence of meaning" (118).

4. The novel has been frequently compared to *The Adventures of Huckleberry Finn*. A reviewer in the *English Journal* says: "Surely without intending to, in *Rich in Love* Humphreys has written a modern *Huck Finn* narrated by a young woman who is at least as vividly portrayed as Huck. Lucille is a loving and lonely creation whose journey is an emotional one, and throughout its course she sheds light on our times, our feelings, our lives" (83). For further discussion of the ways in which *Rich in Love* revises *Huckleberry Finn*, see Kreyling 118–19 and Henley 83.

5. See Walker 313.

6. Michael Kreyling aptly points out that it isn't "sexual politics that will be changed.... Lucille is also engaged in a rethinking of southern cultural politics.... Lucille is the dynamiter's daughter; she knows just where to place the charge to bring the whole construction to the ground" (119).

7. See Bennett 45.

Chapter Five

1. According to interviewer Dannye Powell, Humphreys was told this same thing by her mother. "It was supposed to perturb me," says Humphreys. "But I just lit up and ran and put it in the novel" (183).

2. Reviews of the novel have been consistently positive, although some objections have been raised to the characterization of Lucille and to the ending of the novel. For negative reviews see Wickenden 46 and Steinberg 58. Positive responses include Chappell 9 and Malone 389.

3. Or as Michael Kreyling puts it, "In Humphreys's postmodern South there is no simultaneity of real and replica; in *Rich in Love* nothing but simulacra are available in the search for meaning" (116). However, Lucille "has an eye for the sideshow of

Chapter Six

1. Lynda Hart says that "Allison writes to 'save her life,' for she is Bone, and she is Bone's witness, the one who arrives to listen after the girl has been waiting for a long time" (202). Allison is both character and witness, actor and audience, the knowledge of which gives Bone's survival and quiet triumph at the end of the novel new resonance.

2. Debora Horvitz says the novel emphasizes "the crucial need to understand and integrate one's past, especially when that story derives from and is embedded in sexual/violent trauma" (239). This is particularly important because "trauma works to subvert, if not entirely prevent, precisely this rehabilitative process, especially when its victims are traumatized again by being silenced. Thus each text

becomes a meta-story centered upon the protagonists's search for and acquisition of story" (239).

3. According to Jillian Sandell, Allison "tempers her portrayal of poverty with the strength and courage of her characters and family members, while also showing their flaws and mistakes" (213). This doesn't eliminate all the potential political problems with writing about working-class characters, however, as the success of the novel reveals "a profound collective desire to engage with the issue of impoverished whites in the United States, while at the same time it suggests a form of disavowal that keeps such issues at arm's length — class issues become safely located in books and popular culture to be consumed as a leisure activity" (216). Still, Allison may come as close as possible to presenting a new way of thinking about the poor, Sandell says. "While many stories about white trash have, until now, participated in a scapegoating function — displaying the ills of society *onto* white trash — by writing from the perspective of queer white trash Allison challenges this stereotype" (226). See also Baker 117, 120 and Reynolds 359.

4. According to Ann Cvetkovich, "By focusing on the mother-daughter relationship, Allison refuses easy dichotomies of victim and perpetrator and explores the complexities of emotional trauma" (368). Of course Bone is not responsible for what happens to her, but neither, entirely, is her mother, who is both "victim and perpetrator." For a detailed discussion of the mother/daughter bond in abusive families, see Jacobs 127.

5. Lynda Hart says that while in her conscious mind Bone retaliates against her stepfather and hopes to be rescued, "her sexual fantasies repeat, magnify, and modify the actual abuse, often transforming it into brilliant scenarios that bear little if any resemblance to her actual experiences..." (180). See also Sandell 220, Cvetkovich 371, and Gilmore 60 for further discussion of Bone's transformative sexual imagination.

6. Jocelyn Donlon says that on Raylene's porch Bone can "begin to define a 'white trash lesbian' identity — a transgressive identity which violates conventional, middle-class, heterosexual porch rituals of romance" (140). She says that the porch "safely situates Bone on the threshold of her emerging identity, positioning her to embrace and to affirm her own transgressiveness and ready to face the world on her own terms" (141). Like its owner, Raylene's house provides a productive space for Bone's growth. For additional commentary on Raylene, see Baker 125.

7. Lynda Hart says that Allison resists "sentimentalizing her ending with Anney Boatwright's heroic rescue of her daughter from her husband's evil grasp" and shows us instead a daughter left " to make her own way in the world profoundly wounded, consumed with rage, and destined probably, to reenact the trauma that we, as readers, are called upon to witness" (179). See Gwin 435 and Gilmore 61 for more positive readings of the ending.

8. As Ralph Wood puts it: "[T]he girl's syntax is collisional, not chiefly because she has failed to learn grammar but because her life has been a series of crashes: one dreadful thing abutting another" (2). Gibbons is compelled to document the "crashes" as they happen; Allison is content to recount them afterward. Gibbons' style more clearly resembles a diary, a quintessential female form. See also Watts 222.

9. Still, some critics, Sharon Monteith in particular, fault Gibbons for not fully developing the character of Starletta. Monteith links the decision to downplay Starletta's role to the *Bildungsroman* form, which results in "an understandable but troubling literary-critical impasse whereby black girls are contained within the first-person narrations of white protagonists" (45). Munafo disagrees with Monteith's assessment. See 54, 59.

10. Makowsky says about this passage that "Ellen is expressing contradictory desires: to return to the womb's safety where she was fed and to take over the

life-sustaining role of the mother's heart-beat and nourishing bloodstream" (104).

11. Munafo interprets the dress scene this way: "On the verge of disillusionment, Ellen both appeals to a higher power and registers its absence; she believes in the cosmic glue that supposedly brings families together while, at the same time, she knows that no such 'natural' bonds exist in her family" (46).

12. See Makowsky 103.

13. See Watts 230.

Chapter Seven

1. Several critics have noticed Ansa's connection to the tradition of African American women's fiction. In *Inventing Southern Fiction*, Michael C. Kreyling says that African American women writers "have unearthed the buried languages of African American folk traditions and community" (109). See also Cherry 2.

2. Although it is part of a proud literary tradition, *Baby of the Family* has not been without controversy, in particular from black writers who find its emphasis on material success and self examination troubling. Thulani Davis, in her essay "Don't Worry, Be Buppie: Black Novelists Head for the Mainstream," says that writers like Ansa and Terry McMillan (*Waiting to Exhale, How Stella Got Her Groove Back*) focus on "the lonely, self-involved journey of the middle-class African American who has access to some little piece of the Dream and is as deeply ensconced in American mass culture as in our boisterous yet closely held black world" (26). Calling their work "[m]ore Bup Art than Black Art," Davis says writers like Ansa have more in common with mainstream white writers, who concentrate on the ordinary person, than they do with the heroic, international, and political work of writers like Toni Morrison. These harsh — and perhaps unfair — criticisms have stunned Ansa. Possibly in response to attacks like this one, Ansa has in recent years insisted on the international nature of her work (Campbell-Spears 1).

3. Speaking about the significance of Lena's caul in an interview accompanying her novel *The Hand I Fan With*, Ansa says she thinks that "all of our citizens, but particularly black folks, have to claim what's ours. We've got to acknowledge who we are as a people, what and where we came from, what we believe in, what got us to where we are today. We've got to stop jettisoning things that are important. ... And to just throw these things over our shoulders, to discard them like so much trash, as Lena's mother did with her child's caul, is suicidal" (472). It becomes Lena's special challenge in the novel to claim what is hers, to extricate herself from her mother's "suicidal" gesture of discarding her caul and its powers and history.

4. Not surprisingly, Lena, who reappears in Ansa's 1996 novel *The Hand I Fan With*, takes over running The Place after her parents' death, and in that novel assumes emotional and financial responsibility for half of Mulberry. Lena says in *Baby* that she will "always wear high-heeled mules and good-looking dresses like her mother did and not worry one bit about the smell of cigarette smoke and grease from the grill," and *The Hand I Fan With* finds her at 45 doing those very things (121).

5. As Nagueylati Warren puts it, Ansa "oppose[s] the prevailing images of motherhood, choosing instead to depict resistant mothers in [her] fiction" (182). Ansa, she says, "employs irony, satire, and paradox to unravel the stereotyped notions of motherhood," especially in her second Mulberry novel *Ugly Ways*, where the difficult mother Mudear Lovejoy is reviled and finally understood by her three daughters (193). In *Baby of the Family*, Nellie McPherson is just the first of Ansa's problematic mother figures.

6. Clearly the role of mothers, both biological and surrogate, in girls' psychological development continues to interest Ansa. She told interviewer Sharon Smith Henderson in 1999 that she is at work on

a new novel called *You Know Better* (published in 2002) that features a nineteen-year-old main character from Mulberry who has "no sense of herself" (67). All LaShandra Pine wants to do is get to Atlanta and be in a music video. Ansa says that the story is a "cautionary tale" for women — with and without children — who have "passed on nothing" to the girls who have come after them, who have "sat back and let it happen." She sees it as her duty "to rescue the LaShandras and all the rest of our children" (68). LaShandra is a contemporary Lena, one who has no sense of family or self respect, who literally and symbolically has left Mulberry; she could in fact be Lena's daughter.

Chapter Eight

1. Leigh Gilmore blurs the line between fictionalized works based on life stories, such as Allison's *Bastard Out of Carolina*, and explicitly autobiographical works like *Ecology*. For a detailed discussion of this issue see Gilmore 45–69.

2. Reviewers have complained about the abrupt introduction of religion into the narrative. "We are a hundred pages into the book before learning that Ray was raised with a Christianity so austere that she wasn't allowed to don pants, cut her hair, watch TV, swim, play sports, date — even wear sandals," says the critic from the *New York Times* (Horwitz 3). Another reviewer says that the knowledge of her family's fundamentalism "jars our perspective because nothing prior to this mention has indicated such a belief" (Paulson 179). This reaction may stem from their ignorance of Southern culture, rendering them unable to recognize the clues, given both in the photographs and throughout the narrative, to Ray's fundamentalist background. For example, the fact that the girls are wearing dresses as they play with go carts in a photograph inside the front cover would be a clear signal to anyone familiar with fundamentalist practice that these girls belong to one of the several Old Testament-adhering Protestant sects in the South.

3. Shirley Neuman has written extensively about the representation of the mother's body in daughter's autobiography. See especially 56–75. For other discussions of the relationships between mothers and daughters in female autobiography see Benstock 12, Malin 1, and MacKethan 63.

Chapter Nine

1. According to Barbara Bennett, the critic who has written most extensively about McCorkle, McCorkle's works are concerned with the same conflicts dealt with by her Southern female precursors Harper Lee, Carson McCullers, Eudora Welty, Flannery O'Connor, and Katherine Anne Porter: "independence versus dependence, femininity versus strength, the nurturing of others in direct conflict with preservation of self, purity and virginity in opposition to sexual freedom and expression" (*Understanding* 9). Nevertheless, "her history is often private rather than a history shared by a collective Southern consciousness"(9). For further discussion of the ways in which contemporary Southern writers like McCorkle rewrite Southern traditions of family and home, see Joan Schultz 83.

2. The first-person reflective narrative style, which is employed in both *The Cheer Leader* and *Ferris Beach* is similar to the one used by Harper Lee in *To Kill a Mockingbird*, but McCorkle adds her own variations. Jo, for example, shifts from first to third person when she moves from a relatively integrated personality to a more dissociated one, and Kate's tone is decidedly less nostalgic than Scout's. While the first-person voice does create a sense of intimacy and link the characters to their (in these cases Southern) environments, McCorkle seems, through her use of perspective shifts and ironic tone, to insist on a certain degree of distance.

3. For further discussion of Jo's rebel-

lion against the old code of behavior and morality, see Pierce 22.

4. McCorkle has told interviewers that she wrote *The Cheer Leader* in part to dismantle stereotypes about cheerleaders (McCord 107).

5. For a slightly less optimistic view of the ending see Walker 92–93.

Chapter Ten

1. For further discussion of circularity and the relationship of the island to the self in the novel, see Smedman and Goforth.

2. The debate about Paterson's conventionality has been quite heated. June Agee and James MacGavran are critical of what they see as her capitulation to traditional gender stereotypes, while Roberta Trites sees Paterson deconstructing society's confusion about gender. Paterson has reacted strongly against MacGavran and others, saying that she respects women who choose more traditional roles. For a discussion of the ways in which Paterson is replicating actual historical conditions for women in *Jacob*, see Hubler 88–89.

3. See Mills 236 for an analysis of foster children in young adult literature.

4. For a detailed description of the use of unreliable narration in *Jacob Have I Loved*, see Nikolajeva.

5. Chaston discusses the ways in which Sara Louise's reading affects her Romantic view of the world (100–103).

6. See Schmidt 72 for the importance of home for Paterson's characters.

7. Bosmajian and Hubler discuss the sexual dimension of racism in Taylor.

8. For a discussion of the ways in which identity formation is affected by family dynamics in ethnic families, see Khorana 54–56.

9. For more on the ways in which Cassie overcomes the various attempts to silence her, see Trites 49–51.

10. See Bosmajian for the symbolic differences between novels in the series.

11. Bosmajian discusses the equivocal role Bradley plays in the novel (143, 153–54).

12. Bosmajian has an interesting reading of Cassie's response to the assault (157).

13. Karen Smith describes this balancing well (273).

14. For an elaboration of the ways in which Voigt manipulates traditional conventions surrounding the family, see Clark 198–200.

15. For a fascinating article on the ways in which *Homecoming* rewrites the traditional orphan story, See Clark. James Henke and Gloria Jamison discuss the ways in Voigt uses Greek myths in order to transform a realistic (and rather grim) narrative into something more profound. For another discussion of Voigt's use of myth, see Jamison and Wolf.

Bibliography

Agee, June M. "Mothers and Daughters: Gender-Role Socialization in Two New-bery Award Books." *Children's Literature in Education* 24 (1993): 165–83.

Allison, Dorothy. *Bastard Out of Carolina*. New York: Dutton, 1992.

_____. *Skin: Talking About Sex, Class & Literature*. Ithaca, NY: Firebrand, 1994.

_____. *Two or Three Things I Know for Sure*. New York: Plume, 1996.

Ansa, Tina McElroy. *Baby of the Family*. New York: Harcourt, 1989.

_____. *The Hand I Fan With*. New York: Random House, 1996.

_____. "An Interview with Tina McElroy Ansa." *The Hand I Fan With*. Paperback reprint edition. New York: Anchor, 1998: 469–75.

_____. "Sea Island Daughter." *Essence* 26 (1995): 49.

_____. *Ugly Ways*. New York: Harcourt, 1993.

_____. *You Know Better*. New York: Morrow, 2002.

Applebee, Arthur N. *Literature in the Secondary School Classroom: Studies of Curriculum and Instruction in the United States*. Urbana: NCTE, 1993.

Arnold, Edwin T. "An Interview with Lee Smith." In Tate 2001 (q.v.), Tate 1–18.

Baker, Moira P. "'The Politics of They': Dorothy Allison's *Bastard Out of Carolina* as Critique of Class, Gender, and Sexual Ideologies." In Folks and Folks (q.v.), 117–41.

Barnes, Linda Adams. "Telling Yourself into Existence: The Fiction of Kaye Gibbons." *Tennessee Philological Bulletin* 30 (1993): 28–35.

Baym, Nina. "The Madwoman and Her Languages: Why I Don't Do Feminist Theory." *Tulsa Studies in Women's Literature* 3 (1984): 45–59.

Bell, Pearl K. "Southern Discomfort." *New Republic* 19 (1988): 38–41.

Benfer, Amy. "Lost Boys." *Salon*, 5 Feb. 2002. <http://www.salon.com>.

Bennett, Barbara. *Comic Visions, Female Voices: Contemporary Women Novelists and Southern Humor*. Baton Rouge: Louisiana State University Press, 1998.

_____. "Making Peace with the (M)other." In Folks and Folks (q.v.), 186–200.

_____. "'Reality Burst Forth': Truth, Lies, and Secrets in the Novels of Jill McCorkle." *Southern Quarterly* 36 (1997): 107–122.

_____. *Understanding Jill McCorkle*. Columbia: University of South Carolina Press, 2000.

Bennett, Tanya Long. "The Protean Ivy in Lee Smith's *Fair and Tender Ladies*." *Southern Literary Journal* 30 (1998): 76–95. *Literature Online*. Georgia Southern University Library, 12 Dec. 2003. <http://lionreference.chadyck.com/>.

Benstock, Shari. "The Female Self Engendered: Autobiographical Writing and Theories of Selfhood." In Brownley and Kimmich (q.v.), 3–13.

Betts, Doris. "Introduction." In Inge (q.v.), 1–8.

_____. "Tyler's Marriage of Opposites." *The Fiction of Anne Tyler*. Ed. C. Ralph Stephens. Jackson: University Press of Mississippi, 1990. 1–15.

Blais, Ellen A. "Gender Issues in Bobbie Ann Mason's *In Country*." *South Atlantic Review* 56 (1991): 107–18.

Bloom, Lynn Z. "Jill McCorkle." *Contemporary Fiction Writers of the South*. Ed. Joseph M. Flora and Robert Bain. Westport, CT: Greenwood, 1993. 295–302.

Bosmajian, Hamid. "Mildred Taylor's Story of Cassie Logan: A Search for Law and Justice in a Racist Society." *Children's Literature* 24 (1996): 141–60.

Bourne, Daniel. "*Artful Dodge* Interviews: Lee Smith." In Tate 2001 (q.v.), 40–56.

Brinkmeyer, Robert H., Jr. "Finding One's History: Bobbie Ann Mason and Contemporary Southern Literature." *Southern Literary Journal* 19 (1987): 22–33.

Brooks, Peter. *Reading for the Plot: Design and Intention in Narrative*. Cambridge, MA: Harvard University Press, 1984.

Brown, Joanne, and Nancy St. Clair. *Declarations of Independence: Empowered Girls in Young Adult Literature, 1990–2001*. Lanham, MD: Scarecrow, 2002.

Brownley, Martine, and Allison Kimmich, eds. *Women and Autobiography*. Wilmington: Scholarly Resources, 1999.

Brownstein, Rachel M. *Becoming a Heroine: Reading about Women in Novels*. New York: Viking, 1982.

Brumberg, Joan Jacobs. *The Body Project*. New York: Random House, 1997.

Buchanan, Harriette, C. "Lee Smith: The Storyteller's Voice." In Inge (q.v.), 324–345.

Burns, Ann, and Thompson, Bibi. "First Novelists: 90 New Novels for Fall and Winter." *Library Journal* 14 (1989): 52–58.

Butler, Judith. *Gender Trouble: Feminism and the Subversion of Identity*. New York: Routledge, 1990.

Byrd-Cook, Linda J. "Reconciliation with the Great Mother Goddess in Lee Smith's *Saving Grace*." *Southern Quarterly* 40 (2002): 97–112.

_____. "Toward Healing the Split: Lee Smith's *Fancy Strut* and *Black Mountain Breakdown*." In Folks and Folks (q.v.), 201–219.

Campbell-Spears, Tiffany. "Interview with Tina McElroy Ansa," 2 July, 2001. <htttp://www.geocities.com/~cullars/jan-mar01/ansa.htm>.

Carroll, Rebecca. "Tina McElroy Ansa." *I Know What the Red Clay Looks Like: The Voice and Vision of Black Women Writers*. New York: Carol Southern Books, 1994. 18–33.

Carroll, Virginia Schaefer. "Re-Reading the Romance of *Seventeenth Summer*." *Children's Literature Association Quarterly* 21 (1996): 12–19.

Chappell, Fred. "Good Girls Can Turn Out Well." Rev. of *Rich in Love*, by Josephine Humphreys. *New York Times Book Review*, 13 Sept. 1987: 9.

Chaston, Joel D. "Pine Groves and Pumpkin Patches: Katherine Paterson's 'Secret Gardens.'" In Smedman and Chaston (q.v.), 63–86.

Cherry, Joyce. "Tina McElroy Ansa." *Contemporary African American Novelists: A Bio-Bibliographical Critical Sourcebook.* Ed. Emmanuel S. Nelson. Westport, CT: Greenwood, 1999. 1–5.

Chodorow, Nancy. *The Reproduction of Mothering: Psychoanalysis and the Sociology of Gender.* Berkeley: University of California Press, 1978.

Christopher, Renny. "Working-Class Literature's Challenge to the Canon." *The Canon in the Classroom: The Pedagogical Implications of Canon Revision in American Literature.* Ed. John Alberti. New York: Garland, 1995. 45–55.

Clark, Beverly Lyon, and Melvin J. Friedman, eds. *Critical Essays on Carson McCullers.* New York: G. K. Hall, 1996.

Clark, Dorothy G. "Edging Toward Bethlehem: Rewriting the Myth of Childhood in Voigt's *Homecoming.*" *Children's Literature Association Quarterly* 25 (2001): 191–202.

Conarroe, Joel. "Winning Her Father's War." Rev. of *In Country. New York Times Book Review,* 15 Sept. 1985: 7.

Costello, Brannon. "Swimming Free of the Matriarchy: Sexual Baptism and the Feminine Individuality in Eudora Welty's *The Golden Apples.*" *Southern Literary Journal* 22 (2000): 82–93.

Crowe, Chris. *Presenting Mildred D. Taylor.* New York: Twayne, 1999.

Curry, Renee R. "'I Ain't No FRIGGIN' LITTLE WIMP': The Girl 'I' Narrator in Contemporary Fiction." *The Girl: Constructions of the Girl in Contemporary Fiction by Women.* Ed. Ruth O. Saxton. New York: St. Martin's, 1998. 95–105.

Cvetkovich, Ann. "Sexual Trauma/Queer Memory: Incest, Lesbianism, and Therapeutic Culture." *GLQ* 2 (1995): 351–77.

Davis, Jingle. "A Longleaf Salvation: South Georgia Writer Chronicles a Life and Landscape in *Ecology of a Cracker Childhood.*" *Atlanta Journal & Constitution,* 19 Dec. 1999: M1+.

Davis, Thulani. "Don't Worry, Be Buppie: Black Novelists Head for the Mainstream." *Village Voice Literary Supplement* 85 (May 1990): 26–29.

DeMarr, Mary Jean, and Jane S. Bakerman. *The Adolescent in the American Novel Since 1960.* New York: Ungar, 1984.

Donlon, Jocelyn Hazelwood. "'Born on the Wrong Side of the Porch': Violating Traditions in *Bastard Out of Carolina.*" *Southern Folklore* 55 (1998): 133–44.

DuPlessis, Rachel Blau. *Writing Beyond the Ending: Narrative Strategies of Twentieth-Century Women Writers.* Bloomington: Indiana University Press, 1985.

Durham, Sandra Bonilla. "Women and War: Bobbie Ann Mason's *In Country.*" *Southern Literary Journal* 22 (1990): 45–52.

Dwyer, June. "New Roles, New History and New Patriotism: Bobbie Ann Mason's *In Country.*" *Modern Language Studies* 22 (1992): 72–78.

Eakin, Paul John. *How Our Lives Become Stories: Making Selves.* Ithaca: Cornell University Press, 1999.

Eckard, Paula Gallant. "The Prismatic Past in *Oral History* and *Mama Day.*" *MELUS* 20 (3) (1995): 121–135. *Literature Online.* Georgia Southern University Library, 3 Nov. 2003. <http://lionreference.chadwyck.com>

[Review of] *Ecology of a Cracker Childhood. Publishers Weekly,* 18 Oct. 1999: 63–64.

Elmore, Jenifer B. "Jill McCorkle." *The History of Southern Women's Literature.* Ed.

Carolyn Perry and Mary Louise Weaks. Baton Rouge: Louisiana State University Press, 2002. 599–603.

Erkkila, Betsy. *The Wicked Sisters: Women Poets, Literary History and Discord.* Oxford: Oxford University Press, 1992.

Evans, Elizabeth. *Anne Tyler.* New York: Twayne, 1993.

Evoy, Karen. *"Marilee:* 'A Permanent Landscape of the Heart.'" *Mississippi Quarterly* 36 (1983): 569–78.

Fine, Laura. "Gender Conflicts and the 'Dark Projections' in Coming of Age White Female Southern Novels." *Southern Quarterly* 36 (1998): 121–29.

Fine, Michelle, and Pat Macpherson. "Over Dinner: Feminism and Adolescent Female Bodies." *Disruptive Voices: The Possibilities of Feminist Research.* Ed. Michelle Fine. Ann Arbor: University of Michigan Press, 1992: 175–203.

Flax, Jane. "The Family in Contemporary Feminist Thought: A Critical Review." *The Family in Political Thought.* Ed. Jean Bethke Elshtain. Amherst: University of Massachusetts Press, 1982. 223–53.

Folks, Jeffrey J., and Nancy Summer Folks, eds. *The World Is Our Home: Society and Culture in Contemporary Southern Writing.* Lexington: University Press of Kentucky, 2000.

Frye, Joanne S. *Living Stories, Telling Lives: Women and the Novel in Contemporary Experience.* Ann Arbor: University of Michigan Press, 1986.

Fuss, Diana. *Essentially Speaking.* New York: Routledge, 1989.

Gallop, Jane. *The Daughter's Seduction: Feminism and Psychoanalysis.* Ithaca: Cornell University Press, 1982.

_____. *Thinking Through the Body.* New York: Columbia, 1988.

_____. "Reading the Mother Tongue: Psychoanalytic Feminist Criticism." *Critical Inquiry* 13 (Winter 1987): 314–29.

Garbarino, James. *Lost Boys: Why Our Sons Turn Violent and How We Can Save Them.* New York: Free Press, 1999.

Gibbons, Kaye. *Ellen Foster.* Chapel Hill, NC: Algonquin, 1987.

_____. "My Mother, Literature, and Life Split Neatly into Two Halves." *The Writer on Her Work.* Vol. II. Ed. Janet Sternburg. New York: Norton, 1991. 52–60.

Gibson, Mary Ellis. "Family as Fate: The Novels of Anne Tyler." *Critical Essays on Anne Tyler.* Ed. Alice Hall Petry. New York: G.K. Hall, 1992. 165–74.

Gilchrist, Ellen, Josephine Humphreys, Gloria Naylor, and Louise Shiver. "Do You Think of Yourself as a Woman Writer?" Panel Discussion. Ed. Willard Pate. *Furman Studies* 34 (1988): 2–13.

Gilligan, Carol. *In a Different Voice: Psychological Theory and Women's Development.* Cambridge, MA: Harvard University Press, 1982.

_____. "Joining the Resistance: Psychology, Politics, Girls and Women." *Michigan Quarterly Review* 29 (1990): 501–36.

Gilmore, Leigh. *The Limits of Autobiography: Trauma and Testimony.* Ithaca: Cornell University Press, 2001.

Glasgow, Ellen. *Barren Ground.* Garden City, NY: Doubleday, Doran, 1933.

_____. *The Sheltered Life.* Garden City, NY: Doubleday, Doran, 1932.

Godine, Amy. Rev. of *Ecology of a Cracker Childhood. Orion* 18 (1999): 74–75.

Gofoth, Caroline R. "The Role of the Island in *Jacob Have I Loved.*" *Children's Literature Association Quarterly* 9 (1984–85): 176–78.

Greenway, Betty. "'Every Mother's Dream': Cynthia Voigt's Orphans." In Iskander (q.v.), 127–131.

Grosskurth, Phyllis. "The New Psychology of Women." *New York Review of Books*, 24 Oct. 1991: 25–32.

Grover, Jan Z. "Real Places." Rev. of *Ecology of a Cracker Childhood*. *Women's Review of Books* 17 (2000): 9–10.

Gullette, Margaret Morganroth. "Anne Tyler: The Tears (and Joys) Are in the Things." Reprinted in *The Fiction of Anne Tyler*. Ed. C. Ralph Stephens. Jackson: University Press of Mississippi, 1990. 97–109.

Gurian, Michael. *The Wonder of Boys*. Los Angeles: J.P. Tarcher, 1997.

Gwin, Minrose. "Nonfelicitous Space and Survivor Discourse: Reading the Incest Story in Southern Women's Fiction." *Haunted Bodies: Gender and Southern Texts*. Ed. Anne Goodwyn Jones and Susan V. Donaldson. Charlottesville: University of Virginia Press, 1997. 416–40.

Hall, Joan Wylie. "Arriving Where She Started: Redemption at Scrabble Creek in Lee Smith's *Saving Grace*." *Pembroke Magazine* 34 (2002): 91–99.

Hankins, Leslie Kathleen. "Alas, Alack! Or a Lass, a Lack? Quarrels of Gender and Genre in the Revisionist Kunstlerroman: Eudora Welty's *The Golden Apples*." *Mississippi Quarterly* 44 (1991): 391–409.

Harper, Mary Turner. "Merger and Metamorphosis in the Fiction of Mildred D. Taylor." *Children's Literature Association Quarterly* 13 (1988): 75–80.

Harrison, Suzan. "'The Other Way to Live': Gender and Selfhood in *Delta Wedding* and *The Golden Apples*." *Mississippi Quarterly* 44 (1991): 49–67.

Hart, Lynda. *Between the Body and the Flesh: Performing Sadomasochism*. New York: Columbia University Press, 1998.

Havens, Lila. "Residents and Transients: An Interview with Bobbie Ann Mason." *Crazy Horse* 29 (1985): 87–104.

Heilbrun, Carolyn. *Writing a Woman's Life*. New York: Norton, 1988.

Henderson, Sharon Smith. "An Interview with Tina McElroy Ansa." *Kalliope* 21 (1999): 61–68.

Henke, James T. "Dicey, Odysseus, and Hansel and Gretel: The Lost Children in Voigt's *Homecoming*." *Children's Literature in Education* 16 (1985): 45–52.

Henley, Ann. "Space for Yourself: Nadine Gordimer's *A Sport of Nature* and Josephine Humphreys' *Rich in Love*." *Frontiers* 13 (1992): 81–89.

Henning, Barbara. "Minimalism and the American Dream: 'Shilo' by Bobbie Ann Mason and 'Preservation' by Raymond Carver." *Modern Fiction Studies* 35 (1989): 689–98.

Herion-Sarafidis, Elisabeth. "Interview with Lee Smith." Tate. 92–103.

Hill, Dorothy Combs. "An Interview with Bobbie Ann Mason." *Southern Quarterly* 31 (1992): 85–118.

_____. "An Interview with Lee Smith." In Tate 2001 (q.v.), 19–28.

_____. *Lee Smith*. New York: Twayne, 1992.

Hirsch, Marianne. *The Mother/Daughter Plot*. Bloomington: Indiana University Press, 1989.

Homans, Margaret. *Bearing the Word: Language and Female Experience in 19th-Century Women's Writing*. Chicago: University of Chicago Press, 1986.

Horvitz, Deborah. "'Sadism Demands a Story'": Oedipus, Feminism, and Sexuality in Gayl Jones's *Corregidora* and Dorothy Allison's *Bastard Out of Carolina.*" *Contemporary Literature* 39 (1998): 238–61.

Horwitz, Tony. "In Praise of the Blue-Tailed Mole Skink." Rev. of *Ecology of a Cracker Childhood. New York Times*, 9 Jan. 2000. *Proquest*, 21 Sept. 2001. <http://proquest.umi.com/pqdweb?RQT=306&TS=1013112229>.

"How Schools Shortchange Girls: Executive Summary." The American Association of University Women Education Foundation. 1992: 1–8.

Hubler, Angela E. "Beyond the Image: Adolescent Girls, Reading, and Social Reality." *NWSA Journal* 12 (2002): 84–99.

_____. "Can Anne Shirley Help 'Revive Ophelia'"? *Delinquents and Debutantes: Twentieth-Century American Girls' Cultures.* Ed. Sherrie A. Innes. New York: New York University Press, 1998. 266–284.

Humphreys, Josephine. "My Real Invisible Self." *A World Unsuspected: Portraits of Southern Childhood.* Ed. Alex Harris. Chapel Hill: University of North Carolina Press, 1987. 1–13.

_____. *Rich in Love.* New York: Viking, 1987.

Hunter, Dianne. "Hysteria, Psychoanalysis, and Feminism: The Case of Anna O." *The (M)other Tongue: Essays in Feminist Psychoanalytic Interpretation.* Eds. Shirley Nelson Garner, Claire Kahane, and Madelon Sprengnether. Ithaca: Cornell University Press, 1985. 89–115.

Inge, Tonette Bond, ed. *Southern Women Writers: The New Generation.* Tuscaloosa: University of Alabama Press, 1990.

Irving, Katrina. "'Writing It Down So That It Would Be Real': Narrative Strategies in Dorothy Allison's *Bastard Out of Carolina.*" *College Literature* 25 (1998): 94–107. *Proquest*, 1 Oct. 1999. <http://proquest.umi.com/pqdweb?RQT=306&TS=1013111 424>.

Iskander, Sylvia P., ed. *The Image of the Child: Proceedings of the 1991 International Conference of the Children's Literature Association.* Battle Creek, MI. The Children's Literature Association, 1991.

Jackson, Shelley M. "Josephine Humphreys and the Politics of Postmodern Desire." *Mississippi Quarterly* 47 (1994): 275–85.

Jacobs, Janet Liebmann. "Victimized Daughters: Sexual Violence and the Empathic Female Self." *Signs* 19 (1993): 126–41.

Jameson, Gloria. "The Triumph of the Spirit in Cynthia Voigt's 'Homecoming,' 'Dicey's Song,' and 'A Solitary Blue.'" *Triumphs of the Spirit in Children's Literature.* Ed. Francelia Butler and Richard Rotert. Hamden, CT: Library Professional Publication, 1986. 3–14.

Jardine, Alice. *Gynesis: Configurations of Woman and Modernity.* Ithaca: Cornell University Press, 1985.

Johnson, Claudia Durst. *"To Kill a Mockingbird": Threatening Boundaries.* New York: Twayne, 1994.

Johnson, Diane. "Southern Comfort." *New York Review of Books*, 7 Nov. 1985: 15–17.

Jones, Anne Goodwyn. "The World of Lee Smith." *Southern Quarterly* 22 (1983): 115–39.

Kalb, John D. "The Second 'Rape' of Crystal Spangler." *Southern Literary Journal* 21 (1) (1988): 23–30.

Kanoza, Theresa. "Mentors and Maternal Role Models: The Healthy Mean Between

Extremes in Anne Tyler's Fiction." *The Fiction of Anne Tyler.* Ed. C. Ralph Stephens. Jackson: University Press of Mississippi, 1990. 28–39.

Kearns, Katherine. "From Shadow to Substance: The Empowerment of the Artist Figure in Lee Smith's Fiction." *Writing the Woman Artist: Essays in Poetics, Politics, and Portraiture.* Ed. Suzanne W. Jones. Philadelphia: University of Pennsylvania Press, 1991. 175–95.

Kennan, Randall. "Sorrow's Child." Rev. of *Bastard out of Carolina. Nation* 255 (1992): 815–16. *Proquest,* 1 Oct. 1999. <http://proquest.umi.com/pqdweb?RQT= 306&TS=1013111424>.

Khorana, Meena. "The Ethnic Family and Identity Formation in Adolescents." *The Child and the Family.* Ed. Susan R. Gannon and Ruth Anne Thompson. New York: Pace, 1988: 52–58.

Kindlon, Daniel J., and Michael Thompson. *Raising Cain: Protecting the Emotional Life of Boys.* New York: Ballantine, 1999.

Kinney, Katherine. "'Humping the Boonies': Sex, Combat, and the Female in Bobbie Ann Mason's *In Country.*" *Fourteen Landing Zones: Approaches to Vietnam War Literature.* Ed. Phillip K. Jason. Iowa City: University of Iowa Press, 1991. 38–48.

Kleinfeld, Judith. "Why Smart People Believe that Schools Shortchange Girls: What You See When You Live in a Tail." *Gender Issues* 16 (1998): 47–63. *Proquest,* 2 Feb. 2002. <http://proquest.umi.com/pqdweb?RQT=306&TS=101311179>.

Krasteva, Yonka. "The South and the West in Bobbie Ann Mason's *In Country.*" *Southern Literary Journal* 26 (1994): 77–90.

Kristeva, Julia. "Women's Time." *The Kristeva Reader.* Ed. Toril Moi. New York: Columbia University Press, 1986. 187–213.

Kreyling, Michael C. *Inventing Southern Fiction.* Jackson: University Press of Mississippi, 1998.

Lanier, Parks, Jr. "Psychic Space in Lee Smith's *Black Mountain Breakdown.*" *The Poetics of Appalachian Space.* Ed. Parks Lanier, Jr. Knoxville: University of Tennessee Press, 1991. 58–66.

Lee, Harper. *To Kill a Mockingbird.* New York: Warner, 1960.

L'Engle, Madeleine. "Do I Dare Disturb the Universe?" *Innocence and Experience: Essays and Conversations on Children's Literature.* Ed. Barbara Harrison and Gregory Maguire. New York: Lothrop, Lee & Shepard, 1987. 215–223.

Lesser, Ellen. "Voices with Stories to Tell: A Conversation with Jill McCorkle." *Southern Review* 26 (1990): 53–64.

Loewinsohn, Ron. "The World Across the Street." Rev. of *Ferris Beach. New York Times Book Review,* 7 Oct. 1990: 10.

Loewenstein, Claudia. "Unshackling the Patriarchy: An Interview with Lee Smith." *Southwest Review* 78 (1993): 486–505. *Academic Search Premier.* EBSCO Georgia Southern University Library, 29 Oct. 2003. <http://www.epnet.com/>.

Lyons, Bonnie, and Bill Oliver. "An Interview with Bobbie Ann Mason." *Contemporary Literature* 32 (1991): 448–70.

MacCann, Donnarae. "The Family Chronicles of Mildred D. Taylor and Mary E. Mebane." *Journal of African Children's and Youth Literature* 3 (1991): 93–104.

MacKethan, Lucinda H. "Artists and Beauticians: Balance in Lee Smith's Fiction." *Southern Literary Journal* 15 (1982): 3–14.

_____. *Daughters of Time: Creating Woman's Voice in Southern Story*. Athens: University of Georgia Press, 1990.

MacLeod, Anne Scott. *American Childhood: Essays on Children's Literature of the Nineteenth and Twentieth Centuries*. Athens: University of Georgia Press, 1994.

Magee, Rosemary M. "Continuity and Separation: An Interview with Josephine Humphreys." *Southern Review* 27 (Fall 1991): 792–802.

Makowsky, Veronica. "'The Only Hard Part Was the Food': Recipes for Self-Nurture in Kaye Gibbons's Novels." *Southern Quarterly* 30 (1992): 103–12.

Malin, Jo. *The Voice of the Mother: Embedded Maternal Narratives in Twentieth-Century Women's Autobiographies*. Carbondale: Southern Illinois University Press, 2000.

Malone, Michael. "Rich in Words." Rev. of *Rich in Love* by Josephine Humphreys. *Nation* 10 Oct. 1987: 388–89.

Mason, Bobbie Ann. "Big Dreams for *Little Women*." *Salon*, 5 April 1999. <http://www.salonmagazine.com>.

_____. *The Girl Sleuth: A Feminist Guide*. Old Westbury: The Feminist Press, 1975.

_____. *In Country*. New York: Harper, 1985.

_____. *Midnight Magic: Selected Stories of Bobbie Ann Mason*. New York: Ecco Press, 1998.

Mason, Mary G. "The Other Voice: Autobiographies of Women Writers." In Olney 1980 (q.v.), 207–35.

McCord, Charlene R. "'I Still See with a Southern Eye.' An Interview with Jill McCorkle." *Southern Quarterly* 36 (1998):103–12.

_____. "Interview with Lee Smith." In Tate 2001 (q.v.), 153–77.

McCorkle, Jill. *The Cheer Leader*. Chapel Hill, NC: Algonquin, 1984.

_____. *Ferris Beach*. Chapel Hill, NC: Algonquin, 1990.

McCullers, Carson. *The Heart is a Lonely Hunter*. Cambridge: Riverside, 1940.

_____. *The Member of the Wedding*. Boston: Houghton Mifflin, 1946.

McDonald, Kathleen. "Talking Trash, Talking Back: Resistance to Stereotypes in Dorothy Allison's *Bastard out of Carolina*." *Women's Studies Quarterly* 2 (1998): 15–25.

McGavran, James Holt. "Bathrobes and Bibles, Waves and Words in Katherine Paterson's *Jacob Have I Loved*." In Smedman and Chaston (q.v.), 123–135.

Megan, Carolyn. "Moving Toward Truth." Interview with Dorothy Allison. *Kenyon Review* 16 (1994): 71–83.

Millichap, Joseph. "Josephine Humphreys." *Contemporary Fiction Writers of the South: A Bio-Bibliographical Sourcebook*. Ed. Joseph M. Flora and Robert Bain. Westport, CT: Greenwood, 1993: 244–54.

Mills, Claudia. "Children in Search of a Family: Orphan Novels Through the Century." *Children's Literature in Education* 18 (1987): 227–39.

Moi, Toril. *Sexual/Textual Politics: Feminist Literary Theory*. London: Meuthen, 1985.

Molarsky, Mona. "Back in the World." Rev. of *In Country* by Bobbie Ann Mason. *Nation* 18 January 1986: 57–58.

Monteith, Sharon. "Between Girls: Kaye Gibbons' *Ellen Foster* and Friendship as a Monologic Formulation." *Journal of American Studies* 33 (1999): 45–64.

Munafo, Giavanna. "'Colored Biscuits': Reconstructing Whiteness and the Boundaries of 'Home' in Kaye Gibbons's *Ellen Foster.*" *Women, America, and Movement.* Ed. Susan L. Roberson. Columbia: University of Missouri Press, 1998: 38–61.

Myers, Thomas. "Dispatches from Ghost Country: The Vietnam Veteran in Recent American Fiction." *Genre* 21 (1988): 409–28.

Natov, Roni. "Mothers and Daughters: Jamaica Kincaid's Pre-Oedipal Narrative." *Children's Literature* 18 (1990): 1–16.

Nesanovich, Stella. "The Early Novels." *Anne Tyler as Novelist.* Ed. Dale Sawak. Iowa City: University of Iowa Press, 1994: 15–32.

Neumann, Shirley. "'Your Past ... Your Future': Autobiography and Mothers' Bodies." *Genre Trope Gender: Critical Essays by Northrop Frye, Linda Hutcheon, and Shirley Neuman.* Ottawa: Carleton University Press, 1992: 53–86.

Nikolajeva, Maria. "The Art of Self-Deceit: Narrative Strategies in Katherine Paterson's Novels." In Smedman and Chaston (q.v.), 18–40.

Olney, James, ed. *Autobiography: Essays Theoretical and Critical.* Princeton: Princeton University Press, 1980.

_____. "Autobiography and the Cultural Moment: A Thematic, Historical, and Bibliographical Introduction." In Olney 1980 (q.v.), 3–27.

_____. "Some Versions of Memory/Some Versions of Bios: The Ontology of Autobiography." In Olney 1980 (q.v.), 236–67.

Orenstein, Peggy. *SchoolGirls: Young Women, Self-Esteem, and the Confidence Gap.* New York: Doubleday, 1994.

Parrish, Nancy C. *Lee Smith, Annie Dillard, and the Hollins Group: A Genesis of Writers.* Baton Rouge: Louisiana State University Press, 1998.

_____. "Lee Smith." *The History of Southern Women's Literature.* Ed. Carolyn Perry and Mary Louise Weaks. Baton Rouge: Louisiana State University Press, 2002. 575–78.

Paterson, Katherine. *The Great Gilly Hopkins.* New York: Harper, 1978.

_____. "Heart in Hiding." *Worlds of Childhood: The Art and Craft of Writing for Children.* Ed. William Zinsser. Boston: Houghton Mifflin, 1990. 147–77.

_____. *The Invisible Child: On Reading and Writing Books for Children.* New York: Dutton, 2001.

_____. *Jacob Have I Loved.* New York: HarperCollins, 1980.

_____. *A Sense of Wonder: On Reading and Writing Books for Children.* New York: Plume, 1995.

Paul, Lissa. "Enigma Variations: What Feminist Theory Knows about Children's Literature." *Signal* 54 (1987): 186–202.

Paulson, Michael. Rev. of *Ecology of a Cracker Childhood. Georgia Review* 54 (2000): 178–79.

Pearlman, Mickey. "A Conversation with Josephine Humphreys." *South Carolina Review* 22 (Spring 1990): 121–24.

Petry, Alice Hall. *Understanding Anne Tyler.* Columbia: University of South Carolina Press, 1990.

Pierce, Todd. "Jill McCorkle: The Emergence of the New South." *Southern Studies* 5 (1994): 19–30.

Pipher, Mary. *Reviving Ophelia: Saving the Selves of Adolescent Girls.* New York: Grosset/Putnam, 1994.

Pollack, William S. *Real Boys: Rescuing Our Sons from the Myths of Boyhood.* New York: Random House, 1998.

Porter, Michael. *Kill Them Before They Grow: The Misdiagnosis of African American Boys in America's Classrooms.* Chicago: African American Images, 1998.

Powell, Dannye Romine. "Josephine Humphreys." *Parting the Curtains: Interviews with Southern Writers.* Winston-Salem, NC: Blair, 1994. 182–95.

Prajznerova, Katerina. *Cultural Intermarriage in Southern Appalachia: Cherokee Elements in Four Selected Novels by Lee Smith.* New York: Routledge, 2003.

Presley, Delma Eugene. "Carson McCullers and the South." In Clark and Friedman (q.v.), 99–110.

Price, Joanna. "Remembering Vietnam: Subjectivity and Mourning in American New Realist Writing." *Journal of American Studies* 27 (1993): 173–86.

Quiello, Rose. "Breakdowns and Breakthroughs: The Hysterical Use of Language." *Anne Tyler as Novelist.* Ed. Dale Sawak. Iowa City: University of Iowa Press, 1994. 50–64.

Raper, Julius Rowan. "*Barren Ground* and the Transition to Southern Modernism." In Scura (q.v.), 146–161.

Raver, Anne. "A Georgia Daughter's Lullaby of the Pines." *New York Times*, 27 Apr. 2000: F1.

Ravitch, Diane. "Girls are Beneficiaries of Gender Gap." Brookings Institution, 6 Feb. 2002. <http://www.brook.edu.>.

Ray, Janisse. *Ecology of a Cracker Childhood.* Minneapolis: Milkweed Editions, 1999.

Reid, Suzanne Elizabeth. *Presenting Cynthia Voigt.* New York: Twayne, 1995.

Reynolds, David. "White Trash in Your Face: The Literary Descent of Dorothy Allison." *Appalachian Journal* 20 (1993): 356–72.

Ridley, Clifford. "Anne Tyler: A Sense of Reticence Balanced by 'Oh, Well, Why Not?'" *Critical Essays on Anne Tyler.* Ed. Alice Hall Petry. New York: G.K. Hall, 1992. 24–27.

Robertson, Mary F. "Anne Tyler: Medusa Points and Contact Points." Reprinted in *Contemporary American Women Writers: Narrative Strategies.* Ed. Catherine Rainwater and William J. Scheik. Lexington: University of Kentucky Press, 1985. 119–42.

Rosowski, Susan J. "The Novel of Awakening." *The Voyage In: Fictions of Female Development.* Ed. Elizabeth Abel, Marianne Hirsch, and Elizabeth Langland. Hanover, NH: University Press of New England, 1983. 49–68.

Rothstein, Mervyn. "Homegrown Fiction." *New York Times Magazine.* 15 May 1988. 50, 98–102.

Ryan, Barbara T. "Decentered Authority in Bobbie Ann Mason's *In Country*." *Critique* 31 (1990): 199–212.

Sandell, Jillian. "Telling Stories of 'Queer White Trash': Race, Class, and Sexuality in the Work of Dorothy Allison." *White Trash: Race and Class in America.* Ed. Matt Wray and Annalee Newitz. New York: Routledge, 1997. 211–30.

Sayers, Valerie. "The Girl Who Walked with Ghosts." Review of *Baby of the Family. New York Times Book Review*, 26 Nov. 1989: 6.

Saxton, Ruth O. "Crepe Soles, Boots, and Fringed Shawls: Female Dress as Signals of Femininity." *Anne Tyler as Novelist.* Ed. Dale Sawak. Iowa City: University of Iowa Press, 1994: 65–76.

Schmidt, Gary D. *Katherine Paterson*. New York: Twayne, 1994.

Schultz, Joan. "Orphaning as Resistance." *The Female Tradition in Southern Literature: Essays on Southern Women Writers*. Ed. Carol S. Manning. Champaign: University of Illinois Press, 1993. 89–109.

Scura, Dorothy M., ed. *Ellen Glasgow: New Perspectives*. Knoxville: University of Tennessee Press, 1995.

Sexton, Anne. *Selected Poems*. Ed. Diane Wood Middlebrook and Diana Hume George. Boston: Houghton Mifflin, 1988.

Shelton, Frank. W. "The Necessary Balance: Distance and Sympathy in the Novels of Anne Tyler." *Critical Essays on Anne Tyler*. Ed. Alice Hall Petry. New York: G.K. Hall, 1992. 175–83.

Smedman, M. Sarah. "'A Good Oyster': Story and Meaning in *Jacob Have I Loved*." In Smedman and Chaston (q.v.), 9–17.

Smedman, M. Sarah, and Joel D. Chaston., eds. *Bridges for the Young: The Fiction of Katherine Paterson*. Lanham, MD: Scarecrow, 2003.

Smith, Karen Patricia. "A Chronicle of Family Honor: Balancing Rage and Triumph in the Novels of Mildred D. Taylor." *African American Voices in Young Adult Literature. Tradition, Transition, Transformation*. Ed. Karen Patricia Smith. Metuchen, NJ: Scarecrow, 1994. 247–76.

Smith, Lee. *Black Mountain Breakdown*. New York: Putnam, 1980.

_____. "Driving Miss Daisy Crazy; or, Losing the Mind of the South." *Studies in the Literary Imagination* 35 (2002): 117–126.

_____. *Fair and Tender Ladies*. New York: Putnam, 1988.

_____. *The Last Day the Dogbushes Bloomed*. Harper & Row, 1968; Reprint, Baton Rouge: Louisiana State University Press, 1994.

_____. *Oral History*. New York: Putnam, 1983.

_____. *Saving Grace*. New York: Putnam, 1995; Reprint, New York: Ballantine, 1996.

_____. *Something in the Wind*. New York: Harper & Row, 1971.

Smith, Rebecca. *Gender Dynamics in the Fiction of Lee Smith: Examining Language and Narrative Strategies*. San Francisco: International Scholars Publications, 1997.

Smith, Sidonie. "Construing Truth in Lying Mouths: Truthtelling in Women's Autobiography." In Brownley and Kimmich (q.v.), 33–52.

Smith, Virginia A. "On Regionalism, Women's Writing, and Writing as a Woman: A Conversation with Lee Smith." In Tate 2001 (q.v.), 65–77.

Sommers, Christina Hoff. *The War Against Boys*. New York: Simon & Schuster, 2000.

Spencer, Elizabeth. "A Southern Landscape." *The Stories of Elizabeth Spencer*. New York: Doubleday, 1981. 41–52.

_____. "Sharon." *The Stories of Elizabeth Spencer*. New York: Doubleday, 1981. 283–90.

_____. "Indian Summer." *The Stories of Elizabeth Spencer*. New York: Doubleday, 1981. 381–400.

Spivak, Gayatri Chakravorty. "Three Feminist Readings: McCullers, Drabble, Habermas." In Clark and Friedman (q.v.), 129–42.

Stacey, Judith. "On Resistance, Ambivalence and Feminist Theory: A Response to Carol Gilligan." *Michigan Quarterly Review* 29 (1990): 537–46.

Stein, Rachel. *Shifting the Ground: American Women Writers' Revisions of Nature, Gender, and Race*. Charlottesville: University Press of Virginia, 1997.

Steinberg, Sybil. "Rich in Love." Rev. of *Rich in Love* by Josephine Humphreys. *Publishers Weekly*, 10 July 1987: 58.

Stewart, Matthew C. "Realism, Verisimilitude, and the Depiction of Vietnam Veterans in *In Country*." *Fourteen Landing Zones: Approaches to Vietnam War Literature*. Ed. Phillip K. Jason. Iowa City: University of Iowa Press, 1991. 166–79.

Stover, Jim. "Recommended Fiction of the 1980's." Rev. of *Rich in Love* by Josephine Humphreys. *English Journal* 79 (1990): 83.

Sweeney, Susan Elizabeth. "Intimate Violence in Anne Tyler's Fiction: *The Clock Winder* and *Dinner at the Homesick Restaurant*." *Southern Literary Journal* 28 (1996):79–94.

Tarr, Anita. "To 'Endure the Loss of Paradise': Katherine Paterson's Modernist Endings for a Postmodern World." In Smedman and Chaston (q.v.), 254–567.

Tate, Linda, ed. *Conversations with Lee Smith*. Jackson: University of Mississippi Press, 2001.

_____. *A Southern Weave of Women: Fiction of the Contemporary South*. Athens: University of Georgia Press, 1994.

Taylor, Mildred D. "Newbery Award Acceptance." *The Horn Book* 53 (1977): 401–09.

_____. *The Road to Memphis*. New York: Dial, 1990; Reprint, New York: Puffin, 1992.

_____. *Roll of Thunder, Hear My Cry*. New York: Dial, 1976; Reprint, New York: Puffin, 1991.

_____. *Let the Circle Be Unbroken*. New York: Dial, 1981; Reprint, New York: Bantam, 1989.

Trites, Roberta Seelinger. "Feminist Dialogics in Katherine Paterson's Novels." In Smedman and Chaston (q.v.), 41–52.

Tyler, Anne. *A Slipping-Down Life*. New York: Knopf, 1970.

_____. *The Clock Winder*. New York: Knopf, 1972.

_____. *Dinner at the Homesick Restaurant*. New York: Knopf, 1982.

_____. "Women Writers: Equal but Separate." Rev. of *Literary Women,* by Ellen Moers. *The National Observer*, 10 Apr. 1976: 21.

Voelker, Joseph C. *Art and the Accidental in Anne Tyler*. Columbia: University of Missouri Press, 1989.

Voigt, Cynthia. *Dicey's Song*. New York: Atheneum, 1982; Reprint, New York: Ballantine, 1991.

_____. *Homecoming*. New York: Atheneum, 1980.

Wagner-Martin, Linda. "Glasgow's Time in *The Sheltered Life*." In Scura (q.v.), 196–203.

Walker, Elinor Ann. "Dizzying Possibilities, Plots, and Endings: Girlhood in Jill McCorkle's *Ferris Beach*." *The Girl: Constructions of the Girl in Contemporary Fiction by Women*. Ed. Ruth O. Saxton. New York: St. Martin's, 1998. 79–94.

_____. "Josephine Humphreys' *Rich in Love*: Redefining Southern Fiction." *Mississippi Quarterly* 47 (Spring 1994): 301–315.

Walsh, William J. "Lee Smith." In Tate 2001 (q.v.), 29–39.

Warren, Nagueylati. "Resistant Mothers in Alice Walker's *Meridian* and Tina McElroy Ansa's *Ugly Ways*." *Southern Mothers: Fact and Fictions in Southern Women's Writing*. Ed. Nagueylati Warren and Sally Wolff. Baton Rouge: Louisiana State University Press, 1999. 182–202.

Watts, Linda. "Stories Told by Their Survivors (and Other Sins of Memory): Survivor Guilt in Kaye Gibbons's *Ellen Foster*." In Folks and Folks (q.v.), 220–31.

Welty, Eudora. *The Golden Apples*. New York: Harvest, 1949.

Westling, Louise. "Tomboys and Revolting Femininity." In Clark and Friedman (q.v.), 155–65.

White, Leslie. "The Function of Popular Culture in Bobbie Ann Mason's *Shiloh and Other Stories* and *In Country*." *Southern Quarterly* 26 (1988): 69–79.

Wickenden, Dorothy. "What Lucille Knew." Rev. of *Rich in Love* by Josephine Humphreys. *New Republic* 19 Oct. 1987: 45–46.

Wilhelm, Albert E. "An Interview with Bobbie Ann Mason." *Southern Quarterly* 26 (1988): 27–38.

Winther, Marjorie. "M*A*S*H, Malls and Meaning: Popular and Corporate Culture in *In Country*." *Literature* 4 (1993): 195–201.

Wolf, Virginia. "The Linear Image: The Road and the River in the Juvenile Novel." *Proceedings of the Thirteenth Annual Conference of the Children's Literature Association*. West Lafayette, IN: Purdue, 1988. 41–47.

Wood, Ralph C. "Gumption and Grace in the Novels of Kaye Gibbons." *Christian Century* 109 (1992): 842–46. *Proquest*, 1 Oct. 1992. <http://proquest.umi.com/pqd web?RQT=306&TS=1013112229>.

Index

Adolescence: alienation from peers 75, 112; anticipation 76; anxieties 131, 137, 142; emotions 113, 129, 132; limitations 15; optimism 1, 8, 13, 34, 42, 72, 85, 129, 142, 143; secrecy 37, 75, 79–81, 122, 132, 149, 150, 162; self-consciousness 75–76; troubled girls 1, 7–10
The Adventures of Huckleberry Finn 175*n*
African American Culture 104–5, 154–64, 177*n*
Agee, June 179*n*
Allison, Dorothy 2, 4, 23, 83. 105, 116, 173*n*, 175*n*, 176*n*, 178*n*; *Bastard Out of Carolina* 4, 65, 83–97, 102, 139, 178*n*; *Skin* 83, 87; *Two or Three Things I Know for Sure* 87–88
Ansa, Tina 2, 4, 22, 103, 116, 177*n*; *Baby of the Family* 4, 103–14, 150, 160, 177*n*; *The Hand I Fan With* 110, 177*n*; *Ugly Ways* 177*n*; *You Know Better* 178*n*
Arnold, Edwin T. 23
Association of American University Women Study "How Schools Shortchange Girls" 171*n*
Autobiography 118–20, 178*n*

Baker, Moira P. 176*n*
Bakerman, Jane S. 172*n*
Baltimore, MD 3
Barnes, Linda 97–98

Baym, Nina 11; The Madwoman and her Languages" 11–12
Bell, Pearl 102
The Bell Jar 131
Benfer, Amy 171*n*
Bennett, Barbara 131, 136, 137, 173*n*, 174*n*, 175*n*, 178*n*
Benstock, Shari 178*n*
Betts, Doris 6, 20, 42, 173*n*
Bildungsroman 3, 52, 59–61, 97, 108, 130, 156, 165, 174*n*, 176*n*
Blais, Ellen 60, 174*n*, 175*n*
Bloom, Lynn 136
Bosmajian, Hamid 179*n*
Bourne, Daniel 23
Bridgeport, CN 164–66
Brinkmeyer, Robert H., Jr. 69, 174*n*
Brooks, Peter 172*n*
Brown, Joanne 15
Brownstein, Rachel M. 172*n*
Brumberg, Joan 171*n*; *The Body Project* 171*n*
Buchanan, Harriette 25, 173*n*
Butler, Judith 7, 10; *Gender Trouble* 10–11
Byrd-Cook, Linda J. 173*n*

Carolinas 4
Carroll, Virginia Schaefer 14, 104
Chappell, Fred 175*n*
Chaston, Joel 179*n*

Cherry, Joyce 104, 177*n*
Chodorow, Nancy 2, 8, 9; *The Repro-*
duction of Mothering 9
Christopher, Renny 84–85
Clark, Dorothy 169, 179*n*
Conarroe, Joel 174*n*
Cormier, Robert 145; *The Chocolate War*
145
Costello, Brannon 172*n*
Crisfield, MD 167
Crowe, Chris 155, 163
Curry, Renee 85
Cvetkovich, Ann 176*n*

Daly, Maureen 14; *The Seventeenth Sum-*
mer 14
Davis, Jingle 116
Davis, Thulani 177*n*; "Don't Worry, Be
Buppie: Black Novelists Head for the
Mainstream" 177*n*
DeMarr, Mary Jean 172*n*
Donlon, Jocelyn 176*n*
Durham, Sandra Bonilla 174*n*
Dwyer, June 174*n*

Eaken, Paul John 118–19
Edelman, Gerald M. 119
Elmore, Jenifer 130–31
Erkkila, Betsy 172*n*
Evans, Elizabeth 173*n*, 174*n*
Evoy, Karen 172*n*

Fadiman, Clifton 173*n*
Fairy tales 149–50, 163, 179*n*
Family: dysfunctional 25, 37, 53, 122;
ethnic 154–57, 179*n*; reification of
12–13, 85–86, 100, 172*n*; rewriting/
redefining 4, 14, 39, 42–43, 47, 49,
51, 53, 55–58, 68, 72, 78, 80–82, 87,
89, 91, 99, 100–4, 107, 114, 122–24,
134–37, 142, 147–48, 150, 154, 164–
65, 169, 179*n*
Fine, Michelle 172*n*
Flax, Jane 12
Fundamentalism 36–39, 124, 178*n*
Fuss, Diana 172*n*

Gallant, Paula 23
Gallop, Jane 12, 172*n*; *The Daughters*
Seduction 12; *Thinking Through the*
Body 172*n*

Garbarino, James 171*n*
Gender: as performance 7, 10–11, 15,
62–64; resisting stereotypes 24, 26,
28–29, 47, 50, 75, 82, 91, 100, 145,
158–59, 164, 173*n*, 174*n*, 178–79*n*
Georgia 103, 106, 111, 115
Gibbons, Kaye 2, 4, 83, 105, 116, 130,
172*n*, 176*n*; *Ellen Foster* 4, 83–86,
97–102, 139, 149; "My Mother, Liter-
ature and Life" 97
Gibson, Mary Ellis 173*n*
Gilchrist Ellen 6
Gilligan, Carole 2, 8, 119, 171–72*n*; *In a*
Different Voice 9
Gilmore, Leigh 118, 176*n*, 178*n*
Glasgow, Ellen 18, 172*n*; *Barren Ground*
18–20; *The Sheltered Life* 19
Godwin, Gail 6
Goforth, Caroline R. 179*n*
Grau, Shirley Ann 6
Greeno 172*n*
Grosskurth, Phyllis 171*n*
Grover, Jan Z. 117
Gulette, Margaret Morganroth 56, 173*n*,
174*n*
Gurian, Michael 171*n*
Gwin, Minrose 85–86, 91–92, 176*n*

Hall, Joan Wylie 173*n*
Hankins, Leslie Kathleen 172*n*
Harrison, Susan 172*n*
Hart, Linda 175*n*, 176*n*
Henderson, Barbara 104, 107
Henderson, Sharon Smith 177*n*
Henke, James 179*n*
Henley, Ann 175*n*
Henning, Barbara 64
Hill, Dorothy Combs 21, 35, 59, 60,
172*n*, 173*n*
Homans, Margaret 172*n*
Home 4, 8, 31, 48, 51, 55, 86, 98, 102,
106, 134, 141, 143, 146–47, 149–50, 154,
155, 158, 162–64, 166–69, 173*n*, 178*n*
Horvitz, Deborah 175*n*
Horwitz, Tony 117, 178*n*
Hubler, Angela 16, 179*n*
Humphreys, Josephine 2, 4, 22, 84, 116,
175*n*; "My Real Invisible Self" 74;
Rich in Love 4, 35, 65, 71–82, 136,
151, 174*n*, 175*n*
Hunter, Diane 172*n*

Hurston, Zora Neale 105; *Their Eyes Were Watching God* 105

Jackson, Shelley 73, 78
Jacob and Esau 152
Jacobs, Janet Liebmann 176*n*
Jamison, Gloria 179*n*
Jardine, Alice 7, 172*n*
Johnson, Claudia Durst 172*n*
Johnson, Diane 174*n*
Jones, Anne Goodwyn 26, 173*n*

Kalb, John D. 173*n*
Kanoza, Theresa 173*n*, 174*n*
Karr, Mary 6
Kearns, Katherine 173*n*
Keller, Helen 137
Kenan, Randall 96
Kentucky 3, 59, 16, 63, 156
Khorana, Meena 179*n*
Kincaid, Jamaica 172*n*; *Annie John* 172*n*
Kindlon, Daniel 171*n*
King, Martin Luther, Jr. 125–26
Kleinfeld, Judith 171*n*
Krasteva, Yonka 174*n*, 175*n*
Kreyling, Michael 173*n*, 175*n*, 177*n*; *Inventing Southern Fiction* 177*n*
Kristeva, Julia 172*n*; "Women's Time" 172*n*

Lee, Harper 18, 172*n*, 178*n*; *To Kill a Mockingbird* 19

MacGavran, James 179*n*
MacKethan, Lucinda 2, 24–25, 30, 119, 173*n*, 178*n*
Macpherson, Pat 172*n*
Makowsky, Veronica 97, 176*n*, 177*n*
Malin, Jo 119, 178*n*
Malone, Michael 175*n*
M*A*S*H 61–62, 175*n*
Mason, Bobbie Ann 3, 22, 84, 105, 116, 130, 173*n*, 174*n*, 175*n*; *The Girl Sleuth: A Feminist Guide* 174*n*; *In Country* 3–4, 35, 57–69, 99, 174*n*, 175*n*; *Midnight Magic* 57
Mason, Mary 119
McCann, Donnarae 158
McCord, Charlene R. 130, 173*n*, 179*n*
McCorkle, Jill 2, 17, 22, 129–30, 142–43, 172*n*, 178*n*; *The Cheer Leader*

5, 22, 28, 130–36, 140, 143, 169, 178*n*, 179*n*; *Ferris Beach* 5, 36, 136–143, 151, 178*n*, 179*n*
McCullers, Carson 18, 130, 172*n*, 178*n*; *The Heart Is a Lonely Hunter* 19; *The Member of the Wedding* 19
McDonald, Kathleen 85
McMillan, Terry 177*n*; *How Stella Got Her Groove Back* 177*n*; *Waiting to Exhale* 177*n*
Megan, Carolyn 87
Memphis, TN 161, 163
Milkweed Press 116
Millichap, Joseph 74
Mills, Claudia 179*n*
Moi, Toril 172*n*
Molarsky, Mona 174*n*
Monteith, Sharon 176*n*
Morrison, Toni 105, 177*n*; *The Bluest Eye* 105
Motherhood/Mothers: absent 71, 72–73, 88; ambivalence toward 110, 125, 178*n*; critique of maternalism 11–13, 172*n*; distant 25, 78–79, 131; distracted 58; influence of 98–99; love for 88–89; maternal language 172*n*; monstrous 54; neglectful 28, 87–88, 95–96; redefined 165; reproduced 9–10; surrogate 42, 110, 137–49, 177–78*n*; transformative experience of 49, 52–53, 173*n*
Munafo, Giavanna 98, 99, 102, 176*n*, 177*n*
Myers, Thomas 174*n*

Natov, Roni 172*n*
Naylor, Gloria 105; *Mama Day* 105
Nesanovich, Stella 49, 173*n*
Neuman, Shirley 178*n*
Newbery Award 155
Nikolajeva, Maria 179*n*
North Carolina 3, 22, 36, 44, 129–30

O'Connor, Flannery 130, 178*n*
Olney, James 118
Orion magazine 117

Parrish, Nancy 24, 25, 172*n*, 173*n*
Paterson, Katherine 5, 14, 145–49, 179*n*; *The Great Gilly Hopkins* 145, 146, 149–50, 154; *The Invisible Child* 146, 147,

148; *Jacob Have I Loved* 145, 146, 150–
54, 179*n*; *A Sense of Wonder* 146, 147;
Worlds of Childhood 148, 151, 154
Paul, Lissa 15
Paulson, Michael 116, 178*n*
Pearlman, Mickey 72–73
Petry, Alice Hall 173*n*, 174*n*
Phillips, Jayne Ann 6
Pierce, Todd 130, 136, 137
Pipher, Mary 1, 2, 8–9, 119; *Revising
Ophelia* 1, 8, 136
Pollack, William 171*n*, 174*n*
Porter, Katherine Anne 130, 178*n*
Porter, Michael 171
Powell, Dannye 3, 73–74, 175*n*
Prajznerova, Katerina 24, 173*n*
Pregnancy: forcing action 48, 58; limit-
ing options 63–64
Price, Joanna 174*n*, 175*n*

Quiello, Rose 173*n*

Rape 26–29, 31, 95–96, 139–40
Raper, Julius Rowan 172*n*
Raver, Anne 116
Ravitch, Diane 171*n*
Ray, Janisse 2, 5, 22, 115, 173*n*, 178*n*;
Ecology of a Cracker Childhood 5, 17,
115–27, 178*n*
Reid, Suzanne Elizabeth 164, 169
Reynolds, David 176*n*
Ridley, Clifford 41
Robertson, Mary F. 43
Rosowski, Susan J. 13, 172*n*; "The Novel
of Awakening" 13–14
Ryan, Barbara T. 60

St. Claire, Nancy 15
Sandell, Jillian 176*n*
Saxton, Ruth 174*n*
Schmidt, Gary 147, 179*n*
Schultz, Joan 178*n*
Sexuality: abuse 83, 87, 93, 175*n*, 176*n*;
disappointing 133; as liberating force
32, 34–35, 37, 38, 141, 173*n*; as limi-
tation 159–62; secrecy about 80–81;
stigmatized 109; virginity 29
Shelton, Frank W. 173*n*, 174*n*
Sibling rivalry 151–54
Smedman, Sarah 179*n*
Smith, Karen 179*n*

Smith, Lee 2, 3, 21–40, 130, 173*n*; *Black
Mountain Breakdown* 22, 26–27, 30–
34; *Fair and Tender Ladies* 22, 34–36,
173*n*; *The Last Day the Dogbushes
Bloomed* 22, 24–27, 39; *Saving Grace*
22, 36–40; *Something in the Wind*
27–30
Smith, Rebecca 21, 25, 27, 30, 39,
173*n*
Smith, Sidonie 118
Smith, Virginia 172*n*
Sommers, Christine Hoff 171*n*; *The War
Against Boys* 171*n*
The South: Bible Belt 147–48; comfort
foods 134; disappearing way of life
22–24, 57, 58, 61, 69, 116, 126–27,
130, 175*n*; home/heritage/sense of
place 106, 146–48, 155–56, 178*n*;
lost causes 148; New South 61, 130;
regional identity 172–73*n*, 174*n*;
resisting the patriarchy 34, 39, 42–43,
85–86, 148; Southern gothic 130;
Southern literary tradition 17–20,
178*n*
Spencer, Elizabeth 18–20, 172*n*
Stacey, Judith 172*n*
Steinberg, Sybil 175*n*
Stewart, Matthew C. 175*n*
Sweeney, Susan Elizabeth 56

Tarr, Anita 149
Tate, Linda 173*n*
Taylor, Mildred D. 5, 14, 105, 145,
154–56; *The Road to Memphis* 145,
154, 156; *Roll of Thunder, Hear My
Cry* 145, 154, 155, 156, 157; *Will the
Circle Be Unbroken* 145, 154, 156,
157–58
Thompson, Michael 171*n*
Trites, Roberta 179*n*
Tyler, Anne 3, 22, 41–56, 72, 84, 105,
116, 168, 172*n*, 173*n*; *The Clock
Winder* 22, 49–53, 65, 174*n*; *Dinner
at the Homesick Restaurant* 1, 53–56;
A Slipping-Down Life 22, 44–49

Vietnam 58–69
Voigt, Cynthia 5, 14, 145, 164–65, 179*n*;
Dicey's Song 145, 165, 168–69; *Home-
coming* 145, 164–68, 169
Volker, Joseph 44, 173*n*, 174*n*

Wagner-Martin, Linda 172*n*
Walker, Alice 6
Walker, Elinor Ann 175*n*, 179*n*
Walsh, William 25, 34
Warren, Nagueylati 177*n*
Watts, Linda 176*n*, 177*n*
Welty, Eudora 18, 147, 178*n*; *The Golden Apples* 19
White, Leslie 61, 175*n*

White Trash 61, 84–85, 94, 97, 121–22, 176*n*
Wickenden, Dorothy 175*n*
Wilhelm, Albert E. 174*n*
Wolf, Virginia 164
Wood, Ralph 176*n*

Yeats, William Butler 135; "Among School Children" 135–36